Write Yourself In

Write Yourself In

**THE DEFINITIVE GUIDE
TO WRITING SUCCESSFUL
COLLEGE ADMISSIONS ESSAYS**

Eric Tipler

Simon Element

NEW YORK   LONDON   TORONTO   SYDNEY   NEW DELHI

SIMON
ELEMENT

An Imprint of Simon & Schuster, LLC
1230 Avenue of the Americas
New York, NY 10020

First Simon Element trade paperback edition June 2024

SIMON ELEMENT is a trademark of Simon & Schuster, LLC

Simon & Schuster: Celebrating 100 Years of Publishing in 2024

For information about special discounts for bulk purchases, please contact Simon &
Schuster Special Sales at 1-866-506-1949 or business@simonandschuster.com.

The Simon & Schuster Speakers Bureau can bring authors to your live event. For
more information or to book an event, contact the Simon & Schuster Speakers
Bureau at 1-866-248-3049 or visit our website at www.simonspeakers.com.

Interior design by Ruth Lee-Mui

Manufactured in the United States of America

1 3 5 7 9 10 8 6 4 2

Library of Congress Cataloging-in-Publication Data has been applied for.

ISBN 978-1-6680-5521-2
ISBN 978-1-6680-5522-9 (ebook)

For Chris Weller (1948–2005),

my high school English teacher,

who cared enough about her students

to teach us how to write

Contents

I picked up a pen
And wrote my way out

—Lin-Manuel Miranda, Nasir Jones, David Brewster,
Egbert Nathaniel Dawkins III, and Ramon Ibanga, Jr.,
"Wrote My Way Out," *The Hamilton Mixtape*

I only went out for a walk, and finally concluded to stay out
till sundown, for going out, I found, was really going in.

—John Muir, circa 1901, in *John of the Mountains:
The Unpublished Journals of John Muir*

Preface

When I started writing this book five years ago, my goal was to help high school students write better essays and gain admission to colleges where they would flourish. I wanted to create something informative and useful: the guidebook I wish I'd had when I was an eager, anxious high school senior.

Fast-forward to 2024. Who could have predicted how much more of a need there would be, just five years later, for informed guidance on college admissions? Families today are more confused and worried than ever about the admissions process, which is not surprising, given that it becomes more confusing, complicated, and competitive each year. "It's so different from when we were kids!" is a refrain I often hear from frustrated parents. American higher education is in the midst of major structural and ideological transformations, and selective college admissions aren't just changing; they're front and center in national debates and controversies.

So before we start talking about applications, I want to help teens and their parents understand the journey they're about to undertake. We'll do this by looking at how three recent events have transformed the admissions landscape, each of them heightening the focus on college admissions essays.

The first transformative event occurred in 2020, when the COVID-19 pandemic led most colleges to drop their long-standing requirements for standardized tests such as the SAT and ACT. At some universities, the

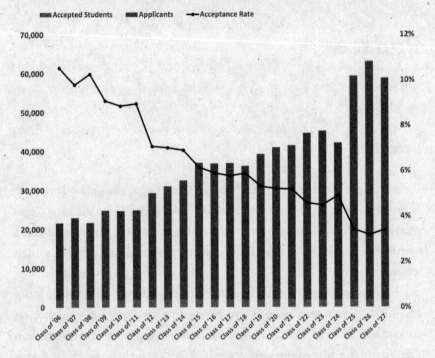

Harvard Undergraduate Acceptance Rate, Classes of 2006-2027

Note the 50% increase in applicants between the classes of 2024 and 2026.

number of applicants increased by as much as 50% in just two years. Acceptance rates plummeted, accelerating the trend toward higher selectivity that had been under way for decades. And with test scores for many students gone, college essays—already a top factor in admissions—became even more important.

Three years later, just as the numbers were starting to stabilize post-COVID, the second momentous event happened: the US Supreme Court struck down affirmative action programs at Harvard University and University of North Carolina. That ruling, part of an ongoing national conversation around diversity and access in higher education, quickly upset the fundamentals of college admissions. Colleges responded by changing their admissions practices, while students recalibrated their odds at the top schools. Yet because the Supreme Court allowed students to continue writing about personal experiences connected to race, even more attention—in the media, in high schools, and in admissions committee rooms—was directed toward the essays.

The year 2023 also gave us a third transformative event: the widespread availability of AI chatbots like ChatGPT. In the 2023–2024 admissions cycle, many high school seniors continued to write their own application essays; others used chatbots to write and revise. On the opposite side of the table, colleges began experimenting with using AI to review applications.

It seems likely that admissions officers ended up reading a lot of ChatGPT-generated essays during what the *New York Times* called "the first full academic year of the post-ChatGPT era." It seems equally likely that most of those essays didn't do much good for the kids who submitted them, at least at selective colleges. ChatGPT may be able to write strong analytical essays—one Harvard undergraduate found that her professors gave ChatGPT mostly As and Bs on freshman writing assignments—but it's not yet good at writing narrative stories in a distinctive, personal voice. Regardless, AI is poised to transform how essays are written and evaluated, at the same time as essays are playing an elevated role in admissions decisions.

WHAT'S CHANGED SINCE WE WERE KIDS?

BACK IN THE DAY	THE CURRENT LANDSCAPE
Harvard Class of 1999: • 17,847 applicants • 2,112 admissions • 11.8% acceptance rate	**Harvard Class of 2026:** • 61,220 applicants • 1,954 admissions • 3.2% acceptance rate
University of Pennsylvania Class of 2004: • 18,815 applicants • 4,280 admissions • 22.7% acceptance rate	**University of Pennsylvania Class of 2025:** • 56,333 applicants • 3,202 admissions • 5.7% acceptance rate
University of Michigan Class of 2002: • 59.0% acceptance rate	**University of Michigan Class of 2025:** • 20.1% acceptance rate

The New Landscape

Put together, these events have rapidly accelerated two trends that were already underway.

The first is **greater selectivity**. Admissions rates today at most of the country's selective colleges are much lower than they were five, ten, or twenty years ago. When I applied to Harvard in 1995, the admissions rate was just under 12%. By 2019, it had fallen to 4.9%, and in 2022, it dropped even further to 3.2%, a trend that played out at many other selective schools as well (see chart on previous page).

The flip side of higher selectivity is the second new reality: **higher uncertainty**. A decade ago, I could usually forecast—imperfectly but with some accuracy—where my students would get in. Now when I meet with students, one of the first things I tell them is to think broadly about where they're going to apply, because predictions are out the window. Jim Jump, a highly respected past president of the National Association for College Admission Counseling, put it this way:

> A number of years ago, I remember an admissions dean at an Ivy or Little Ivy commenting that if a student is a legitimate candidate for the nation's "elite" colleges and applies to enough of them, they would likely be admitted to one, but perhaps not the one they hoped for. That stopped being the case long ago.

Taken together, increasing selectivity and uncertainty have changed the way kids apply to competitive schools. Gone are the days when a student with good grades could simply look at the top thirty schools in the *U.S. News & World Report* rankings, find a handful that looked appealing, and just apply there. If a teen does that these days, there's a very good chance that they will not get in anywhere.

The good news, however, is that there are *many* excellent, lesser-known colleges and universities where a student can get a world-class education, surround themselves with friends who will motivate and inspire them, and set themselves up for success in life. So it's vital for each student to begin the process by thinking deeply about what *they* want in a college, then applying to a wide range of schools (including reach, target, and safety) that would be a good fit for *them*, regardless of the rankings. That's why this book includes a section on "Introspection" (see appendix I) so teens can start their process by exploring their own goals, needs, and aspirations, as well as strategies for finding great schools beyond the rankings (see chapter 7 and appendix I).

A Way Forward

Now more than ever, applying to college in the United States is complex. One key to your success—as well as your sanity—is to clearly identify the things you can control and the things you can't.

When a student sits down to write their essays, much of the application is already out of their control. Freshman through junior year grades are done, as are most of their activities. Hopefully the student has already asked teachers for recommendations (if not, do it now!), but they have little to no control over what their teachers will write. Applicants also have no control over who else is applying that year and what each college's institutional priorities happen to be. (Do they want more in-state students? More out-of-staters? A kid from every state in the union? More women, more engineering majors, more oboists?)

All of that is completely out of applicants' hands, so there's no point worrying about it. Really, just let it go!

Instead, focus on what you *can* control—namely, your test scores (if you choose to submit them), your senior year grades (they matter, especially in the regular decision round), the list of schools you apply to (more on that later), and of course, your essays.

Taken together, those four factors will help you reach your goal: a college where you will flourish. And so, with best wishes for the journey ahead, I humbly present a road map to your college admissions essays.

ERIC TIPLER

Cold Spring, New York

January 2024

Introduction

The college essay. Like homecoming and the prom, it's a rite of passage in American education. Your essay may feel like the summation of your high school career, a chance—or a challenge—to tell it all in 650 words or less. College essays inspire fear, dread, and, when done well, awe.

But what exactly is a college essay? How do you write it? How do you write one that doesn't suck? More important, how can you write one that will help persuade a team of admissions officers—the gatekeepers—to admit you to the school of your dreams?

These are questions I've been thinking about for nearly thirty years.

I thought about them as a high school senior, when I wrote essays that got me admitted Early Action to Harvard, then to Princeton, Stanford, and the University of Virginia. I thought about them when I taught at Thomas Jefferson High School for Science and Technology, in Alexandria, Virginia, one of the top high schools in the country. I thought about them when I applied to graduate school at Yale, got in, and was later awarded a full scholarship. And I've thought about them over the past ten years as a writing tutor and essay coach in New York City, one of the most competitive regions for college admissions on the planet.

This guide is filled with tips, tricks, strategies, and approaches garnered from many years of thinking about and teaching writing. Knowledge is power. This book contains a lot of power because it unpacks the admissions process and will help you understand it in ways that few high school students do.

My first goal in writing it is to help you understand how the process works. I wrote this book because I am passionate about helping equalize opportunities, which I believe is the key to the American Dream. I believe that the more people who understand the process, the better. After all, you shouldn't have to have insider connections to understand how the game works. A meritocracy can truly work only when the rules are known to all.

Most college admissions officers, in fact, would probably agree. Though college admission *is* competitive and can sometimes feel like a battle, the schools are not your enemy. Most AdComs (university lingo for "admissions committee") are made up of genuinely nice, caring people who want students to thrive. But they are also extremely busy; admissions officers have to read and analyze thousands of applications per year. Their primary job is to recruit, sort through, and select students—not to educate them about the process.

In addition to teaching you about how essays will be used in admissions, I also hope that reading this book will bring a little more ease—and maybe even some joy—to a process that can be stressful, confusing, and fraught with self-doubt. After all, this is a process where you're asked to put your best foot forward, to show off your best qualities, and, yes, sometimes even to "sell" yourself. Yet presenting yourself at your best is very different from pretending to be someone else, and it can sometimes be easy to confuse the two.

Putting Your Best Foot Forward

To understand the difference, think of your Instagram profile. When you select pics for Instagram, you instinctively look for images that present you at your best. Yet you also want to make sure that the pictures actually look like you and not like someone else. If a friend of yours started posting pics of some gorgeous model and pretending to be that person or started tagging themselves in places they'd never visited, that would be weird, creepy, even a bit dishonest, right?

The same principle applies to college admissions. Presenting yourself at your best will get you the attention that you need and, in this case, deserve.

Over the course of this book, you will learn how to present yourself at your best in the rarefied, peculiar world of selective college admissions. You'll learn how the admissions process works and how misunderstandings of the process can create problems for you. You'll also learn the specific qualities that admissions officers are looking for and that you already possess—although you may not realize it yet! And finally, you will learn step-by-step tactics for writing your essays: the main college essay (widely known as the "Common App personal essay"), as well as supplemental essays for various schools.

Along the way, you'll read excerpts from actual essays that helped students get into some of the top colleges in the country and see advice from admissions officers at major schools.

Keep in mind that the advice in this book is focused on *selective* schools, which for our purposes means undergraduate programs with a less than 30% admissions rate.* If you're applying to a community college or to a university with a high acceptance rate (say, greater than 70%), some of what's in here may be overkill. However, these strategies will be *extremely* useful if you're applying for honors programs at large state universities. They can also make a big difference in scholarship applications, which are nearly always competitive.

The Best School for You

Before we dive in, I want to explain my other goal in writing this book, which is all about making the college admissions process work for you. Put simply:

I want to help you get into a college where you will flourish.

---

*As you explore articles and websites about college admissions, you're likely to run into a range of terms such as "selective," "highly selective," "very selective," "most selective," "not selective," and so on. There are no universally agreed-upon definitions for these categories, so I'll keep things simple and stick with "selective."

What do I mean by "flourish"? I mean being in a school where you will be happy, where you will feel safe and supported, where you will also be pushed and encouraged to grow, learn, develop, and become your best self. If you're lucky, you had this experience in high school. Even if you didn't, it's still possible in college.

Now, "flourishing" is not the first word that comes to mind when most people think about college admissions. Instead, most of us tend to think about it in terms of getting into the most prestigious college we can.

There's nothing wrong with prestige, and I would never urge someone to settle for less than what they can accomplish. Indeed, as a graduate of both Harvard and Yale it would be hypocritical for me to say that going to a prestigious school hasn't impacted my life.

But prestige isn't everything. Harvard happened to be a great school for me at age seventeen, but many of my friends, especially those who were premed, were miserable. At our twenty-year reunion, one of them told me flat out that she would never send her own kids there.

My sister, on the other hand, went to a less prestigious but still excellent, highly selective small school, Pomona College. She had an incredible experience there, attended a top grad school, and is now a professor of political theory. Most Fortune 500 CEOs did not go to Ivy League schools for their undergrad studies. And if I were to go back to college now, I wouldn't go to Harvard again, because the person I am today would flourish in a smaller school, with a warmer community and closer relationships with faculty.

The reality is that if you are admitted to a selective school, public or private, you're going to get a great education. You'll also get to enjoy the college experience that is unique to American education. That experience, however, varies widely among big, medium, and small schools, urban and rural schools, research-focused universities and student-centered colleges. Like plants, different people flourish in different environments. My hope is that you will use the ideas and knowledge, the power in this book, to find a school where you, too, will flourish.

Your Road Map to Success

You do, of course, need to get admitted to that school. And if you want to write essays that will help you get in, you need to have an understanding of the admissions process—and the role your essays will play in that process—*before* you start writing.

Chapters 1 and 2 of this book, therefore, will give you a crash course in how the college admissions process works. You'll learn about the people who make admissions decisions, how your essays are used in that process, and perhaps most important, you'll learn what admissions committees are looking for.

The remainder of the book is devoted to helping you write those essays. In chapter 3 you'll develop a strategy for planning and writing all your essays. Chapter 4 is devoted to the personal essay, which is the primary essay that you'll submit to most schools. Chapters 5 through 7 will help you master the supplemental essays that you'll write for applications to specific schools, and in chapter 8 you'll learn how to apply these writing strategies to scholarship essays.

Throughout the book, you'll find guidance on using AI chatbots such as ChatGPT to assist you at different stages of the process. You'll also find tips on how the 2023 Supreme Court affirmative action ruling impacts what you should say in your essays, as well as how you need to say it.

You Can Do It!

In high school, many of us were led to believe that we always needed to do more, be more, achieve more. But the truth is, you are good enough just the way you are. If you've made it through middle and high school, done your best inside and outside the classroom, and reached the point where it's time to write your college essays, you have done enough and deserve success.

Now your task is to tell your authentic story and to do so in a way that highlights qualities you already have that selective colleges are looking for.

Trust me, those qualities are there; you just need to learn how to recognize them. This book will help you do that.

Believe in yourself. You're about to embark on an exciting journey, and I'm honored to be one of your guides along the way.

A practical tip: Hopefully you're reading this book well in advance of your admissions deadlines! But if your applications are due in a week or less, stop reading and skip to chapter 3. Come back and read the first two chapters later, once you have a plan.

A Note to Parents

Applying to college is hard for students. It can also be unexpectedly difficult for parents. I've seen hard-boiled moms and dads, from Wall Street bankers to janitors, freak out when their kids are about to fly the coop. The process can be especially challenging when you're going through it for the first time. (If you have multiple kids, take heart: it gets easier.)

Essays are one of the first steps in this journey, so I'd like to reassure you up front that it's going to be okay. Yes, it will be uncomfortable, even painful at times. Your child is preparing to leave home, which will stir up emotions. Excitement, anticipation, and fear are normal parts of this process. So is grief.

Yet if your kid is reflective, self-disciplined, and pragmatic (e.g., they don't apply only to Ivy League schools), it's going to work out. It may not work out exactly as they—or you—expect, and it may take longer than you want it to, but it will work out.

As a parent, your biggest challenge during the college application process will be to let go. You want to give your child space to navigate their own process, while at the same time being there to catch them if they fall. You want to provide the support and resources they might need, and you want to be tuned in to what's going on, so you can help them redirect the ship if it goes off course.

A metaphor I often use when speaking about this process is a board of directors. In a well-functioning corporation or nonprofit, the board members do not get involved with day-to-day business. Instead, they put good people into key roles, then work with the organization's leadership to plan strategy. The board meets regularly to keep an eye on things, and if things go off course, they will redirect, holding leaders accountable when necessary.

That's your role here: you're the board, and your child is the CEO of their college process. In many ways, of course, this is a natural evolution in the role you've been playing over the past few years, as your teen developed independence while still relying on you more than they cared to admit.

If you'd like more specific guidance on how you can be helpful (and avoid being harmful) in this process, here are some dos and don'ts.

Dos

1. **Start talking about college early.**

   Your kid may have been talking about college since elementary school, or they may never have brought it up. Either way, they're probably thinking about it.

   Sophomore year is a good time to—gently—start the conversation, and you definitely want to be talking about schools and the application process by the midpoint of junior year.

2. **Help your child set and stick to a timeline.**

   Ideally your child will start working on their college essays the summer before senior year (see page 50 for a more detailed timeline). If they haven't started writing by Labor Day, consider intervening to help them get back on track.

3. **Encourage them to research many schools, and take them on college visits.**

   When kids take the time to research a variety of colleges, they gain a clearer sense of where they'll thrive. A campus visit can be the best way to discover if a particular school is right for your child; once they've spent an hour or two on campus, they'll usually know in their gut if it's a good fit.

   If campus visits aren't manageable for your family, virtual visits are the next best thing. In addition, many admissions offices will be happy to put your child in touch with current students, which can be a great way to learn more about a school.

   One red flag to watch out for: if your child stays narrowly focused on one or two highly competitive schools for a long period of time, i.e., several months or more. With admissions more competitive now than ever, that is a setup for disappointment. Encourage them to think broadly and to take the time to figure out what they want. The reality is that there are many schools where they will flourish.

4. **Help them find the support they need.**

   Different kids need different levels of support. Some will benefit from SAT/ACT tutoring, an essay coach, even a private college admissions counselor. Others prefer to navigate the process themselves, perhaps with help from the counselor at their high school.

Instead of trying to read their mind, ask your teen, "What support do you need?" and offer some options. Have a conversation, use your best judgment, and work within your means to connect them with resources.

For example, parents of children who've just been through this process are likely to have suggestions for private tutors and counselors. If not, the Independent Educational Consultants Association (IECA), a nonprofit association, maintains a list of admissions counselors who have completed a certification process at https://www.iecaonline.com/. Most youth and community centers—and many high schools—offer free or low-cost assistance, such as SAT tutoring and help with the essays.

5. **Read the essays when they're done. Make sure that they convey your child's personality.**

Most kids will want to write their essays without your input. Then, when they're done or nearly done (or if they get stuck), they will suddenly want you to read them.

That moment—when they're ready for you to take a look—is a time where you can be especially helpful. Read their essays. Make sure they are well written: clear, organized, and free of grammatical errors. Most important, make sure that they reflect your child—the young person you know and love—at their best.

Some of the most transformative feedback I've gotten from parents happened when the kid's essay was good . . . but didn't sound quite like their child. Maybe the kid was trying to be too formal and had sacrificed their voice. Maybe he hadn't admitted how scared he was at one point, or maybe she was underselling her strengths. Either way, the essay wasn't quite reflecting the child's personality and character.

If that happens, speak up. Your teen may, of course, need to hear this feedback from someone else. But you are in the best position to see if it's needed, because you know them better than anyone.

Don'ts

1. **Don't write the essays for them.**

   This goes without saying, and it's against the rules, but it happens. Writing your child's essays or paying someone else to do so *might* give them an edge. But very often it backfires, because admissions officers read thousands of these things per year. They are experts, and unless you work in admissions, teach high school English, or write teen fiction, you are not. Most admissions professionals can sniff out adult writing from miles away.

   Even if you get really lucky and an admissions officer doesn't catch the fraud, writing your child's essays for them will undermine their self-confidence and possibly damage your long-term relationship with them.

2. **Don't rewrite the essays once they've written them.**

   As long as you're judicious, your child's essays can benefit from your feedback, ideas, and light edits. But resist the temptation to rewrite large portions of their essays. Instead, if you see problems, explain why you think major rewrites are needed. Or—even better—steer them to someone who can help them revise it, such as an English teacher or tutor.

   Writing this, I'm reminded of a student I once worked with who was brilliant but shy. Over the course of two months, I watched her slowly come out of her shell as she discovered and told her own story in her essays. Then, forty-eight hours before the deadline, her mother came in and rewrote everything. I've never seen a teenager crumble and deflate so quickly. Don't be that parent.

3. **Don't tell them what to write about.**

   Most parents have ideas about what their kid should write about in their college essays. It's fine to suggest topics, and you should definitely help if they're lost or steer them to adults who can (tutors, teachers, counselors, relatives, or others). But in the end, leave the decision to them.

4. **Don't insist on your point of view.**

   Some of the most painful parent-child conflicts I've seen in this process have arisen when a parent insists that the child tell a story the way the parent remembers it or when they insist that a child highlight an event that the child doesn't think is important.

There are two things to keep in mind here. First, remember that your child is likely to have a different memory of most events than you do, even moments that you shared. Something that may have seemed pivotal to you may not have registered for them. Or the kid may have thought it was a big deal at the time, but in the intervening years it's receded into the background.

Second, remember that these essays will focus on their high school years. You probably spent a lot of time with your kid in early childhood and were privy to all of the highlights. However, with a few exceptions, that period is not what they'll be writing about in these essays.

Instead, they'll be telling stories from a time when they've been going through the adolescent process of individuation, developing lives of their own. They may choose to focus on events that you weren't there for—not because you were a bad parent, but because they occurred during a band trip, an after-school activity, or that cool summer program you pushed them to try.

Let them tell their own story.

They Need You, Even If They Don't Know It

As in so much of adolescence, your child needs you now more than ever. They just need different things than in the past. Right now, they need for you to stand back and give them some space. They also need you there in the background, keeping an eye out for them if and when they screw up. Your kid probably knows this at some level, but it's hard for most teens to admit it.

Supporting them in this way is a big ask, and for most parents, it's not easy. But the more you're able to do it, the more they'll develop confidence and independence as they prepare to leave home. In the process, you will also be building the foundation for a strong, adult relationship with them for many years to come.

PART I

The Task at Hand

CHAPTER 1

Know Your Audience

AdCom Psychology 101

> If you don't know where you are going, you'll end up someplace else.
> —YOGI BERRA

If you want to write essays that will help you get into college, it's crucial to have an understanding of the admissions process, as well as the role essays play in them, *before* you start writing.

Over many years of teaching, interviewing applicants, speaking with admissions officers, and advising hundreds of students on their applications, I've been shocked to learn that most applicants have very little idea why they're actually writing these essays or how the essays are used in the admissions process.

This is an enormous problem, and it's a big part of why I wrote this book. During high school, it leads families to waste time and money on pursuits that kids don't really care about and drives already anxious teenagers to stress out over the wrong things. When application time comes, it inspires students to write admissions essays that fail to help them—or may even hurt them.

The goal of this chapter is to help you understand who will be reading the essays, how they use them, and what the admissions process actually looks like. Once you have that knowledge, you will be way ahead of most other high school students.

Know Your Audience—The "Who"

Imagine that you are a college admissions officer somewhere in the wintry wilds of New England.

It's an early morning in February, the dead of winter, and the height of admissions season. Outside it's still dark; you're just finishing your coffee and still waking up.

On your desk sits a folder for the 2,425th applicant you'll be reading this season. On the tab of the folder is the student's name. Inside, a ream of papers waits for your review: the student's transcript, a printout of their SAT/ACT scores, recommendations from teachers, maybe a letter from their high school's college counselor.

And of course . . . the essays.

Just by looking at the grades, level of rigor in the coursework, and test scores, you'll be able to make a rough assessment as to whether the student will be a competitive applicant at your school. And if the answer is yes, the next most important question in your mind will be: Who is the person behind all these numbers?

That's where the essays come in. After all, though you will probably never meet this student in person, you and your colleagues are tasked with making the potentially life-altering decision of whether to offer them one of the very limited spots at your school.

What Exactly Is an Admissions Committee?

In a classic *Simpsons* episode (like many nerds of my generation, I'm a fan) Homer causes a nuclear meltdown and must go back to college to keep his job. He's in luck: Mr. Burns, his boss, has a chair at Springfield University. Quick cut to a Springfield U. admissions committee meeting, where we see a group of mostly bald, middle-aged men in jackets and ties, sitting around a table, smoking cigars, and heatedly discussing Homer's candidacy in what appears to be a wood-paneled room.

I love this scene, because when we hear the words "admissions committee," something like that often comes to mind. But aside from the

Real AdComs look more like this stock photo.

debates—which do happen and can get heated—that's not the reality these days. The modern admissions committee, or "AdCom" in university parlance (universities, like most bureaucracies, love fake words), looks more like the photo above.

Today, nearly all committees at selective American schools are diverse in many ways: race, ethnicity, gender, sexual identity, and more. A typical committee might consist of ten to forty people, and committee members are often young adults in their twenties and thirties, many of them recent graduates.

There will usually be some more experienced folks running the show; they may be older alumni of the school or perhaps professional educators hired from the outside. Either way, they will have decades of experience in college admissions. And while professors occasionally serve on committees or evaluate student submissions in certain fields (e.g., the arts), most admissions decisions are made by admissions professionals.

How Are the Essays Used?

The AdCom Is Your Friend

Though it may seem counterintuitive, the truth is that committee members are on your side, *especially* when it comes to the essays.

What do I mean by that? Now that you know who'll be reading your essays, take a moment to think about them as people. Nearly all of them are folks who genuinely care about their school, about education, and about their community. Younger AdCom members are often recent graduates who loved their college so much that they decided to stick around and work in the admissions office for a few years.

These people are not looking for you to make mistakes in your essays; in fact, it's exactly the opposite. The reason the essays are there is so that admissions officers have a chance to see positive qualities that might not show up in other parts of your application. When they read the essays, they are looking to give you points, not take them away, to give you credit for the good things you've done instead of docking you for things you didn't do.

Although they will certainly notice grammatical, syntactical, and similar mistakes—proofreading and revising are therefore *very* important—most admissions officers approach these essays with an open heart. They're looking for reasons to vote *for* a student and admit them, not reasons to deny them admission.

In this way, essays are quite different from the SAT, where wrong answers are literally designed to trick you into choosing them. (In test design circles—the Educational Testing Service, the College Board—wrong answers are called "distractors," and the right answer is called the "key.") Unlike standardized tests, the goal of the essays has always been to give applicants an additional chance to show how good they are—to demonstrate qualities, accomplishments, and skills that tests don't necessarily reveal.

That last point is *very* important to keep in mind: **Admissions officers read these essays looking for reasons to admit you, not for reasons**

to reject you. Most people don't realize that the process works this way, which can easily lead to essays that miss the mark.

The Process: What Happens Once You Click "Submit"

Once your application arrives at a selective college or university's admissions office, it will go through some variation of the following process.

1. **Initial sorting.** Many selective schools organize their admissions regionally. So the first thing that happens is that your application will be grouped with others from your region and assigned to an admissions officer, who will do the first read.

2. **First read.** In the weeks following your submission, the admissions officer or officers assigned to your file will do a first read of your portfolio. They'll look over your transcript, activities, recommendations, test scores, and, of course, your essays.

   Though every school handles this differently, based on that first read, you'll be formally or informally placed into one of three categories: likely reject, likely admit, or undecided.

   The "likely rejects" are the clear "nos": people who don't meet the college's academic admissions requirements or are way behind the pack in grades, extracurriculars, course rigor, and other aspects. Sadly, it's clear from the beginning that they won't be going far in the process.

   The "likely admit" pile is typically small. Almost no one is admitted to a selective school without at least *some* committee discussion. But there is usually a small pool of applications where it's clear the discussion is going to be pretty short. Depending on the school's selectivity, if you are a nationally ranked athlete with great grades, Malala, or, in the words of one admissions officer, "a high-testing All-State bassoonist," you may end up in this pile.

   Because that "likely admit" pool is usually so small, most candidates who are eventually admitted are in the third category:

"undecided." For the purposes of this book, this is the category we care most about. It's the category where you're most likely to end up if you have a strong application, and it's also the category where your essays are going to make the most difference.

3. **Committee meeting.** After being reviewed by an individual admissions officer, each application is then taken to the entire admissions committee and discussed. Some discussions are quite short. Other times, the committee debates a single candidate for more than an hour.

   At many schools, the admissions officer who first reads your application will present it—and therefore you—to the larger group. In some ways they are functioning like your advocate, a bit like a lawyer in a courtroom trial. Though the rest of the committee will typically have seen your essays, at most schools they won't have had time to read them as closely as the initial reader.

   This step is quite important to remember when you're working on your essays. Why? Because **one of the most powerful things you can do in your essays is to give your readers evidence and arguments that they can use to support your candidacy in discussions with other admissions officers** and ultimately in the committee meeting.

4. **Vote.** Finally, the committee will vote on your candidacy: admit, reject, wait-list, or—in the early round—defer. Sometimes the vote will happen immediately. Other times, depending on what the applicant pool looks like, they will take a "wait-and-see" approach, tabling your application and voting on it once other applications have been discussed.

That's pretty much it. Keep in mind that this process will be repeated at every college you apply to. Also keep in mind that it will vary—sometimes significantly—from college to college.

For example, some schools have two or more officers do the first read; then they exchange views on the application before moving it on to the committee. At other schools, there are multiple committees devoted to reading applications from students with different interests or backgrounds. The University of California, which consists of UCLA, Berkeley, and the other UC schools, has a number of idiosyncrasies, such as not using teacher recommendations. And some schools repeat the rounds described above multiple times, until they've "shaped" their incoming class to meet their institutional priorities.*

In general, however, the process will be some variation of: initial sorting, first read, committee meeting, vote!

So What Do They Want?

Now that you know *who* will be reading your essays, *how* they'll be using them in the admissions process, and *what* that process looks like, in the next chapter we'll drill down one more level and answer the biggest question of all: What are admissions officers looking for?

Should I Use ChatGPT to Write My College Essays?

In the years to come, the college admissions cycle of 2023–2024 will likely be remembered not only as the year affirmative action was struck down—which was huge—but also as the year artificial intelligence made its way into college admissions.

We seem to be entering the Age of AI, which brings with it both promise and peril. AI can do lots of great things, and it's getting more powerful every day.

But it's not perfect. For example, a chatbot programmed to generate meal recipes for supermarket shoppers didn't just come up with some unappealing ideas, such as "Oreo vegetable stir-fry"; it also created a drink recipe that, if prepared according to the bot's instructions, would create

---

*For clarity and brevity, I've simplified the process here. For a more thorough discussion by a journalist who spent a year inside the admissions offices of several competitive schools, check out the excellent book *Who Gets In and Why: A Year Inside College Admissions* by Jeffrey Selingo.

chlorine gas—a highly toxic substance that can damage your lungs or even kill you.

While college essays are unlikely to kill you, it's important to keep in mind that AI, although it often writes in an authoritative tone, is far from perfect and has the potential to be harmful.

When it comes to college admissions, I think this is a case where the kids are a step ahead of the grown-ups. Most teens today are using AI in their personal or academic lives, while the admissions industry, which generally moves slowly, has been slow to address ChatGPT. As of this writing, the Common App had not yet released any guidance for students about ChatGPT (I wouldn't be surprised if it released guidance in mid-2024). Some colleges offered advice to applicants on how to use or avoid AI; others didn't. More quietly, admissions offices at some schools have started using AI to evaluate applications.

So the question of the day is: Should you use ChatGPT to write your college application essays? If by that you mean prompting ChatGPT to write an essay and then pasting that essay into the Common App, the answer is a clear, hard no, for two reasons.

The first is ethical. Every time you submit a college application through the Common App, you digitally sign a statement attesting that "all information submitted in the admission process—including this application and any other supporting materials—is my own work, factually true, and honestly presented." Submitting an AI-generated essay is a clear violation of that, in the same way that submitting an essay written by another person would be.

If you're not swayed by the ethical concerns, there's an equally powerful, practical reason not to submit an AI-generated essay: ChatGPT is not very good at writing college essays, at least not yet. It *is* good at writing grammatically correct, well-structured paragraphs and essays, but they tend to be generic, relatively boring, and occasionally inaccurate. ChatGPT essays will also lack the most important elements college admissions officers are looking for: your voice and details about your life.

As Rick Clark, the executive director of undergraduate admissions at Georgia Tech, put it:

Colleges want applications that are full of details, specifics, and insight into who you are, how you think, what you have learned, and what you care about.

Simply put, that is not a task that today's AI chatbots are especially good at. Will that stop some people from using ChatGPT to write their essays? Of course not, and I have no doubt that colleges will be receiving thousands of AI-generated essays this year, especially in applications submitted the night before the deadline.

However, the students that submit them may be wasting their application fee, because those essays are unlikely to do their authors much good.

The good news, however, is that even though AI isn't very good at writing the essays themselves, it can be a powerful and useful tool throughout your application process. You'll find some ethical, practical suggestions for using chatbots throughout this book, such as brainstorming essay topics (page 75) and creating your list of schools (page 265).

The other bit of good news is that there is a simple way to figure out if you're using it safely or not: **you should never copy and paste anything from ChatGPT into your essays**. Instead, treat ChatGPT as you would a collaboration partner or interlocutor—the same way you might ask for ideas and advice from a friend, parent, or teacher. You can learn from your "conversations" with ChatGPT, but your work ultimately needs to be your own.

This approach, by the way, is inspired by the forward-thinking, tech-savvy undergraduate admissions office at Georgia Tech (led by the same Rick Clark). The staff there collaborated with Georgia Tech faculty to develop some of the best and earliest guidance on using AI, back in August 2023. Here's what they had to say:

In the same way you would not copy directly from any other source you may incorporate into the writing process, you should not copy and paste directly out of any AI platform or submit work that you did not originally create. Instead, approach and consider any interaction with an AI tool as a learning experience that may help you generate ideas, provide alternative phrasing options, and organize your thoughts. Ultimately, we want to read and hear your unique and valuable writing style.

The use of ChatGPT is an evolving story, of course, and the one thing we can be certain about is that it will change. My hunch, however, is that this kind of advice will continue to be a useful heuristic for AI. If you try to get a chatbot to do your thinking for you, you're setting yourself up for trouble. If, on the other hand, you use it as an assistant, it can help you achieve your goals.

CHAPTER 2

The Top Ten Qualities Admissions Officers Look For

1. Achievement
2. Maturity and Personal Growth
3. Community Engagement
4. Passion
5. Intellectual Curiosity
6. Creativity
7. Leadership
8. Resilience
9. Empathy
10. Fit

Most people think they know what colleges are looking for: stellar grades, perfect test scores, and an extracurricular list longer than a CVS receipt.

To an extent, of course, they are. Admissions committees at selective colleges love achievements, and it's hard to get into a top school without them.

But they're not everything. As an Ivy League admissions officer once explained to me, "Each year we could admit a class made up entirely of valedictorians with perfect SAT scores. But we don't, because it would be a disaster."

Colleges are communities, and admissions committees are looking to put together a diverse group of students who will thrive together. They also admit people, not numbers, and are highly trained to look for human characteristics behind those well-polished résumés.

So what are they looking for? **Admissions officers want to know whether you can succeed inside and outside the classroom, how you would contribute to their community, and if you'd flourish at their school.** They're also looking for *you*—some sense of your unique spark or spirit that makes you tick.

That may sound abstract and difficult to put into an essay. So here is a list of the top ten personal qualities that admissions officers at selective schools are looking for, along with tips on how you can highlight them in your essays.

One note: Though I can guarantee that you possess all ten of these qualities to some degree, you do *not* need to shine in all ten areas! Very few high school students (or adults, for that matter) do. Instead, look for a few of these qualities you can see most clearly in yourself. They will be the ones you want to highlight in your applications.

1. Achievement

First and foremost, selective colleges are looking for achievement. As you may already know, they're looking for achievement in two categories: (a) academic, and (b) nonacademic (or extracurricular).

Let's start with academic. Colleges are institutions of education, which is why your high school transcript is the single most important item in your admissions portfolio.

Literally. If you're a junior and you're reading this book instead of studying for that chemistry test tomorrow, put this book down and start studying! Your grades and the rigor of your courses are by far the most significant factors in college admissions. If you don't believe me, listen to the Harvard admissions officer who quipped, "A good essay can heal the sick; it can't raise the dead."*

Test scores also function as markers of academic achievement. Not only do admissions committees like to see outside verification of your academic performance, but standardized tests help them compare kids from different high schools in different parts of the country.

It's important to note that America's approach to testing is in the midst of major changes, with the pandemic shifting most schools—at least for now—to test-optional and test-blind admissions. However, many admissions officers still prefer to see test scores, and when you don't submit SAT or ACT scores, AP tests can be an especially important sign of academic achievement.

The second type of achievement—extracurricular—is often used to differentiate students with solid grades and test scores. If your transcript gets you in the door, what you do outside the classroom will help move you to the top of the pile.

Typically, selective colleges are looking for some mixture of depth and breadth. As most high schoolers know, your activity list (along with your résumé if a college requests it) is an important way of showing your achievement, especially if you can list leadership positions, awards, and other such factors. All of those are concrete examples of what some admissions officers call "demonstrated excellence."

How will this affect your essays? Obviously, a lot of your achievement will be documented in the other parts of your application, so there's no need to rehash it in the essays. Don't waste valuable essay space on things that are already listed elsewhere! Instead, when it comes to achievement, use your essays to do two things:

---

*Or believe national surveys of four-year colleges in 2019 and 2023 by the National Association for College Admission Counseling, which found that—both years—the top three factors in admissions decisions for incoming freshmen were: grades in college prep courses, grades in all courses, and strength of high school curriculum.

1. **Craft a narrative.** Many students applying to selective schools have a lot of achievements, especially extracurricular ones, and it may not be clear to the committee how they fit together. An admissions officer will rightfully ask: "Why is the student doing all these things? Are these activities just padding? Who is the person behind these clubs and titles?" A good essay will help the admissions officer put all the pieces together, one of the most important things you can do in your essays.

2. **Draw attention to achievements that might be overlooked.** For example, being cocaptain of the volleyball team is impressive. But if you also broke your tibia sophomore year and spent six months rehabbing in grueling pain while still keeping your 4.0 average, that's extraordinary. It's the kind of achievement you can talk about in an essay, because it won't be obvious from your list of activities.

Activity: List three achievements from the last three years that meant something to you, whether they seem large or small. How does each relate to your passions and priorities in life?

_____

_____

_____

_____

_____

_____

2. Maturity and Personal Growth

While achievement is obviously a factor in college admissions, some people are surprised to learn just how important maturity and personal growth are. Especially when it comes to your personal essay, they might just be the most important characteristics on this list.

That's because maturity and personal growth are entirely internal; you can't list them on a transcript or résumé. So what are they, and how do you talk about them in a 650-word essay?

Let's start with maturity. That word can mean a lot of things—physical maturity, emotional maturity, and so on—so you want to have a concrete understanding of what colleges are looking for.

When it comes to maturity, colleges are looking for students who, even though they're teenagers, have begun to develop a sense of their own values. Selective schools want to admit young people who have the ability to self-reflect, who can slow down enough to articulate who they are, what they care about, and the impact they want to have on the world.

One thing they're *not* looking for is adults. That's why deeply introspective essays written by well-meaning parents usually bomb: a forty-five-year-old has a *very* different level of maturity than a seventeen-year-old does.

Personal growth, on the other hand, is simply the process of developing maturity. Ideally, that's what happening to you as a teenager: you're growing up physically, emotionally, and mentally.

How can you demonstrate these qualities in an essay? Once again, the best approach is "Show, don't tell." Use your essays to illustrate turning points in your life, moments when something changed in how you see the world, yourself, or others. Have the courage to show a younger version of yourself being immature—and then show how you grew up. That difficult thing you went through last year: How did it change you? Are there things you believe or value now that you didn't even care about freshman year? More broadly, how have you grown and developed as a person over the last three years?

Most of us don't go around thinking about these questions, so your first instinct might be that you don't have anything to say. If that's the case, I urge you to dig deeper. Adolescence is a time of huge change, so I can guarantee that you have grown and changed over the last few years. Taking the time to slow down and reflect on that growth is, for many students, one of the most rewarding parts of the college essay process. It also makes for great essays.

Activity: How have you matured since freshman year of high school? What do you care about now that you didn't care about then? Do you see the world differently? What events, people, or ideas caused these changes?

_____

_____

_____

_____

_____

_____

3. Community Engagement

Will she contribute something, somewhere, somehow?

—Harvard College Office of Admissions and
Financial Aid, *Interviewer Handbook*

In addition to achievement and maturity/personal growth, another key quality colleges are looking for is community engagement.

To understand why engagement matters, think of the process from an admissions officer's perspective. They hold the keys to a garden filled with incredible opportunities: classes, research facilities, clubs, athletic teams, brilliant professors, and more. It's far more than any one person could take advantage of in just four years—or in a lifetime, for that matter.

Those opportunities are a limited resource, however, because there are a finite number of spots in each class. So in a very real way, each admissions officer is a gatekeeper. Their job is to admit students who will take advantage of the incredible resources their school has to offer, and a key question they're asking is: **"What will this person contribute to our community?"**

Community engagement is a great way for an admissions officer to assess this. As with achievement, past results can be an indicator of future performance. If you have great grades but sat in your bedroom playing Fortnite for the last four years, it stands to reason that you might do the same in college. Do you think Stanford wants to admit people who never leave the dorm? No! They want students who will go outside and get involved in campus life.

Although engagement will certainly show up in your activity list, your essays can help you highlight the ways you've engaged with the world around you that matter most. In fact, you can use any of your essays to tell the story behind one or more of your more important commitments.

As with achievement, you can use the essays to craft a broader narrative. All the different things that you do—what holds them together? Whether it's a unique passion or curiosity or a commitment to social justice, what motivates you to step outside and get involved? If you can answer those questions, you'll take a huge step forward toward defining yourself in the admissions officer's imagination.

Activity: Name one or two communities that are important to you. Think broadly; a community could be your school, family, team, neighborhood, religious organization, or any other group of people. How have you engaged with this community over the past few years?

_____

_____

_____

_____

_____

_____

4. Passion

The next few traits, beginning with passion, may be a bit less obvious than the first three. They also contradict the popular myth that the top colleges are looking for overachieving, high-testing robots.

How to Talk About Passion

I first realized how much I had to learn about passion about fifteen years ago, when I was living in San Francisco and feeling lost in my career.

One night I went out with some friends and met a guitar player who, like me, was passionate about music. At some point during our conversation, he surprised me by asking, seemingly out of the blue, "Wow you really like opera, don't you?"

What? How did he know that?

"What do you mean?" I asked.

"Well," he responded, "you just mentioned opera and your eyes lit up."

Though we may not always recognize our own passions, others can usually identify them because **the things you are passionate about are the things that make your eyes light up.**

Colleges are looking for people who know what they're passionate about and who *pursue those passions*. In part that's because exploring one's passions is what the liberal arts experience is all about: finding your interests and digging in, learning more about them, debating and growing and understanding. Admissions officers like to see students who have started this process in their own lives and want to keep going.

Passion, of course, is not completely separate from achievement and engagement. Colleges want people who have passions that they go out and pursue through courses, clubs, volunteering, teams, and more. In the admissions process, as in life, few things are more impressive than someone who has found their passion and is committed to pursuing it.

As you might guess, once we start talking about passion, we are in territory where your essays are crucial. It's nearly impossible to demonstrate passion through lists and numbers alone; your essays are the ideal place to talk about your passions. What are they? Where did they come from? And most important, what have you done to pursue them?

A word to the wise, however: don't overuse the phrase "My passion is _____." In the words of one Ivy League admissions officer, the word "passion" can sometimes become "so cliché as to be almost meaningless."

Instead, follow the classic writing advice "Show, don't tell." Use your words to describe how you explore and pursue your passions, creating a specific feeling for your reader: that spark you feel when someone's eyes light up because they're excited about something, whether it's opera, football, or test tubes. If your essays can do that, they will get an admissions officer excited about you and your candidacy.

> **Activity:** What are the two or three pursuits, causes, or ideas you're most passionate about? What makes your eyes light up? How have you pursued those passions, inside or outside school?
>
> _____
>
> _____
>
> _____
>
> _____
>
> _____
>
> _____

5. Intellectual Curiosity

Like passion, intellectual curiosity is one of the softer qualities that admissions officers are looking for.

Let's be clear: "soft" doesn't imply easy. In the words of Jeremy Hunter, a professor at Claremont Graduate University, "There are hard skills, and then there are the hardest skills." Demonstrating intellectual curiosity in your essays is challenging, which is one reason why essays that do it well often rise to the top.

Intellectual curiosity is a genuine interest in ideas and learning. Why is this important? Remember that colleges are academies: centers of learning, study, and knowledge. In many cases they exist primarily to further human knowledge—Yale's motto, "Lux et Veritas," means "Light and Truth"—and the university is looking for students who value the life of the mind.

Intellectual curiosity is a quality that becomes increasingly important as you move up the ladder in terms of college prestige and selectivity, which makes sense, when you think about it, because the best universities are global centers of scholarship. They want students who care deeply about the life of the mind.

Like passion, intellectual curiosity can be hard to quantify. Aside from your interview, your essays may be the only place you can demonstrate it in your application.

How can you do this? By writing essays that show what you're curious about! If you have achievements that demonstrate intellectual curiosity, highlight them. For example: What ideas from authors or about scientific theories are so fascinating that you've written papers about them, done research on them, or taken summer classes to investigate them?

Just as important, you can let the committee inside your unique thinking process, showing them how your mind works. Lots of people love Shakespeare. If you do, too, why? What is it that interests you about Amy Tan, Malcolm X, or Rosalind Franklin (the female scientist who was key to discovering the structure of DNA)? When you approach a math or physics problem or start building a robot, what exactly is it that gets you excited and helps you overcome the fear of the unknown? Colleges want people who can answer these questions.

Activity: What ideas or topics ignite your intellectual curiosity? What are your favorite classes, and what topics have you most enjoyed? Have you ever done a research project about something that you couldn't wait to learn more about?

_____

_____

_____

_____

_____

_____

6. Creativity

Many of us approach college essays with the idea that they are supposed to be "creative." We all have different ideas of what creativity is in our writing. For some, it means being shocking, witty, or even cloying.

While flashy writing can get an admissions officer's attention, it's not necessarily going to help you get admitted, because flash and cuteness are not typically desired qualities in college admissions.

Creativity in a deeper sense, however, is a quality that schools—and liberal arts colleges in particular—value, foster, and seek out in applicants.

For our purposes, creativity means imagination: the ability to come up with new ideas. Happily, all of us are creative. If you are a painter, you'll demonstrate creativity through your art. Athletes use creativity to win games and navigate team dynamics, scholars show creativity in their research, and leaders of every stripe need creativity to motivate others toward common goals. Showing your creativity in your essays will help show readers who you are.

For example, if you're an artist, write about your process. What's it like for you to paint? What do you put into each painting and why? Are you inspired by ideas? Other people? Nature?

If you're an athlete, how have you had to think creatively to win games, interact with your team, and overcome challenges that arise? Success in group settings requires social creativity, which is part of why businesses like to hire former athletes; they tend to be solution oriented and can think on their feet.

The best way to approach creativity in your essays is integrative: show the committee how it relates to your passions and achievements, how it blends with the other qualities on this list.

Activity: Where does creativity show up in your life? This could be at school, in activities, on the sports field, at work, or in activities you pursue in your free time.

_____

_____

_____

_____

_____

_____

7. Leadership

Most selective colleges are looking for students who have demonstrated leadership in one way or another. In fact, most universities see leadership as part of their mission. The University of Michigan's mission statement includes "developing leaders and citizens who will challenge the present and enrich the future," whereas Harvard's is succinct: "The mission of Harvard College is to educate the citizens and citizen-leaders for our society."

Hopefully you will have demonstrated some leadership through clubs and other activities. As you surely know, official roles such as president, captain, and founder are all good ways of showing leadership.

Your essays can be a great place to highlight your leadership qualities, and—even better—to **make a statement about what leadership means to you.** For example, lots of kids have been captains of sports teams. What did being captain or cocaptain of your team mean to you? What were some of the challenges you faced, and how did you overcome them? What kind of leader do you want to be, on your team and in your life?

Just as important, colleges are aware that leadership happens in many different ways. You want to think broadly and creatively here. Maybe you've been a leader academically: being a thought leader in classes, helping other students out when they struggled, or leading in the laboratory. Or, as *Mean Girls* brilliantly illustrated on-screen, social groups have leaders who affect the happiness and well-being of everyone around them. We can be leaders at home, in our extended families, at camps, in religious communities—really, anywhere people come together.

The point is that even if you're not class president, you've probably shown leadership somewhere in your life. If you can highlight that in your essays, colleges will take note.

Activity: What does leadership look like for you? List two or three ways you've been a leader at school, home, work, in your community, at a church/synagogue/mosque/temple, or in any other setting.

_____

_____

_____

_____

_____

_____

---

8. Resilience

Resilience, determination, or "grit" is in some ways a corollary of maturity. Resilience, defined as a "capacity to recover quickly from difficulties," shows up when you bounce back from setbacks, overcome obstacles, persist in the face of challenges, and think creatively to achieve your goals.

Resilience is also closely tied to adversity; not only can you develop resilience *through* adversity, resilience can help you to *overcome* adversity. And although both concepts have long been important in admissions, the 2023 Supreme Court affirmative action ruling shone an even brighter spotlight on them. In fact, immediately after the Court released its opinion, President Joe Biden issued a national call for universities to take adversity into account. Many colleges also introduced new supplemental essay prompts, such as one from Columbia University asking applicants to "describe a barrier or obstacle you have faced and discuss the personal qualities, skills or insights you have developed as a result" that specifically addressed adversity and thus resilience.*

Like maturity, resilience will rarely be visible in your transcript or test scores. Achievements can be the result of determination and grit, but it's your job to show in your essays how you have overcome adversity in your life.

In successful college essays, resilience is often revealed in how you've overcome obstacles. When you started that science experiment and it failed, did you give up? Or did you keep going, revising your hypothesis or trying a different approach? When you were cut from the basketball team, did you quit, or did you start going to the gym and practicing lay-ups every morning?

For students from historically marginalized backgrounds—and for kids for whom a racial, ethnic, gender, or sexual orientation/identity minority status is an important part of their identity—situations in which you overcome societal obstacles can make for powerful essays. They can be great ways of talking about your identity, and for students of color, they can be a compelling way of writing about race in a post–affirmative action world.

---

*So many, in fact, that it represents a new genre of supplemental essay. I call it the "Contributions/Lived Experience" essay, because your task is to discuss how your lived experiences shaped you into the person you are today. You'll find a step-by-step guide to writing these essays in chapter 6, starting on page 149.

When you're writing about resilience, the key is to find a balance between being real about the obstacles you faced (adversity) and showcasing your efforts to overcome them (resilience). Though few admissions officers want to read a sob story, most will be moved by someone who fights to surmount the challenges that life has thrown in their way.

Activity: What are the biggest challenges you've faced over the last few years, both inside and outside of school? How did you overcome them?

_____

_____

_____

_____

_____

_____

9. Empathy

Ten years ago, I would not have described empathy as a top quality admissions officers are looking for. But a lot has changed in this country since 2014. Today, universities are thinking very seriously about their role in fostering a democratic society in which people must listen to, learn from, and understand the views of others.

For the purposes of college admissions, empathy can show up in two ways. The most obvious is by caring about others and responding to their needs. You might show this kind of empathy through volunteering to help those less fortunate than yourself. You could also show it by making time to listen to friends and family members when they're going through difficult times or by fighting for a more just society through protests, fundraising for worthy causes, advocating for new laws, and other forms of activism.

The second type of empathy, which you could call "intellectual empathy," is the ability to tolerate, understand, and learn from points of view that are different from one's own. Many schools are now asking essay questions that specifically address this quality. For example, a recent Brown University essay required students to "Tell us about a time you were challenged by a perspective that differed from your own. How did you respond?"

As the Brown prompt suggests, the best way to show empathy is through a situation in which you displayed it. Maybe it was in the midst of community service, or in a heated class discussion, or in the way you tried to include all perspectives while leading your school's robotics club. All kinds of empathy are important and worth writing about in your essays.

Activity: What have you done to help others—people you know or perhaps people you'll never meet? When and where have you encountered ideas and perspectives different from your own?

_____

_____

_____

_____

_____

_____

10. Fit

When I was doing Harvard alumni interviews, a question I was told to keep in mind was "Is this someone I could see myself having a conversation with in the dining hall?" It's a great question, since so much of undergraduate education takes place in conversation with other students. At Harvard, specifically, most kids are thoughtful, intelligent, and unafraid of sharing their ideas and opinions. It's not a place where wallflowers are going to be happy.

That question gets to the heart of fit, which is one of the most intangible qualities of all. Yet as admissions officers make their final decisions, it can become one of the most important—especially at highly selective schools.

Each college has a unique character—its own personality, if you will. Each school also has a unique set of academic and extracurricular offerings. Colleges are looking for students who understand what they're offering, who want that, and who will integrate well into their communities.

How can you show your fit in your essays? The first step is to do your research. Take time to visit college websites and learn about their academic offerings, their values, and the kind of community they foster. For example, not all Ivies offer the same academic programs. Harvard has a world-class economics program but no undergraduate business major (Harvard Business School is graduate only), whereas Penn has a top undergraduate business program. Yet a former Harvard admissions officer told me, "I can't tell you how many people would apply to Harvard saying that they wanted to study business. We don't do that, go to Penn!"

College visits are also an excellent way to discern fit. I've found that most young people know within ten minutes of stepping onto a campus whether they'd want to go there or not. If you feel that spark when you visit a school, take some time to do your research and articulate exactly *why* you want to go there. If you can show that in your essays, admissions officers will take notice.

Activity: Name one college that you're excited about. What makes that school unique, and why would you be a good fit there? If you can't answer those questions, go online and do twenty minutes of research on the school, then answer them.

_____

_____

_____

_____

_____

_____

It All Adds Up to *Personality*

When you put all ten factors together, what do you end up with? Personality, which is your ultimate goal in the essays: to give the reader a sense of your character.

Your personality is your own unique way of being human in this crazy world. Believe it or not, college admissions officers really do want to see your personality. Every student they admit will possess some subset of these ten qualities—leadership, achievement, community engagement, and so on—but only you will have your own unique way of living them.

Personality is also why ChatGPT, although it can be a useful tool in your journey, is unlikely to write an essay that will help you get into a selective college. AI may be able to churn out paragraphs of grammatically correct prose, but it does not yet have the ability to show something authentic about *your* individual personality.

Focus on telling your story. The more honest and vulnerable you can be in your essays, the more clearly your personality will shine through, the more powerful your application will be, and the more likely it is that you will be admitted.

What About Diversity?

Diversity is a major force in college admissions, so why isn't it on this list? Simply put, diversity plays a different role in the admissions process than these other personal qualities, so you'll need to handle it differently in your writing.

All of the ten qualities listed above are internal, personal characteristics that could be possessed by any human. In any individual, these traits may be affected and shaped by that person's race, gender, sexual orientation, religion, family, and economic status, yet they can also exist independently of those factors.

When talking about diversity in college essays, the challenge is finding a way to discuss your own identity that is relevant to the college application process. The solution: when you write about any aspect of your identity that might add to the diversity of a college community—be it gender, race, ethnicity, sexual identity, religion, economic status, or any other factor—write about it in relationship to these ten qualities.

For example: How has growing up Black in your community affected your approach to leadership? Did it lead to challenges in which you showed resilience? Did realizing that you were gay or trans force you to mature faster than you might have otherwise? In what ways has your sexual or gender identity shaped your ability to empathize with others? How has your Latinx heritage helped you serve the communities that matter most to you?

Although this has long been my advice to students, some details in the 2023 Supreme Court landmark ruling on two cases—*Students for Fair Admissions, Inc. v. President and Fellows of Harvard College* and *Students for Fair Admissions, Inc. v. University of North Carolina*—have made this approach more important than ever. The Harvard decision, often called the "affirmative action ruling," struck down the use of race as a factor in college admissions. In practical terms, that means college admissions officers can no longer use information from race and ethnicity checkboxes to decide who is admitted.

But the decision also specifically allowed colleges to continue taking into account *an applicant's discussion of race*—i.e., writing about it in essays—as long as that discussion directly relates to race-neutral traits such as the ten we've just explored.

Here is the relevant passage from the majority opinion:

> Nothing in this opinion should be construed as prohibiting universities from considering an applicant's discussion of how race affected his or her life, be it through discrimination, inspiration, or otherwise.

In other words, you can still write about race in your essays. But there's a catch:

> A benefit to a student who overcame racial discrimination, for example, must be tied to *that student's* courage and determination. Or a

benefit to a student whose heritage or culture motivated him or her to assume a leadership role or attain a particular goal must be tied to *that student's* unique ability to contribute to the university.

In other words, the Court decided that a "benefit," or a leg up in the admissions process, must be given to you based on your personal qualities, skills, or other ways you, as an individual, would contribute to a college community. (Many colleges then introduced a new supplemental essay that prompts you to do exactly that; you can read more about it in chapter 7, page 149.)

There are many things I don't like about this decision, such as how it places an uncomfortable onus on teenagers of color to explain how complex social forces such as racism have shaped them into the people they are today. That is hard stuff for adults to grapple with, let alone teenagers. Further, I don't think applicants should feel pressured to write about any particular aspect of their identity in order to get into a good school. Instead, everyone—especially young people—should have full power and agency to choose whether they want to discuss their identity (or not), and only around the people with whom they want to share it.

However, this ruling is now the law of the land. The good news is that if you're reading this book, you have the tools to write strong, effective essays regardless of your race, gender, or sexual orientation. When you find ways to relate your identity to these ten factors with honesty and candor, you will write essays that highlight both your identity *and* your personality. When done well, these are often the essays that cause admissions officers to sit back and go, "Wow!"

You Are Better than You Know

As you reflect on these personal qualities, you may be freaking out. "I don't have that one," you say. "I don't have enough achievements or enough leadership or . . ."

Don't worry about that, because the truth is that you do. Sure, if you don't have any activities, your grades are Bs, and you're applying to

Princeton, you're probably not going to get in. But maybe Princeton isn't the best school for you. It's highly competitive, stressful, and full of over-achievers; there's a good chance you'd be happier somewhere else.

What's important is that you *do* have something from each of these categories in your life and that there are going to be a few areas in which you shine. I know this because I've worked with hundreds of students from all walks of life. As we talk through their stories, there's always material there, and it's always more than the student thought they had.

Being a teenager is hard, and by the time you're seventeen you've accumulated enough life experience that you have things to talk about in your essays. Remember that these essays aren't even that long! It's 650 words for the personal essay, then a few hundred words of supplemental essays for each school. At this point in your life, you have something rich to talk about. I promise.

A final tip to keep in mind: as you explore how these qualities play out in your own life, have the courage to be vulnerable. It doesn't matter how many awards and achievements you have; if you aren't able to show some vulnerability and let the committee into the person behind the mask, your essays are never going to sing. It's the hardest thing to do in a process that's constantly asking you to put your best foot forward, yet ironically, it's also the best way to present yourself in a compelling light, show your true personality, and get admitted.

Writing the Essays

CHAPTER 3

Your Plan of Action

"Begin at the beginning," the King said.

—LEWIS CARROLL, *Alice in Wonderland*

So you're ready to dive into your college essays! Where should you begin?

In part, that depends on what month it is. If you have an application due in the next two weeks, write your résumé now (see appendix II for samples), then go directly to chapter 4 and start working on your personal essay. In a "crunch" situation like this, you need to begin writing ASAP. The more revisions you can get through, the better.

If, however, you have more time—relax and congratulate yourself! The process determines the product. The more time and energy you have, the better your essays will be.

YOUR COLLEGE APPLICATION TIMELINE

TIMEFRAME	WHAT TO DO
Junior year: fall semester	• Start brainstorming your college list • Prep for the SAT/ACT
Junior year: spring semester	• Top priority: keep those grades high! • Begin visiting colleges • Take the SAT or ACT • Start researching scholarships, costs, and financial aid • Ask two teachers for recommendations
Summer before senior year	• Create a list of schools you want to apply to, including potential EA/ED schools • Write your résumé • Ask 1 or 2 people to be on your committee • Start writing your essays in mid-July or early August • By Labor Day, complete the Common App personal essay and supplemental essays for one school
Senior year: fall semester	• Finish writing your supplemental essays • Finalize your EA/ED list and RD list • Fill out the FAFSA and CSS Profile • Apply for admission, financial aid, and scholarships!
Senior year: spring semester	• Watch for admissions decisions from schools • Review your offers and pick a school • Relax and enjoy senior spring; just be sure to keep your grades up (a college can rescind its offer if your grades tank!)

When Should I Start Writing?

July and August are good times to begin. The timeline above represents an effective and healthy approach for most students. Not everyone is going to follow it exactly. Don't sweat it if you're a bit ahead or behind at some points. Rather than a do-or-die prescription, this timeline is more of a Platonic ideal that you want to aim for.

One thing you might notice is that I don't recommend starting your essays until the summer before senior year. It's true that some English teachers and counselors tell their students to start writing earlier, e.g., spring of junior year. Though that can be a fine time to review the principles of college essays or to learn skills like the telling one's own story, it's not a very good time to write a college essay, and I find that it rarely produces material of value.

Why is that? If you're on an honors/AP track and aiming for a selective college, junior year will likely be one of the most stressful periods of your life. Though I sincerely wish it were otherwise, that is the reality in the United States right now. Your focus needs to be on making good grades and keeping your sanity as you dive into activities.

That's why junior year is not the best time to do the kind of deep reflection and introspection that a good college essay process requires. Just as important, a lot of maturing happens during junior year. For most teens, the summer that follows is a time to reflect on and process—mentally, emotionally, and spiritually—the personal growth that's just happened, as well as the reality that they're one year away from leaving their home and family of origin (that's big stuff!).

In addition, many students have a transformative experience the summer between junior and senior year—maybe at a camp, maybe as part of a research project, maybe on a trip or in conversations with family—that helps frame where they want to go to college and why. College visits during the summer can also help students focus their desires and make their aspirations more concrete.

Taken together, these factors combine to give you a sense of purpose, direction, and maturity that will result in better essays. That's why I find that mid-July and early August are the perfect times to start on these essays. You've had time to recover from the stress of junior year, hopefully you've done something fun and rewarding and interesting in the first half of the summer, and by now you have both the bandwidth and the energy to really devote yourself to a process that will involve self-reflection, introspection, and hard work.

A Few Words on Your College List

This may be a college essay guidebook, but ideally the process of writing yourself in begins well before you start typing your personal statement.

You probably already know that when you apply to selective colleges, you should apply to a range of schools: reach schools (less than 25% chance of admission), target schools (25 to 75% chance of admission), and likely or "safety" schools (greater than 75% chance admission).* You may also know that it's wise to apply to twelve to fifteen colleges, roughly an equal mix of reach, target, and safety. That list of twelve to fifteen schools is your college list, and it's worth investing some time and energy in it.

Most teens (understandably) tend to focus on their dream schools, which are usually in the reach category. Yet college admissions have become so competitive and unpredictable that it's crucial to think just as carefully about your target and likely schools.

That's why I recommend starting your college application process by identifying what *you* want in a college. If you read chapter 2, you already know what colleges are looking for; now it's time to flesh out the other half of the equation. Once you can articulate your own goals and priorities—be they academic, extracurricular, geographic, social, or something else entirely—you'll be able to find a wide range of schools where you could flourish.

So before beginning your essays, turn to appendix I (page 263), where you'll find a short writing activity designed to help you figure out what you want in your college experience. That appendix also includes tips on finding schools to fill out your list, including ChatGPT-based strategies. Though AI is not yet good at writing admissions essays, it can be a useful tool in your search for schools!

---

*Keep in mind that those numbers refer not to a school's overall acceptance rate but to *your individual chances of getting in*. For example, if a school has a 40% chance of admission but your grades place you well below the average GPA of admitted students, it's not a target for you. It's a reach.

Begin with Your Résumé and the Personal Essay

Follow the correct order of categories.

—Marie Kondo

I'm a *huge* fan of the tidying expert Marie Kondo. Her disciplined yet humane approach to tidying—she's been described as a "warrior princess in the war on clutter"—has attracted millions of followers and has some useful lessons for writing college essays.

Instead of quick fixes, Kondo emphasizes the importance of doing things in the "correct order." For her, that means an order that maximizes efficiency, sets you up for success, and helps you do your best work. When cleaning out your house, for example, she has you start with books, which are relatively easy to sort and dispose of, before moving on to things that are harder to part with, like clothes, photographs, and mementoes.

There's a correct order to writing your college essays, too. I recommend that students follow this one:

1. Your résumé
2. The personal essay
3. Supplemental essays for your first school
4. Supplemental essays for your remaining schools, one at a time

Why is this the correct order?

To start with, putting together a résumé is both useful and less daunting than starting with an essay. At minimum, your résumé should list all activities you've done since ninth grade, both during the school year and in the summer. It should include the years you did those activities, any leadership roles you held, and any honors and awards you've earned. Many students choose to include their junior and senior year coursework and test scores as well; the typical résumé is two to three pages long. (There are two sample résumés in appendix II, as well as tips on putting together your résumé and activities list. Refer to those to get started.)

Setting down all your activities and honors on one page will give you a clear overview of everything you did in high school and will also jog your memory about things you may have forgotten. (Wait, didn't I do chess club in ninth grade? And I was band treasurer in tenth grade, right?) Though you won't need to submit a résumé to every college, you will find yourself referring to it throughout the process—so do it first!

Next, the essays. We start with the personal essay because, as you learned in chapter 2, your application is a portfolio: a collection of materials (transcripts, test scores, essays, recommendations) that work together to paint a picture of you.

The personal essay is the keystone of that portfolio. It's the first place admissions officers will turn to get a sense of who you are as a person; the human behind the numbers. It's also one element that will appear in nearly every application you submit. Your portfolio will be strongest if you start at the center with your personal essay, getting it in solid shape before you move on.

The supplemental essays come last, and it's important that you approach them one school at a time. There are two reasons for this. One is that you can often reuse or adapt material you've written for one school to another school, because many of the prompts are quite similar. It's common, for example, for schools to ask for a short essay about an activity you did in high school. It's absolutely fine to write one essay and reuse or adapt it for other schools.

The other reason is that if you start working on too many schools at once, it's easy to become confused about what you've written about for one school versus another. For example, the most common supplemental essay is the Why Our School essay, which requires you to do some research about what a school offers and why it's right for you. I've seen students try to research two or three schools at once and quickly get confused and overwhelmed. Your mind works much better—and the process will be much more peaceful—if you take the schools one at a time.

Form Your Own Committee

Feedback will make your essays better. Given that your essays will ultimately be read and evaluated by a committee, one of the most empowering things you can do early on is to put together a committee of your own: one or two people who will help you write and revise your essays.

Look for an adult who is college educated and who writes well. That could be an English teacher, counselor, relative, or family friend. Whenever possible, find someone other than your parent or guardian; ideally you will want your parents to read your essays *after* you've finished writing them. But if you don't have other options, a parent or guardian can work fine. So can an older sibling or a friend who's already in college.

Approach this person early in the process, ideally before you start writing, and ask for their help. Explain to them that you'll be working on your college essays and you'd like some feedback as you revise. Most people will be flattered that you're asking for help with such an important piece of your life, and if they have time to help you, they'll probably say yes.

Thank them. And make sure that when you ask for their feedback in the coming weeks and months, you give them enough time to read your essays and respond, ideally a few days. "Can you read this tonight and get back to me?" is unlikely to get you the best feedback, and it's not respectful of the other person's time.

You might also consider asking them to read this book. The more they understand about college essays, the more help they'll be able to offer!

Your Parents and the College Admissions Process

The college application process tends to stir up emotions. It is, after all, a big part of one of the biggest transitions in your life, from childhood to adulthood.

It will be emotional for you, and it's likely to be highly emotional for your parents or guardians as well. Even the best-adjusted, most supportive parents will be going through tons of new feelings as their "baby" prepares to leave the nest and move toward independence.

As much as you can, try to cut your parents some slack. Remember that they are people, too, and expect their fears and anxieties to be brought to the surface. At the same time, be honest and clear with them about your need for independence and space in the process. In the end, these are *your* essays. You—not your parents—will ultimately be attending college next year.

Your Secret Formula: FATP (Form, Audience, Topic, Purpose)

Back when I was in high school and cavemen roamed the earth, my English teacher taught me a powerful framework that I still use to this day. I've used it to write plays, books, musicals, newspaper articles, and blog posts. And in the past ten years, I've seen scores of students use it to get into the college of their choice.

Here are its four components:

- Form
- Audience
- Topic
- Purpose

You'll see these four components throughout the rest of the book. So let's break them down one at a time and see how they apply to your college essays.

1. Form

This one is straightforward, because the form of college essays is clear, simple, and standardized.

First, you will need to write one personal essay of 650 words or less. You may sometimes see this personal essay called the "Common App Essay" because the prompts and format come from the Common Application, a portal for submitting applications online. (The Coalition for College Access, the other main online portal, also asks for a personal essay; most students write one essay and use it for both.)

Second, some schools will ask you to write supplemental essays, ranging from 50 to more than 600 words in length. Some of those essays will be argumentative, i.e., you will need to use evidence to make a case for why a certain school is a good fit for you. Other supplemental essays will be more personal and reflective, like the personal essay.

2. Audience

Your audience is a college admissions committee. It is not your parents, friends, English teacher, or college counselors. Although these people may read your essays and will certainly have opinions on them, they are not your ultimate audience.

Understanding your audience is one of the keys to writing successful essays. Fortunately, if you've read the previous two chapters, you are now an expert on who your audience is and what they are looking for!

3. Topic

When it comes to your college essays, topic is the area where you have the most control. In fact, in many of the essays you can write about almost anything you want.

This freedom means that a lot of care and worry generally goes into figuring out *what* to write about. So the following chapters contain strategies and activities to generate topics that will help you achieve item four: your purpose.

4. Purpose

The purpose of these essays is to get you admitted to college.

It's important to keep that in mind, because it's very easy for other purposes to creep in—especially because our society has so many preconceptions about college essays and what they should or shouldn't be.

For example, some people believe that they should sum up their entire lives in one essay, which is impossible. Others want to write an essay that will make their parents proud or impress their English teacher or college counselor. Still others think that the goal is to make a bold, creative, even shocking impression on their reader, or maybe to use their essays as a forum to make a commentary on the college admissions process itself.

College admissions committees do not want to see any of that. To be clear: while the admissions process can be difficult, even soul-sucking, critiquing it in your essays is unlikely to convince an admissions officer to let you in. Most admissions officers are professional educators who are heavily invested in the college admissions process; their salaries depend on their participation in it. And as you now know, they're looking for specific qualities in these essays.

Several years ago, I had a student whose parents were going through a difficult divorce while he was applying to college. I had a lot of empathy for him, but unfortunately, he decided early on to use his college essays to work through his anger at his parents.

From a psychological point of view, it was admirable that he used writing to process difficult emotions. But it got in the way of his college application process. He had lost sight of the essays' purpose. This student wrote draft after draft of intensely personal, introspective, diary-type material that no one on an admissions committee would ever want to read.

Happily, once he had worked through those feelings, he was able to refocus on the task at hand and write great essays that got him admitted Early Action to several excellent schools.

So keep this in mind: although creativity is encouraged and even necessary, **this is not a creative writing exercise.** These essays will be used in specific ways, by professionals, as part of a decision-making process.

In the end you have one goal in writing your essays, which is to get admitted to a school where you will flourish.

What to Do Next: Résumé, Committee, Essays

If it's spring of junior year or later, now is the time to get started! I suggest that you start thinking about who you will ask to be your committee and that you put together a first draft of your résumé.

Once you're done with those tasks, it will be time to move on to the first essay you will write: the personal essay.

CHAPTER 4

Writing the Common App Personal Essay

Form: 650-word personal essay

Audience: College admissions officers

Topic: A significant moment, interest, or story from your life

Purpose: (1) Show your personal qualities; (2) tell a story that ties your application together

This is it: the big kahuna, the main event, the MOTHER OF ALL ESSAYS! It's the thing your parents and school counselors are talking about when they say "your college essay."

Nearly every high school student has some degree of fear and anxiety around this essay, which is not surprising. The popular mythology, after all, is that in this essay you need to sum up your entire self—everything you've learned and done and grown from and suffered and cried over and achieved in the first seventeen years of your life—in 650 words or less, then send it to a stranger to be read, judged, and evaluated.

Pshew! Just writing that stressed me out.

Fortunately, most of this is malarkey. It simply is not possible to sum up seventeen years of one's life in a two-page essay. However, as you now know, summing up your life is not the goal here. Instead of trying to say *everything*, all you need to do is to tell a story about yourself that highlights the kind of personal qualities that your audience—college admissions officers—is looking for and that shows how you embody them in your own unique, personal way.

Let's break that down a bit and demystify this mysterious essay.

Unpacking the Personal Essay: FATP

> At its heart, the personal essay is a piece of nonfiction writing that shares
> a story for readers that is drawn from the writer's personal experiences.
>
> —Robert Lee Brewer, author and teacher

The **form** of the personal essay is clear and simple: it's a 650-word essay based on personal experience and usually written in a first-person narrative style. Most American colleges—with a few exceptions like the University of California and MIT—require it. The essay length and format come from the Common Application, which is the most widely used platform for undergraduate applications in the country.*

The **audience**, too, is straightforward: the admissions committees of the schools you're applying to. Fortunately, if you've read part I of this book, you are now an expert on what an AdCom is, what they're looking for, and how they will use these essays!

The **topic** of this essay is the trickiest part for most writers, because it's where you're given the least structure. In fact, you have nearly unlimited freedom to write about anything you want—within the bounds of decency and good taste—which, for most people, makes it hard to pick something. That's probably why "What should I write about?" is a big question for most students.

Because of this, the first few exercises in this chapter are devoted to helping you find a topic that works for you. For now, keep in mind that *the topic is not actually the most important part of the essay.* Picking one may seem daunting right now, but the truth is that good—and bad—essays can be written about nearly any topic. Or, in the words of a Yale admissions officer, "The topic matters less than the voice."

Finally, **purpose**. The purpose of this essay is twofold. The obvious and

---

*The other major application platform, the Coalition Application, also requires a 650-word personal essay with similar prompts to the Common App. Since the vast majority of US schools use the Common App, that's what we'll focus on in this chapter, but everything here applies to the Coalition App as well. In fact, you can write one essay and use it for both platforms.

most important purpose is to *show the admissions committee who you are as a person, through story*—to let the committee see who you actually are behind the all the numbers and grades and recommendations and achievements.

The secondary purpose is more subtle: it's to give the committee a narrative that helps them tie your whole application together. The best essays don't just show character; they show character in a way that makes the entire application coherent, smaller parts reflecting a bigger whole.

For example, let's say you have lots of different interests and your résumé reads like a shopping list: chess club, varsity track, band, 4-H, Model United Nations, anime society, and so on. Although selective colleges *are* looking for people with extracurricular engagement, this kind of résumé can risk making you look unfocused.

You might, therefore, choose to focus your personal essay on one particular interest or experience, showing your personal qualities through that. Or you could mention that you have lots of interests, focusing on one while explaining why exploring a diversity of pursuits is important to you. Not only will that make your application look more coherent and focused, it will also show the reader how your interests represent different sides of you and aren't just résumé padding.

So . . . how exactly do you do all of this?

The Writing Process Is Your Friend

Despite all the hype and drama, the reality is that this is an essay just like any other—which means that the best way to write it is the same centuries-old method that has likely been around since ancient Sumerians started carving dashes into stones:

1. Brainstorm
2. Outline
3. Write

Brainstorm, outline, write. I imagine this whole process was lengthier when people were using chisels instead of laptops, although it may have involved more exercise. Fortunately, with today's technology, writing and revising are much easier. And for the purpose of college essays, I'm going to expand this process just a bit, giving you intermediate steps to help you get over the hard parts:

1. Brainstorm
2. Freewrite
3. Outline
4. Write the first draft
5. Revise

Before we do that, however, I want to introduce a core idea to keep in mind for all five stages of this process. More than anything else, it's the key to writing a college essay that will speak to an admissions officer.

Internal Versus External Storytelling

Every good story operates on two levels. There are the things that happen in the outside world, and there are the things that happen inside a character's heart, mind, and soul—usually in response to events in the outside world.

Similarly, the best college essays don't just talk about things that happened; they go a step further and talk about *how* those things affected the writer.

I call this distinction between these two layers—the outer world versus internal psyche—**internal versus external storytelling**. Addressing both of these is the key to writing a college essay that sings.*

For a concrete example, think of the Harry Potter saga. The external story is of a kid with magical abilities who goes to a school for wizards and witches. There, he learns spells, struggles with grades and teachers, makes

---

*For a deeper dive into multiple layers of inner and outer storytelling, check out "The World of a Character" (pages 145–46) in Robert McKee's *Story: Style, Structure, Substance, and the Principles of Screenwriting*. More details on this book in appendix IV.

new friends, and in his spare time battles evil wizards who are trying to take over the world. Ultimately, he and his friends defeat the bad guys.

That's the external story. But what happens internally?

At the beginning, Harry is alone and isolated; he feels unloved. As he starts to make friends, he struggles to trust other people. Internally, he wrestles with constant fears and doubts, wondering whether deep down he is good or evil. Yet by the end of the saga, he's grown and matured. He has more confidence in himself, has learned to trust others. Recognizing how much his parents loved him helps him to move on from the trauma of his parents' death.

That's some pretty heavy stuff for children's novels, right? Yet in the Harry Potter series, as in most good stories, it's the external story that draws us in and keeps us engaged, while the internal story leaves a deep impression in our hearts and minds.

The same is true of your college essays.

For example, that summer you spent at camp or that volunteer work that meant so much to you. What happened to you inside? Why was it so meaningful? Like Harry, how did you learn and grow and change as a person?

These are all questions of the internal story. They are difficult to answer, which is one reason why writing a good college essay is so hard. But I can promise you that the time you invest in answering them will pay off tenfold—both in your essays and in the insights you gain about yourself.

It's this digging deep to find your own, unique internal story and the courage to be vulnerable about it to a stranger that will make your essays shine. It will also leave you feeling good about them, because you'll know that they represent who you truly are.

Now, on to your essays!

Step 1: Brainstorm

Occasionally, someone's first idea for their essay will be what they end up writing about. More often, you'll need to play with some ideas before you find a topic that will really let you "sing."

I recommend you start by doing the following brainstorming exercises. The only requirement is that you *go quickly*. If you stop and think about them too much, you will tie your brain into knots. By working fast, you can bypass your worrying brain and get into the deeper, more instinctual place where the answers are already there, waiting for you.

In fact, I recommend that you don't read these exercises until you're ready to do them. If you're just reading this book for information, skip to the next section and come back when you're ready to dive in.

One last tip: as you're doing the exercises, be sure to **focus on events from your high school years.** Though it can sometimes be effective to use stories from your childhood as introductory material, the strongest personal essays typically center around the writer's high school years. Remember that admissions officers want to know about who you are *now*, not who you were five or ten years ago.

Quieting the Censor

Julia Cameron, a best-selling writer on creativity, uses a powerful metaphor to describe what the brain does whenever we try to come up with new ideas.

According to Cameron, each of us has a strong force inside us that wants to create, to live, to express itself—our creative spirit. We also have another voice in our heads, which she calls "the Censor."

The Censor is a noisy inner critic who is constantly telling us that our ideas aren't good enough, that what we're doing is wrong, or bad, or won't work, etc.

In Cameron's words:

> We are victims of our own internalized perfectionist, a nasty internal and eternal critic, the Censor, who resides in our (left) brain and keeps up a constant stream of subversive remarks that are often disguised as the truth. The Censor says wonderful things like: "You

call that writing? What a joke. You can't even punctuate. If you haven't done it by now you never will. You can't even spell. What makes you think you can be creative?" And on and on.

When the Censor comes up during brainstorming, it can quickly derail the process and trick you into throwing out perfectly good ideas.

To be clear: we don't want to destroy the Censor—or any other part of ourselves, for that matter. Properly channeled, the Censor will become an important ally: your editor. He/she/they will be crucial later in the writing process, when you need to apply a critical lens to your work.

Unfortunately, the human brain does not seem to be designed to create new ideas and edit them at the same time. So it's best to ask the Censor to chill for a bit while you let your creative brain come up with new material. Later, when you need to evaluate and edit, you can invite the Censor to fire up and do its thing.

Finally, keep in mind that while the Censor's self-critical invective can be loud, it's not necessarily correct. As Cameron puts it, "Make this a rule: always remember that your Censor's negative opinions are not the truth."

Before You Begin

Before doing the exercises below, I want you to **write down any ideas you already have for your personal essay.** Don't tell the whole story yet—just make a bulleted list with a few words. The goal is simply to get out any ideas you already have before moving on to new ones.

What if you don't have any ideas yet? Don't worry. Though some people start the process with a topic in mind, many have nothing, zilch, nada. But fear not! That's what the following brainstorming exercises are for.

Brainstorming Exercise 1: Big Turns and Little Turns

Imagine your life as a trail through a lovely forest, starting the day you were born and continuing onward to today. The trail, however, does not follow a straight line. It twists and turns, perhaps to avoid obstacles like mountains and rivers, or maybe to take the scenic route from Point A to Point B.

Looking back over your life's trail, I want you to start remembering two kinds of turning points: big turns and little turns. Big turns are the obvious "big events" in your life: starting at a new school, moving to a new town, joining an activity that became meaningful to you, becoming team captain or winning an award. Big turns are things that other people will probably already know about. Often, they will appear on your résumé.

Little turns, on the other hand, are the more internal, personal moments that others might not know about. Little turns are times when your perspective shifted, you learned something important, or you realized something that would shape the next stage of your life. Maybe it's the car ride home when you suddenly knew you didn't love ballet anymore, or the conversation where you saw, quite clearly, that most of your friendships were shallow, or the moment when you realized that you cared about your family more than anything else in the world. Any of these can be little turns. Often, it's these moments, as well as the actions you take in response to them, that most clearly show who you are.

For this activity, you will visually represent—not list—your big turns and little turns. You could do this through a collage: find an image of a trail or forest that appeals to you, then find images that visually represent your big turns and little turns. Or if you like to draw, paint, or sketch, you can create a path of your own design (Hiking trail? River? Yellow brick road?) and find images that represent each big turn and little turn.

Either way, the important part of this activity is to work with images, not words. Don't worry—you'll be using *lots* of words later, when you start writing! But many of our deepest memories are encoded in sight, smell, and touch. For some, this kind of activity can be the fastest way to access those depths.

Take enough time on your collage, drawing, or painting to create something you're proud of, something that feels like you. Aim for around ten to twelve turns total, approximately equal parts big and little turns. You'll want most of the turns to be from your high school years—the time period your essays will focus on—although it's fine to have a few from your childhood.

Big Turns and Little Turns Activity

1. Create a visual representation of ten to twelve turning points, about equally divided between big and little turns:
   - Big turns: obvious big moments in your life
   - Little turns: smaller moments that were important to you but that other people aren't likely to know about
2. Most turns should be from your high school years; a few can be from before.

Once you're done, look at your work—especially the little turns. They can often make the best essay topics. Are there three or four that you might want to write about? If so, you can move on to the final "Grab Bag" exercise (page 76).

Or maybe this exercise didn't resonate with you. If so, here's a brainstorming activity that will access a different side of your creative mind.

Brainstorming Exercise 2: Five Words

Imagine that you're about to meet an admissions officer from your favorite college. They are a friendly adult in their twenties or thirties who loves learning and is just as excited about their school as you are.

If you had to pick five words to describe yourself as a person, what would those words be?

Write down the first five words that come to mind. Don't worry, you can change them later if you want.

1. _____
2. _____
3. _____
4. _____
5. _____

If you get stuck, below is a list of sample character traits. None of them is any better than others, so don't try to figure out the "best" ones. Instead, use the words that feel most real and honest to you. Remember that this list is *not* exhaustive; feel free to use terms that aren't on it.

A RANGE OF PERSONAL TRAITS

Adventurous	Focused	Meticulous
Athletic	Friendly	Optimistic
Artistic	Funny	Organized
Caring	Generous	Passionate
Committed	Hardworking	Persistent
Compassionate	Honest	People person
Connector	Humble	Practical
Courageous	Humorous	Principled
Creative	Imaginative	Questioning
Curious	Inquisitive	Rational
Dedicated	Inspired	Reliable
Disciplined	Instinctive	Resourceful
Driven	Intelligent	Self-reliant
Efficient	Introspective	Sensitive
Energetic	Introverted	Serious
Enthusiastic	Just	Social
Environmentalist	Kind	Solid
Expressive	Leader	Steady
Extroverted	Logical	Warm
Fair	Loyal	

Got your five words down? Great! Now on to the second part: **for each word, list a couple of stories from your life that show that quality in action.** For example, if two of your words are "creative" and "curious," start by thinking of two or three stories that *show* you being creative. Maybe it's the time you wrote a song, started a club, or painted a mural. Then move on to "curious": How have you expressed your curiosity? Perhaps through a research project, through the way you approach reading, or in the mindset you bring to tutoring middle schoolers. And so on through the list.

Be brief. Use bullet points: "Song I wrote," "Student government," "That time I got lost in the woods." Your goal is to end up with something like:

Word 1: _____

   a. Story 1: _____

   b. Story 2: _____

Word 2: _____

   a. Story 1: _____

   b. Story 2: _____

Word 3: _____
    a. Story 1: _____
    b. Story 2: _____
Word 4: _____
    a. Story 1: _____
    b. Story 2: _____
Word 5: _____
    a. Story 1: _____
    b. Story 2: _____

Once you've finished your list, sit back and take a look. Do you have at least three or four topics that look promising? If so, feel free move on to the final brainstorming exercise, "Grab Bag" (page 76)—unless you still feel as though you need some more ideas, in which case you can try . . .

Brainstorming Exercise 3: Bullet the Prompts

> Prompts are not topics. They are simply questions designed to spark thinking.
>
> —Common App

As you may already know, the Common Application gives you a list of prompts for the main essay. Lots of students get hung up on these prompts, so it's important to understand their raison d'être.

The prompts are there to give you something to write about. More specifically, they're designed to steer you toward crafting essays that reveal how you personally embody the qualities that colleges are looking for: passion, intellectual curiosity, maturity, achievements, and so on.

Think of the prompts, therefore, as a starting point. You can write about literally anything you want, which is why the final prompt is "Share an essay on any topic of your choice." In fact, some admissions officers don't even check to see the prompt you selected! They just ignore it and read your essay.

When writing your essay, don't worry about which prompt you should answer. Instead, find stories from your life that highlight the qualities admissions committees are looking for. Later on, you can figure out which prompt is most relevant to your story and choose it—or just pick the final "grab bag" prompt.

Instead, use the prompts to help you brainstorm. **For each prompt, list two to three stories from your life you could write about.**

As in the first activity, don't write out the whole story. A bullet and a few words are fine. If you can't come up with anything for a particular prompt, don't sweat it. Simply move on to the next one. In this as in any other brainstorming activity, the trick is to keep going.

Note that some of your stories from the previous activities may come up again here. If so, write them down! This is not a problem. **In fact, when a topic comes up multiple times, it's often a sign that it's worth writing about.**

Below are the Common App prompts for 2024–2025. They change periodically—prompt 4 on gratitude was a new addition in 2021—and you can find the latest prompts on the Common App website, www.commonapp.org.

Common App Personal Essay Prompts, 2024–2025 Admissions Cycle

1. Some students have a background, identity, interest, or talent so meaningful they believe their application would be incomplete without it. If this sounds like you, please share your story.

2. The lessons we take from obstacles we encounter can be fundamental to later success. Recount a time when you faced a challenge, setback, or failure. How did it affect you, and what did you learn from the experience?

3. Reflect on a time when you questioned or challenged a belief or idea. What prompted your thinking? What was the outcome?

4. Reflect on something that someone has done for you that has made you happy or thankful in a surprising way. How has this gratitude affected or motivated you?

5. Discuss an accomplishment, event, or realization that sparked a period of personal growth and a new understanding of yourself or others.

6. Describe a topic, idea, or concept you find so engaging that it makes you lose all track of time. Why does it captivate you? What or who do you turn to when you want to learn more?

7. Share an essay on any topic of your choice. It can be one you've already written, one that responds to a different prompt, or one of your own design.

As in the first exercise, you want to end up with something like this:

Prompt 1 _____

   a. Story 1: _____

   b. Story 2: _____

Prompt 2 _____

   a. Story 1: _____

   b. Story 2: _____

Prompt 3 _____

   a. Story 1: _____

   b. Story 2: _____

Prompt 4 _____

   a. Story 1: _____

   b. Story 2: _____

Prompt 5 _____

   a. Story 1: _____

   b. Story 2: _____

Prompt 6 _____

   a. Story 1: _____

   b. Story 2: _____

Brainstorming Exercise 4: Ask ChatGPT for Help

Although you don't want AI to write your essays for you, it can be a useful conversation partner for brainstorming.

The trick here is coming up with good prompts. If you ask ChatGPT a generic question, you'll get information that may or may not be accurate, but definitely will *not* be personal. For example, typing "What's a good college essay topic?" could give you some solid themes such as "Self-Reflection," "Turning Point," and "Passions and Interests." But you won't get guidance on what *you* might actually write about. Instead, the key is to give the AI enough information to come up with essay topics that will be relevant to you, personally. Here are a few ways you can do this.

Playing with AI: Prompts for Brainstorming

- List several of your activities and interests, then ask ChatGPT to suggest ideas for college essays. For example, "I live in Texas, play the trombone, want to major in bioengineering, and love to do watercolor painting. Please suggest some topics for a college essay."
- Paste in your activities list and ask AI to suggest essay topics.
- Paste in your résumé and ask ChatGPT to come up with some essay topics (this has led to some of the most interesting AI-generated suggestions I've seen).
- Describe your college or career goals and ask ChatGPT to suggest some essay topics. For example, "I will be a first-generation college student, and I want to be a doctor who gives back to my community. What are some potential college essay topics?"

As my students and I experimented with ChatGPT over the past year, we found that the results varied. Sometimes it suggested great topics; others were duds. Also, the precise phrasing of the prompts mattered. Questions such as "What should I write about for my college essay?" might prompt ChatGPT to give you a full essay outline, but those outlines tended to be overly simplistic and not particularly useful. However, prompts like "What are some potential college essay topics?" generated interesting ideas. As with everything else AI related, the technology is rapidly evolving, so play with it!

Final Brainstorming Exercise: Grab Bag

If you're like most people, working through these exercises will stir up some memories. Sometimes ideas come up that don't fit neatly into one of the previous activities. This is your chance to write them down. For your final brainstorming exercise, simply answer the following questions:

1. **Are there any additional essay topics that have come to mind?** If so, write them down.
2. **Is there anything particularly meaningful or memorable that happened during your school years?** If it hasn't shown up in one of the previous exercises, write it down.
3. **Is there any time in the past three years when you did something out of the ordinary?** This could include starting a new organization, doing an independent research project, or giving back to your community in some extraordinary way. If so, write it down.

A note on number 3: for our purposes, "out of the ordinary" means atypical for a student at your high school. For example, though the week you spent volunteering in a village in Tanzania may have been meaningful to you personally, it's not likely to be a good college essay topic because many people applying to top schools have done overseas service trips. However, if that week inspired you to take the initiative to start a new service group or club in your hometown, that could be fantastic. Colleges love students who have gone above and beyond to pursue a passion, impacting their community in positive ways.

Your grab bag list may be long or short. Either is fine.

Finishing Brainstorming

Congratulations! You have just taken the first step toward an excellent personal essay.

By now, you will probably have a range of story ideas you can use. There is a very small subset of students (less than 1% in my experience) for whom these exercises simply don't work. If you find yourself completely stuck, turn to appendix I, where you'll find some additional "emergency backup" brainstorming exercises.

However, if these exercises have given you some possible topics, let's move on. You don't want to get caught up in endless brainstorming—or worse, use it as an excuse to avoid writing! It's time for the next stage: freewriting.

Step 2: Freewrite

Now that you have some potential topics, the next step is to start writing. Many people get stuck at this stage, often putting it off for weeks, because they have this idea that they must go from topic to perfectly polished essay.

Reality check: that is impossible. No one, not even Hemingway, can do that. Instead, the next step is to **pick three or four topics from the brainstorming exercises, and freewrite a few paragraphs about each.**

Keep these freewrites short, but not too short. Aim for around a half page, single spaced, per topic—no more than a page. And make sure each freewrite has a beginning, a middle, and an end.

As with brainstorming, it's important to freewrite quickly. It should take no more than two hours in total to write all of your freewrites, ideally less.

What Makes a Good Story?

Most of my career has revolved around telling stories, whether onstage in plays and musicals, on the page in articles and books, or by helping young people tell their stories in college essays. Over time, I've come to believe that there are very few hard and fast "rules" for storytelling. But here is one of them:

Stories have a beginning, a middle, and an end.

To see this in action, think of *The Lord of the Rings* trilogy. At the beginning, Frodo is a hobbit living happily in the Shire. In the middle, he makes new friends and travels to Mordor. At the end (spoiler alert!) he destroys the Ring, returns home, then sails off with the elves.

Of course, many, *many* other things happen in these books. You could look at Frodo's adventures as hundreds—if not thousands—of micro-stories, each with its own beginning, middle, and end. That's why J.R.R. Tolkien is considered a master storyteller: he was able to weave all those stories together into a coherent whole.

Making sense of stories from your own life can be confusing. That's why I recommend you keep things simple: make sure each story has a beginning, a middle, and an end. Not only will it help you organize your ideas, it helps you present them in ways other people can understand them.

By the way, if this seems like a lot of writing now, keep in mind that nothing you create in this process is wasted. Stories that you don't end up using in your personal essay can become the foundation for shorter supplemental essays about your activities, community, and experiences that you'll write later on.

After You Freewrite, Pick a Topic

Once you've completed the freewrites, your next step is to **share them with your committee, i.e., one or two trusted adults or friends.** Send the person the material you've written. Instead of asking "Do you like this?" ask them these questions:

1. Is the freewrite engaging (or potentially engaging)?
2. Does it show who I am as a person?

Whenever possible, get their feedback in person or via phone/Zoom, not by text or email. Listen to what they say, and recall what it felt like to do the writing. Did you feel bored or disinterested as you wrote? If so, your reader will probably feel the same way when they read it. If, however, you felt that you actually wanted to tell the story, it might be a topic worth writing about.

Picking a Topic

Remember the maxim from a Yale admissions officer: "The topic matters less than the voice." The topic you pick should be the one that you will ultimately write the best essay about: an essay that feels like "you," shows your authentic personality, and highlights the personal characteristics that admissions officers want to see.

Although some teens write excellent essays about major, obvious turning points ("big turns"), others have shared that their "Aha!" moment came when they realized that the essay didn't have to be about something big or even about the "right" thing. Instead, they found that when they stopped trying to tell a grand narrative and started writing about small, specific things in their lives, their essays suddenly ended up saying a lot more about them.

With that in mind, here's a checklist to help you evaluate and select a topic for your personal essay.

- ☐ **Are you excited to write about it?** If you find yourself looking forward to telling a particular story, that's a sign it could lead to a strong essay.
- ☐ **Will this story show some of the Top Ten personal qualities in action?** You don't need (or want) to cram all of them in, but a couple of the Top Ten qualities should be reflected in the essay. Note that "in action" means you're not simply pontificating on the meaning of resilience or leadership; you're showing yourself in the process of learning what that quality looks like for you, or you're putting that quality to work in your life.

- ☐ **Is there a focus?** Every compelling personal essay has one central theme, idea, topic, or question that ties it together. Usually, the external story focuses on one or two events in the writer's life. If you want to write about a longer time period, make sure there's a single, strong theme connecting the various events.

- ☐ **Is there change from the beginning of the story to the end?** Remember the one hard-and-fast rule of storytelling: something must change, internally and/or externally.

- ☐ **Is there the potential for a strong internal story?** You may not yet know exactly what your internal story is; that's fine. Most people don't fully uncover theirs until the second or third draft. But in your gut, does the topic feel meaningful to you? If you choose a topic simply because you think it will impress admissions officers, it's unlikely to have a strong internal story.

- ☐ **Does it show personal growth and maturity?** This is the one quality that's key to nearly every good personal essay.

- ☐ **Does it show who I am at age seventeen (or eighteen or however old you are right now)?** The strongest essays usually revolve around the writer's high school years. If you choose to highlight events from your childhood, make sure it's clear to the reader how they shaped you into the person you are today. The admissions committee wants to understand who you are now, not who you were in elementary or middle school.

As you review your freewrites, ask yourself: What are the topics that show me at my best? Do any of these topics show me pursuing things that I'm passionate about, overcoming obstacles, and/or making a difference? Are there stories where my values, the things I care most deeply about, shine through?

If you go through these steps, one or two topics will usually emerge as potential candidates for a 650-word personal essay. When that happens, congratulate yourself! It's time to move on to step 3, which is outlining.

If no topic seems promising yet, that's okay. You have two choices.

One is to go back to your brainstorming exercises and either pick another topic or try a brainstorming exercise you haven't done yet. That's part of why you brainstormed more topics than you will actually need: so you'll have options.

The other is to see if something else comes to mind. Sleep on it for a night. Maybe the act of freewriting will have stirred the pot and you'll wake up with an idea for a new topic, something you didn't think about before. I've seen this happen more often than you might guess.

Conversely, what if you have two or more topics that seem great? Simply follow your gut and pick one. Once you start moving through the next two steps, you'll figure out pretty quickly if your idea is working or not. If not, you're in luck because you have another option to go back to.

As with every step of this process, it's important not to dither too long in search of the "perfect" topic. Though some topics are better than others, there is no one "right" topic. Rather, the quality of your essay will be determined by what you make of the story and how clearly your voice shines through. The "right" topic is the one that you're ultimately able to write a strong essay about, an essay in which your voice and personality shine through.

Congratulations! Freewrite in hand, you're ready to move onto the next step: outlining.

Should I Write About Mental Health Struggles in My Essays?

This is a difficult but important question. In recent years, especially since the pandemic, I've heard more and more students asking about whether they should bring up mental health issues in their essays.

There is a reason they're asking: America is in the midst of a teen mental health crisis. A recent Centers for Disease Control and Prevention (CDC) study showed a whopping 42% of US high school students reporting "persistent feelings of sadness or hopelessness," while 22% had seriously considered suicide that year. Mental health is a big deal, and it affects us all.

Full disclosure: This is a topic that's personal to me. Throughout my life I've had my own ups and downs with mental health, including anxiety, depression, trauma, and PTSD. I've also worked with many students who were going through their own struggles.

Generally, I recommend writing about mental health struggles in college admissions essays only when it will help your candidacy. Usually that means one of two things: either (a) you're framing them as challenges you've already resolved and have learned from and/or (b) you're using them to give context to other parts of your application, such as a year when your grades suffered.

That said, deciding whether to write about your mental health challenges is ultimately a personal decision. There's no "one-size-fits-all" answer. Instead, here are four things to keep in mind.

1. You don't have to write about your mental health.

Your college application is not a confessional. While you *do* need to answer every question honestly and completely, you don't have to tell colleges every single detail about your life. I have not yet seen a prompt that asks, "Have you ever struggled with mental health challenges?" and I don't expect to. Just as you don't have to reveal that you were mean to your sister yesterday or you're secretly jealous of your best friend who has all A's and perfect hair, you don't have to talk about your mental health challenges if you don't want to.

2. Admissions officers are not mental health professionals.

Admissions officers, as you know from chapter 2, are generally smart, well-informed people who care about education. They are not, however, psychologists, psychiatrists, or therapists, and therefore they're not trained to diagnose or treat mental illnesses. Even if they *were* trained in a mental health profession (among the thousands of admissions officers in the country, there are probably a few who also happen to be psychologists or therapists), it's unlikely that they'd be able to assess a student's mental health challenges from the materials presented in a college application.

Since I'm not a mental health professional, either, I turned to someone who is: my friend and colleague Doranna Tindle, a former high school AP English teacher (she used to teach across the hall from me) and principal who is now a licensed social worker. Here's what she had to say:

> An admissions officer is not a clinician and is not equipped to sort through an applicant's trauma history or its aftermath. Nevertheless, we can all appreciate qualities such as self-awareness and self-understanding. If you can explain how adversity or trauma has directly shaped an important skill or capacity of yours, then it is worth including in your essay. If you cannot, then avoid disclosure.

Admissions officers don't have the training to unpack traumatic stories, so one approach you definitely *don't* want to take is to write about your mental health struggles in the hope that an admissions officer can assess whether or not their school could meet your mental health needs or not. They cannot make that assessment. The college admissions system is not set up to perform that function, and it's something you'll need to discern for yourself outside of the application process. Which brings us to the next point . . .

3. Look at the big picture: What do you need?

If mental health struggles are part of your story and you're applying to competitive colleges, make sure you're not missing the forest for the trees. You may need to ask yourself some difficult questions, such as: Would I thrive in an intense, competitive environment? Is college even the right next step for me right now? If so, what kind of support do I need to be successful in school?

Answering these questions is *waaaay* beyond the scope of this book, but I think they're worth asking, in part because the availability and quality of resources for kids with mental health issues can vary widely from school to school. Yale University, for example, recently settled a lawsuit claiming that it had discriminated against students with mental health issues, in part by pressuring students with suicidal thoughts to withdraw. Don't assume that just because a college is prestigious, it will have the resources or the will to give you what you need.

Big picture: Have honest conversations about mental health now with the adults in your life who care about you, like parents, guardians, teachers, and counselors. Find people who are safe to talk to and be honest with them, so you can get the support and care you need.

4. My advice: Write about mental health challenges only if you want to *and* if they support your candidacy.

This brings us back to your applications. Here's what I tell my students: write about your mental health challenges only if they're an important part of your story, if you want the admissions committee to know about them, *and* if they support your candidacy.

Frankly, I don't like giving this advice, because I don't like suggesting that people should be less than fully transparent about anything, especially mental health issues. But the truth is that if you talk about ongoing mental health struggles, there is a very good chance that admissions officers will read them as a red flag.* At many schools, writing about mental health issues supports a student's candidacy only when the story is that they have fully resolved the problem and they have evidence to show it (improved grades, extracurricular participation, and so on).

If you do choose to write about your mental health, it's important to include a lot of context. For example, if you were diagnosed with depression

---

*I'm not the only one who feels this way. An excellent 2022 guest essay in the *New York Times* describes one student's struggles with whether or not to disclose her mental illness, capturing the difficulty and nuance of this topic. See Emi Nietfeld, "I Edited Mental Illness Out of My College Applications. I'm Not Alone," *New York Times*, December 31, 2022, https://www.nytimes.com/2022/12/31/opinion/college-applications-mental-health.html.

and your grades went down for a bit but then you learned coping strategies and they went back up, that's totally fine. If you learned something important from that experience, that could be a great narrative that might actually help you. But a discussion of ongoing trauma, depression, or anxiety? The sad reality is that disclosing such information could hurt you more than help you in a competitive admissions process.

There is one exception to this rule, and it involves not your personal essay or supplemental essays but a section within the Common App called "Additional Information." There you'll find a prompt reading "Do you wish to provide details of circumstances or qualifications not reflected in the application?"

This is the place to briefly explain how circumstances beyond your control—including but not limited to mental health—impacted something you're not proud of in your academic or extracurricular record. Maybe your grades went down sophomore year before you were diagnosed with ADHD, or maybe you couldn't do any extracurriculars junior year because you were caring for a sick family member. Colleges care about those kinds of extenuating circumstances, and this is the place to talk about them. Even here, though, I always urge students to emphasize growth and progress during and after such struggles, so as not to raise unnecessary red flags.

Finally, it's important to emphasize that I don't think teenagers should have to put this kind of "spin" on their mental health narratives. In fact, I think this is a problem. I wish we lived in a world where we could openly discuss these challenges everywhere, in part because of how shame works. Hiding difficult things often makes them worse. But since this book is about writing essays that will help you get into college, I want you to understand the reality in America today: narratives of triumph over obstacles can help you, but if you talk about unresolved mental health issues, you may be setting yourself up for trouble.

Step 3: Outline

"Mr. Tipler, do I *have* to make an outline?" I hear this question a lot. The answer: No, you don't *have* to make an outline. But I strongly recommend it, because it will save you a lot of time and stress in the long term. It's also an easy way to establish a structure for your essay.

Keep Your Structure Simple

My recommendation: keep it simple. In fact, if you've been following the guidelines in this book, your freewriting already has a structure: beginning, middle, and end.

So what will that look like in your outline and final essay?

Three Options for Structure

In any story—whether it's an essay, movie, or novel—there are essentially three options for overall structure:

1. Start at the beginning
2. Start at the middle
3. Start at the end

Option 1 is the most straightforward: start at the beginning and tell the story to the end. Option 2, which you may have learned as in media res, is the most complicated: start in the middle, then go back to the beginning and take the reader through your story. This usually requires that you retell the middle in a way that seems fresh and also sets up the end— tricky! Option 3 is more complicated than option 1 but still manageable for most writers: start at the end, then rewind back to the beginning and tell us how you got there.

For your essay, I recommend picking option 1 or 3. Why is that? The vast majority of effective college essays start at the beginning, i.e., option 1. It's the most straightforward way of telling a story.

I've also seen quite a few good ones that start at the finish line (option 3) and then rewind. That can be useful if, for example, you want to draw a stark contrast between how things are at the end of the story and how they were at the beginning.

It's very hard, however, to write a compelling 650-word essay that starts *in media res* (option 2)—these types of essays take a lot of storytelling, and you simply have so few words to work with. I have never seen one that worked. Anything is possible, of course. But my recommendation is that you keep it simple and choose option 1 or 3.

Making Your Outline

Now it's time to make your outline! Here are four things to keep in mind.

1. Your outline should have four to six sections (bullets or roman numerals), each of which will correspond to a paragraph in the essay.
2. Those sections are: an opening/introductory paragraph, two to four body paragraphs, and a conclusion.
3. Organize your outline around the story. If you chose option 1, the opening paragraph will be the beginning, the body paragraphs contain the middle and ending, and the conclusion reflects on, contextualizes, or deepens the ending.
4. Keep it short. Four to six bullet points is enough for most people. If you need more structure, use the "long outline" approach described below. Either way, keep your outline less than one page single-spaced.

Sample Outlines: Short and Long

The examples below are from an essay a student of mine wrote some years back. He was an athlete who signed up for the lacrosse team freshman year. Despite some hazing and other bad experiences early on, he stuck with it, eventually became captain, and reorganized his school's lacrosse team to improve its culture.

Here's what a simple outline might look like for his story. As you read it, see if you can imagine it becoming a strong college essay.

Sample Short Outline

- Introduction: Freshman year, joining the team, liking lacrosse but hating the toxic culture
- Sophomore year: Struggling. Deciding the team's values weren't my values, but not sure what to do next
- Junior year: Becoming captain, learning how to be a leader, changing the team's culture
- Senior year: My goals for the team this year, what lacrosse team looks like today
- Conclusion: Applying these lessons to school and community service

That's one approach to outlining. In this case, however, the student wanted more structure in his writing process. So we worked together to craft a longer outline with questions for him to answer in his writing. Here's what it looked like.

Sample Long Outline

i. **[Opening]** Talk about freshman year, coming onto the team. What was it like, both individually for you and in terms of the team culture? What challenges did you face? What did you like about it, what not?

ii. **[Body]** What happened next? What goals did you set for yourself, and how did you follow through on/work toward them? Go into some detail here: be specific, concrete, and honest. The more we see you struggle here, the more powerful the essay (and your triumphs) will be.

iii. **[Body]** What changed over time? How did *you* change, as a player and as a person, *and* how did you work to shift the culture as well? How did you come to realize the things you now believe about leadership, team culture, and how you treat other people?

iv. **[Body]** Now that you're a senior and cocaptain, what are your goals for this year? What legacy do you want to leave behind? What are you proud of? What do you still want to work on?

v. **[Conclusion]** What is the larger impact you want to have on the school community? What have you learned about community, culture, attitude, supporting each other, positivity, etc., from your experiences with lacrosse? How will you share these learnings with the school as a whole?

Reading the second outline, did you notice how the questions addressed both **external story** elements ("What goals did you set for yourself, and how did you follow through on/work toward them?") and the **internal story** ("How did *you* change, as a player and as a person?")? With some digging, that student did a great job writing about both the internal and external in his essay, and he was admitted to several of his top-choice schools.

Hopefully after reading these two outlines, you have a sense of which style will work better for you. If you're not sure, start with the shorter one. You can always come back and write a longer one later if necessary.

Now, write your outline! Remember: no more than one page. If you're scared or stressed, just remember that it doesn't have to be perfect. You're writing a road map, and you'll have many chances to revise in the future.

Done with the outline? Great! It's time to get started on your first draft.

Alternative Essay Structures

There are many ways of structuring a personal essay. Here are the two other structures that are sometimes considered for college essays.

The Braided Essay

A braided essay weaves together two or more strands of narrative, usually by alternating between them. Reading a braided essay, you often feel as though you're reading two separate stories that converge—literally or metaphorically—at the end.

For example:

> I sit outside my house, cold and alone. The rain comes down steadily, yet even though my clothes are drenched, I don't feel wet.
>
> *The bell rings and fifth period begins. Slumping in my desk, I wonder: Was it a good idea to take French IV?*
>
> An hour passes. The rain lightens up, and the sun begins to come out. Was it all a dream, I think?
>
> *Suddenly my French teacher jumps on her desk and begins waving a tricolor flag while shouting "Vive la France!" Yes, I tell myself, French IV was a great idea.*

And so on.

Although I love reading braided essays, I generally don't recommend them for college applications. Why? It is beyond the reach of most high school–level writers—and many adult writers, for that matter—to accomplish everything they need to do in a college essay *and* create an effective braid in 650 words or less. Telling one story in a college essay is hard enough. Telling two? That is tough!

That said, I have seen a *very* small number of braided personal essays that worked. Both of them were written by truly badass writers. If you're a highly skilled and confident writer and you feel up to the challenge, go for it.

The Collage Essay (aka Patchwork Essay, Montage Essay, Segmented Writing)

Whereas the braided essay combines multiple narratives, a collage ("collage," not "college") essay juxtaposes bits of seemingly unconnected material, much like the collages you made in elementary school art class. For example, in a collage essay you might pick five items in your bedroom, then write a paragraph explaining what each item says about you as a person. Ideally there would also be a theme or through line tying all five paragraphs together.

As with the braided essay, I would approach this genre with caution. Unless the collage is built around a story, I advise my students to avoid collage essays for one simple reason: **your entire application is a collage,** i.e., a collection of information about you.

The personal essay is your chance to tie everything together for the admissions officer, and the best way to do that is usually by telling a story. Admissions officers don't want to be the ones connecting the dots, which is what collage essays often require them to do. Instead, they're looking for *you* to tell them who you are in your own words.

Collage essays can be easy to write. They can be cute and flashy, and the structure can sometimes work for other prompts (for example, the University of California personal insight questions). But unless you weave the various elements of the collage into a story with a beginning, middle, and end, it will be tough to give an admissions officer the same sense of personality and maturity that a well-told narrative accomplishes.

Step 4: Write the First Draft

The first draft of anything is s#!t.

—Ernest Hemingway

Write More than You Need

I have good news for you: thanks to the brainstorming, freewriting, and outlining you've already done, you have material, ideas, a potential structure and—just as important—momentum.

Your next task is to write a first draft of the essay. Aim for around 800 to 900 words. Even though the final product will be only 650 words, first you need to get the entire story onto the page. By giving yourself a big canvas, you'll avoid a trap I often see students falling into: worrying that they can't go over 650 words and thus never allowing themselves to write freely.

There is no better way to activate the Censor than to constantly be telling yourself "I can't go over 650 words!" Or, as a dance teacher once told me, "You can't dance with your foot on the gas and the brake pedal at the same time."

Remember that your goal right now is not to create a polished final product. As Hemingway reminds us, first drafts don't need to be great, or even good. Polishing will come later. Instead, your job is to get something down on the page that takes us from the beginning through the middle and to the end.

Two Tricks to Start Writing

To get yourself started, I recommend that you do one or both of the following:

1. **Carve out two hours of uninterrupted time to sit down—alone—and write the draft.** Some call this "Making an appointment

with yourself." Personally, I often block out this time on my phone's calendar app, treating it just as seriously as I would a class, a work commitment, or dinner with a friend.

2. **Pick a time with one person on your committee to review your first draft together.** Maybe you're one of those people who won't get work done unless you have some kind of external accountability. If so, this is a great way to get the ball rolling. Even if you find yourself writing it at 1:00 a.m. the night before your scheduled meeting, that's fine. You're still getting it done! (If this sounds like you, you're not alone. When I'm writing a new play, I always schedule an evening where I invite friends over, serve them dinner, and then we sit in a circle and read the play aloud. Not only do I learn a lot from hearing my words spoken, it is literally the only way I can get myself to finish writing a draft. I know they're coming, and I will be very embarrassed if they don't have anything to read, so I write it!)

What Should I Say?

Once you start writing, you may start asking yourself a more nuanced question: How do I turn my outline into an essay? It's a good question. What follows is an explanation of what needs to go into each section of your essay, as well as examples from essays that worked. Perusing these can be a great way to get your mind turning with some of your own ideas.

I. The Opening

The opening of the essay is simply that: an opening. Its goal is to set the scene while also piquing your reader's interest. Just as the opening of a play or a movie introduces time, place, and characters, your opening needs to ground your reader in your narrative and your themes, which in this case are the personal qualities you want to highlight.

Let's look at a few examples.

Introduction 1

Four players are fighting for the puck. As my teammate gains possession, I race across the ice and receive a hard pass on my stick. Brushing past two defenders, I rush towards the net, drawing the goalie towards me. Then I flip the puck to my teammate, who catches my pass and shoots into the unguarded net. Score!

This is a strong, dynamic opening that starts "on scene": the writer places us on a hockey rink—even though he never uses the word "hockey"—in a moment of action. Reading this, we're engaged, we're energized, and we want to know what happens next.

Just as important, this paragraph sets the stage for the essay to come. Stop and think for a moment: What do you already know about the narrator, just from the opening paragraph?

Well, we can see that he's an athlete, a hockey player. (The gender is not yet clear at this point in the essay—it could have been written by a girl—but in this case it was written by a boy, so I'll use "he" pronouns for the author.) We can infer that he's a strategic thinker, "drawing the goalie toward me," then passing to a teammate.

That last detail also shows us that he's a team player, maybe even a leader. Instead of taking the shot himself, he passes it to a teammate. Creative thinking, orientation toward community, leadership: these are all qualities that admissions officers love.

Diving right into a scene without any introduction is one way of opening an essay. Here's a different approach.

Introduction 2

Some people say I ask too many questions. As a child, my parents would get frustrated because I never answered their questions with a simple "Yes" or "No." Instead, I would always ask, "Why?" I was fascinated with science, so I peppered them with queries such as: Why do our cells divide? Why do I look more like my mom than my dad? But I was also deeply interested in people. Not just helping people—although I care deeply about that—but the "why" of people. I wondered what the biological basis of suffering was and what it meant to be human.

Before you read on, stop for a minute and ask yourself, "What do I already know about this student just from this one paragraph?" If nothing comes to mind, go back and reread it with that question in mind. Then list a few things right now.

1. _____
2. _____
3. _____

It's pretty cool how much we already know, right? We know that this student is curious. She loves science, yet she also has a humanistic interest in helping others and is asking philosophical questions such as what it means to be human.

Personally, I also find myself deeply hooked by the student's energy and creative excitement. There are strong senses of intellectual curiosity and passion—two qualities admissions officers are looking for—even though we're not yet clear precisely *what* she's passionate about. This makes the reader curious, and they want to keep reading. Keep in mind that this essay doesn't have a flashy or shocking "hook" in the traditional sense. Instead, it captures our attention through its energy, curiosity, and vulnerability.

Here's a third and final example.

Introduction 3

Until the age of 16, I was like any other kid, discovering my interests and passions and pursuing them. Basketball and rugby were high priorities. Jazz piano had become something of a mini-obsession. With a wide range of academic interests, I read everything I could get my hands on from ancient history to the history of contemporary art. Then my mother was diagnosed with breast cancer. That changed everything.

This student chooses to open by giving us a brief summary of the first sixteen years of his life. We see that he's a person with varied interests, maybe even a bit of an intellectual. His participation in sports, music, and the humanities hints at engagement, passion, creativity, and intellectual curiosity.

It's also worth mentioning that this kid, unlike the writer of the first introduction, was aiming for schools like UChicago and Columbia. It's not a coincidence that his mini–life summary thus highlights his high-brow intellectual interests—jazz piano, ancient history, contemporary art—alongside athletics.

At the end of the paragraph, he also reveals an important detail: his mother was diagnosed with breast cancer. This instantly raises questions in the reader's mind: What happened to his mother? And how did he respond to that? It also hints at maturity. This is a student who has had to deal with something extraordinary, and we want to see how he has matured as a result.

Thankfully, most high school students have not had a parent who has been diagnosed with cancer. Yet many of us *did* have something unexpected happen during high school that transformed our life or identity in profound ways.

If that's the kind of story you want to tell in your essay, dropping that bomb at the end of the first paragraph can be a good way of setting up the story.

DON'T STRESS ABOUT THE HOOK

Many students get stuck on the opening because they think they have to start with a startling, flashy, or even subversive hook. Often, this is because a well-meaning English teacher gave them this advice.

Don't get caught in that trap. Notice that none of these paragraphs has an especially sexy opening line. The first two don't contain any flashy or startling information. The only jaw-dropper is the cancer diagnosis in the third essay, and that comes near the end. Instead, each of these openings hooks the reader through story and specificity and by hinting at personal qualities admissions officers are looking for—qualities that then need to be developed in the rest of the essay.

For now, focus on telling the story. You don't need a flashy hook. If you decide later on that you want one, that's fine; just make sure it comes from the story itself so that it feels real to the reader.

Finally, if you haven't done so yet, stop here and write your introduction! Then move on to the next part of your essay: the body.

II. The Body

After setting the stage in your opening, you'll want to write a few paragraphs that take the reader through the meat of the story.

Your task here is simple: to tell us what happened.

If you had a life-changing academic experience, what did it involve? If a sport or activity helped you grow as a person, what occurred that caused that growth? What did you do? If there was some experience related to travel or family, what happened? What's the who, what, where, when, why, and how of the action? These are simple questions, but they're hard to answer—especially when writing about yourself.

In theater, I've heard this challenge called the "doughnut problem": there's a hole at the middle of the show, and the hole is the protagonist. There may be lots of fancy, fun things happening onstage (Flashy costumes! Beautiful sets! Thrilling dance numbers!), but if we don't know and care about the central character, it's not going to be a satisfying play.

So here are three strategies to help you create a meaningful central character in your essay—you!—that will leap off the page and speak to admissions officers.

BODY STRATEGY 1: FOCUS ON ACTIONS

Most of us experience life as happening *to* us. We're so busy trying to survive, making sense of the millions of stimuli coming in each day from parents, teachers, friends, social media, etc., that we focus our attention on external forces rather than our responses to them.

This is perfectly normal, as is the fact that we often don't even notice the daily choices we make that shape our lives. Instead, we pay attention to the challenges facing us, then move on to the next problem at hand—and there's always a next problem! Yet in a personal essay or story, it's crucial that the protagonist be active. Especially in an essay that's only 650 words, it's the protagonist's actions that stick with us—the choices they make in response to external stimuli.

So instead of using valuable essay space on a detailed description of what happened *to* you, **focus on what you did**. For some people, it can be helpful to make a bullet list of concrete actions you took in a class/ job/internship/research project/whatever you're writing about. For others, these actions will come up in freewriting or as you're drafting the essay.

Here is a great example of an essay body that is full of actions. This follows Introduction 3 above: the kid who had varied interests until his mother was diagnosed with cancer.

I felt the need to learn everything I could about the disease as quickly as I could. I started by asking my science teachers for information and poring over textbooks. It wasn't enough. Through my mother's treatment, I got to know her oncologist, who was a knowledgeable and encouraging resource. His encouragement prompted me to ask if I could work in his oncology lab. One week after school ended, I began a summer internship that would change my life.

Professor Gandalf's lab is focused on breast cancer research, specifically on the gene LMTK-3. When this faulty gene is expressed, it allows cancer to enter the bloodstream, evade the immune system, and metastasize. His lab investigates how the body regulates LMTK-3 and how its carcinogenic effects might be mitigated.

My first day at the lab was overwhelming. When my new colleagues spoke, the medical terminology sounded like a foreign language, so when I went home that night I read every journal article I could get my hands on. Even then, the following Thursday, when the entire lab met with Professor Gandalf, I could barely understand what the researchers were talking about and became flustered when Professor Gandalf started quizzing me about cancer therapies and signaling pathways that weren't even related to the lab's work. But I continued to read papers, conduct research, and talk to the fellows. As the weeks passed, I not only understood the conversations, I contributed to them.

My primary task was to determine the levels of LMTK-3 protein in test cells—an indicator of our treatments' efficacy. Over the six weeks I was there, I ran the test at least 100 times and was fascinated every time. There are no numbers to analyze, just images, and I had to make judgments based on the relative levels of other proteins. Conducting each test and analyzing the data to figure out the "right" answer gave me immense satisfaction. I was learning about cancer and participating in the journey of discovery.

I was also growing as a scientist. By the end of my second week, I started passing Professor Gandalf's tests. I began to realize that by quizzing me, he was treating me like a medical student. By the end of the summer, the lab's senior fellow invited me to work with him on a new research paper. Suddenly, I was a colleague, not just an intern, and this year I have returned to the lab as a Visiting Researcher to work for Professor Gandalf full-time.

What do you notice in this essay? What stands out to me is how active the writer is. If we were to list all the specific actions he took, the list would include things such as:

- Asking questions
- Reading textbooks
- Signing up for an internship
- Reading journal articles
- Conducting research
- Running tests
- Analyzing data

Notice how each of these bullets starts with a verb: asking, reading, signing up, analyzing, etc. **When writing your body, use action verbs.** They build energy and encourage the reader to picture you doing all these things in their mind.

Taken as a whole, all of these actions combine to show the writer's passion, engagement, intellectual curiosity, and grit. This essay is also very candid about the challenges the student faced, which brings me to the next tip.

BODY STRATEGY 2: FOCUS ON CHALLENGES AND HOW YOU OVERCAME THEM

No one wants to read a story in which the hero magically gets everything they want, without any obstacles. It's not realistic, and it's not interesting. We care about characters when they struggle. Think about it: Who would Luke Skywalker be without Darth Vader? Just another kid on a boring desert planet. A nice guy, maybe, but no real story there.

As you look back on your experience, ask yourself: What challenges did I face? What obstacles got in the way? In the essay you read above, for example, the writer was completely lost at the beginning of his internship. He didn't know anything about scientific research, to the point where he didn't even understand what the people around him were saying.

Similarly, if you were editing your school's yearbook, did you struggle with lack of funding, a small staff, or maybe low interest from the student body? If playing on a sports team, perhaps you struggled with an injury, a history of defeats, or low morale.

Identifying challenges is also useful because they lead directly to actions. Once you've identified the challenges, ask yourself: What actions did you take to overcome them? Did you study more, work harder, ask for help, try a different approach, join a new team, put up posters in the hallways, persuade your friends to help out, and so on?

BODY STRATEGY 3: BE VULNERABLE

Perhaps the most game-changing piece of advice I can give you is this: be vulnerable.

What does that mean? Let's be clear: what I *don't* mean here is being sloppy. College essays are not the place to gush out every feeling you've ever had. That kind of writing can be very useful in poetry, song lyrics, and other highly expressive genres, but it's not going to help you get into college.

Just as important, I *don't* mean that you should write a cringeworthy mea culpa about every flaw, self-doubt, and perceived shortcomings. That ain't gonna get you into college, either.

Instead, it's crucial that you **open up about your doubts and difficulties.** You need to show the reader that you're not perfect, that you *know* you're not perfect, that you have the maturity to see your weaknesses as well as your strengths.

This may seem counterintuitive. After all, isn't the whole college admissions process about putting your best foot forward? Yes, it is. But it's also about showing the reader who you are as a person. No one is perfect. Letting the reader see you make mistakes, doubt yourself, or take wrong turns will help them connect with you and get them on your side. It will also make your essays feel more human, as though they were written by a real person instead of a high-achieving robot.

Show your vulnerability—and end on a high note. Tell the story where you doubted yourself, took a wrong turn, or felt lost…and then summoned up the courage to go on, found your path, or regained your confidence.

An excellent example of the power of vulnerability comes from a former student of mine who loved hockey. You've already read the introduction to his essay (Introduction 1); it opens with "Four players are fighting for the puck."

James had played hockey since early childhood, but in middle school he went through puberty late. In hockey, size matters, and overnight he went from being one of the best players to becoming a little guy who was literally getting pushed around on the ice. Ultimately, however, he worked hard, improved his skills, and emerged from his growth spurt as one of the strongest players on his team. In his early drafts, here's how he told the crucial middle part of his story:

> Then in eighth grade, everything changed. My growth spurt was delayed, so while some of my teammates were now six feet tall, I was still under five feet. For the first time, we began to check each other on the ice, so physical size became more important than ever. Once a

dominant player, I was now a defenseless minnow, surrounded by hungry sharks. Surrounded by larger guys, I was suddenly afraid to go into the corner or fight for a loose puck. I had lost my confidence on the ice, and in hockey, confidence is everything.

I could have quit hockey altogether, but that's not who I am and it's not what hockey has taught me. Instead, I decided to work harder. I began taking more skating lessons, spent more time at the gym, and got up early before school for extra tutorials with my coach.

Not bad, right? But not especially compelling, either. Something wasn't working, and when I talked to James's parents, I learned that he had inadvertently omitted some key details. When things had gotten bad, the coach had told him he might get cut. He had even thought about quitting—walking away from the sport he loved.

Of course he didn't want to write about those things at first. Who would? But once he found the courage to open up about how bad things had truly gotten, the essay came alive. It also became more human. After all, wouldn't *you* want to leave a situation where you're literally getting beat up every day at something you used to be the best at?

Here's his revised essay.

Then, in eighth grade, the unthinkable happened. My growth spurt was delayed, so while some of my teammates were suddenly 6 feet tall, I was still 4'10". Where before I'd been a confident, dominant player, I suddenly felt like a defenseless minnow surrounded by hungry sharks. Not only was I no longer one of the top players, but I had lost my edge and struggled just to keep up with my teammates.

As eighth grade progressed, things went from bad to worse, culminating in the day when my coach pulled me aside and explained that I might not make the team next year. I was crushed. Not only had I lost the most important thing in my life, I was losing my identity. After all, if I wasn't a hockey player, who was I?

I thought long and hard about what to do. I could have moved down to a less competitive team or quit hockey altogether. But if hockey has taught me anything, it's that when you're faced with a challenge, you dig in and work harder. So I began taking more skating lessons, spent more time at the gym, got up at 5:00 a.m. for extra practice sessions.

See the difference? Once he found the courage to be vulnerable, to admit that he had almost been cut, had felt crushed, and had been "losing my identity," the essay came to life. As readers, we care that he then makes the decision to keep going, because we've seen how difficult things truly got for him.

James's final essay was powerful. He was admitted Early Action to his first-choice school, eventually joining the hockey team as a walk-on varsity player.

Vulnerability can also be communicated in more subtle ways. The following is from the body of the essay by the student who wrote Introduction 2. She's the girl who loves asking questions.

The first time I started to sense some common ground among my questions was two years ago at Camp Dream Street, a summer camp for children with chronic illnesses. The camp's goal is to create a normal childhood experience for its campers by mixing them with healthy children. I was a counselor, and I went into the experience— uncharacteristically—with very few questions. Instead, I decided that I was going to protect my campers from harm, no matter what.

My most exuberant camper was Rebecca. She was always smiling and running around the camp. I, however, feared that she would hurt herself. Sure enough, one day as Rebecca was running to the pool, she fell and scraped her knee. Because the campers' conditions were not disclosed to us, I was terrified. Could Rebecca be a hemophiliac? Did she have a chemotherapy port? My mind went racing through all the potential disasters that could result from that one fall.

Rebecca was fine. The nurse gave her a Band-Aid, and she ran cheerfully to her next activity. But I was shaken by my own response and by the assumptions I had made about my "sick" camper. Was I thinking of her as a disease or as a person? What makes someone "normal" or "sick"? I wasn't sure of the answers yet, but for the first time I saw that my questions about science and people might be related . . .

The author of this essay makes several rhetorical moves that show vulnerability without throwing herself under the bus. First, she acknowledges that despite having a flexible, questioning approach to most of life, she went into the camp experience with a rather rigid mindset: "I was going to protect my campers from harm, no matter what."

Describing the incident with Rebecca in the second paragraph, the writer shows her brain racing from one terrible possibility to another, a behavior that psychologists call "catastrophizing." Hemophilia? Chemotherapy port? Without getting too dark, she's revealing the problematic side of a mind—her mind—that asks lots of questions. Sometimes it overreacts and asks questions that are unhelpful.

In the final paragraph, she gives us an honest appraisal of her own behavior. She lets us inside her process of self-reflection and self-criticism that ultimately led to a new insight about her questioning.

Even though she reveals her doubts, uncertainties, even prejudices here, did you find that you actually finish the paragraph with a more positive feeling about her as person? I certainly did—and that's the power of vulnerability.

As a whole, these three paragraphs not only humanize the writer, they also reveal many qualities you want to be showing: intellectual curiosity and maturity, engagement, passion, leadership, and authenticity. With an essay like this, alongside strong grades and extracurricular involvement, it's no surprise that she was admitted ED to Cornell.

Now that you know what to focus on, this a great time to write the body of your essay. Remember: actions, challenges, and vulnerability!

III. The Conclusion

Congratulations! If you made it through the body, you're almost done. In fact, you're further along than you think, because I don't want you to spend too much time on the conclusion right now.

WRITE IT, BUT DON'T SWEAT IT

A good conclusion takes the reader beyond the rest of the essay. Its goal is to wrap up the narrative, give the reader a sense of what you learned/how you grew from those experiences, *and* give a nod to how the events impacted or might impact the rest of your life. However, almost no one is ready to do these things in the first draft. In fact, most writers don't discover their true conclusion until the third or fourth revision of their personal essay.

So don't sweat your conclusion—but don't leave it blank, either! Even if you're not yet sure what you want your conclusion to say, a placeholder conclusion is the first step toward discovering one that will leave your reader singing your praises.

To give you a flavor of what we're aiming for, I want to share the conclusion from one of the essays we've been analyzing in this section. It's from the last excerpt you read: the essay written by the girl who loved asking questions.

After the vignette about the summer camp, this writer told about being introduced to the field of psychology the following summer and falling in love with it. For her, psychology was the first discipline where she found people asking the same kinds of questions as she was—and looking for answers, together. (If you want to read her entire essay, it's in appendix V.) Here is her conclusion:

> Now I see psychology everywhere. I see it in the billboards on Route 17, the menu options at Starbucks, even the design of the new iPhone 7. More importantly, I now know that the kinds of questions that interest me most are the interdisciplinary ones. In college, I want to reach high, think broadly, and do research that goes beyond traditional ways of understanding the world. I want to ask untraditional questions, and I could easily see myself majoring in biology or psychology or even the history of medicine. But whichever direction I pick, I want to continue to ask questions that connect the dots in new ways and broaden our understanding of what it means to be human.

I love this concluding paragraph. I feel the writer's optimism and excitement about where her studies might lead, which gives me a sense of her passion and intellectual curiosity. The conclusion also shows her incorporating her academics into her life—seeing psychology at Starbucks and in her iPhone—and wraps up the narrative with a positive, aspirational tone.

Note, too, what it doesn't do: it does not attempt to offer some radical new insight about what psychology is or to make some grand declaration about the social sciences. Instead, like most good personal essays, it stays *personal*, explaining why psychology is so enlivening for this particular writer.

Finishing Your Draft

Now is a great time to write your conclusion.

Maybe you intuitively have a sense of how you want to end your essay. If so, great! Follow your gut and write it down. If not, **conclude your first draft by answering one or more of the following questions.**

1. What did I learn from this experience?
2. How did I grow from this experience? How did it change or affect the person I am today?
3. From beginning to end, what changed? I.e., what's different now, internally and externally, from how things were in the opening paragraph?
4. What's next? Has this experience affected my goals, dreams, or ambitions? If so, how?

Write your conclusion, and then, after you type the final period at the end of the last sentence—celebrate! Give yourself a break, whether it's ice cream, a hang with friends, or a walk around the block. Not only have you earned it, but it's also wise to give your brain a rest. Put the essay away for a day or two—at least overnight. Let your mind move on to other things, so you can come back to it with fresh eyes for the next stage of the writing process: revision.

Step 5: Revise

Welcome back!

When you pull your essay back out, you have basically two choices. You can:

1. Reread it yourself or
2. Share it with someone else

I recommend you do both.

Start by rereading the essay yourself. Does it say the things you wanted to say? Does it make the main points you wanted to make? Are all the big pieces there? If not, add them in, but don't get too caught up in revision yet. Your goal right now is simply to **revise a bit, then move on to sharing it with someone else.**

Now is when your committee becomes crucial. Start small. Share the essay with your inner circle first: one or two people you trust. As with the freewriting, don't just email it to them and say "Do you like this?"

Instead, ask them a few specific questions, such as the ones below.

How to Solicit Helpful Feedback

Help me help you.

—Jerry Maguire in *Jerry Maguire*

Vague questions such as "What do you think about my essay?" tend to elicit vague, less-than-helpful answers. Instead, ask for feedback with pointed questions, such as:

- Does this sound like me? *(That's the million dollar question!)*
- Does the story flow? Does it have a beginning, a middle, and an end?
- Are there parts that are unclear?

- Where could I cut, and where could I expand?
- What does this essay tell you about who I am as a person?
- What's missing from this essay? What does this essay need to be complete?

Keep in mind that you can request written or verbal feedback. Personally, I nearly always learn more from discussions, so I recommend asking to have a conversation about the essay whenever possible. Conversations can be scary, but they are also much more revealing—and you'll often be pleasantly surprised by the parts of the essay that the reader likes.

How to Handle Feedback

When you get feedback, the first step is to listen to it. Our initial reaction is usually to argue with a person who's criticizing our work, but unless you're trying to get a grade raised, that is rarely helpful. Even if they are wrong, your job is not to convince the reader by talking to them. Your job is to tell the story in your essay.

More important, you need to listen closely to their feedback so you can decide whether you agree with it or not. Though you don't want to be in a rush to dismiss feedback that makes you uncomfortable, you also don't want to blindly accept everything everybody tells you. At the end of the day it's your essay, not theirs.

Sometimes you might be genuinely confused about whether a piece of feedback is a good idea or not. In this case you need multiple perspectives, which is why you have a committee. Share the essay with a few more people. Ask them the same questions you asked the first person and listen to what they say. If multiple people raise the same issue, that's a sign that you need to do some rewriting.

One final note: **it's the other person's job to tell you what's not working, but it's your job to fix it.** Even when people suggest "fixes," take their suggestions with a grain of salt. For example, if somebody says, "Why not talk about a beautiful hike and a waterfall in your introduction?" I wouldn't immediately put waterfalls and rainbows at the beginning of your essay. Instead, ask yourself: "Why does this person think I need a waterfall at the beginning of the essay? What's missing or incomplete that causes them to want that?"

If you can identify the problem that the person is trying to solve with their feedback, then you can come up with a solution that will be yours and yours alone. Maybe it's a waterfall, or maybe it's something even better, a story or image that's personal and unique.

Common Problems in First Drafts

Here are some common problems I see in early drafts of personal essays, along with strategies to address them.

Red Flag 1: Weak Internal Story

This is by far the biggest problem I see in first drafts. Most of us tend to start with the external story, only finding our way to the internal story later on.

The sign of a weak internal story is that although it might be clear what happened, it's not clear how it affected you, changed you, or caused you to grow.

For example, maybe the first draft explains how in tenth grade you took biology, became fascinated with genomics, spent a summer working in a lab, and now want to be a biologist. That's great—but how did the experience change you internally? Did it transform how you see the world? Maybe you have a new appreciation of the importance of science or of the shortcomings of science. Maybe there's a personal angle, e.g., you became interested in genomics because a friend or relative was sick, but the lab experience transformed how you think about disease and wellness.

The options are limitless, and every person will have their own unique story. That's the point. In fact, it's why the internal story is so important:

your internal story is what makes you unique. Most high school seniors have experiences that look similar to many other kids', at least on the surface. But everyone's inside is different. Getting to that is what will make your story pop.

Questions to Ask Yourself If the Internal Story Is Weak or Lacking

- How did I grow from this experience?
- How did this experience change me?
- What did I believe at the beginning of this experience, and what do I now believe at the end?
- What was important to me at the beginning of this, i.e., what were my *values*? What are my values now? How have they changed?
- What were my goals and aspirations at the beginning of the story? What are they now? How have they changed, and why?

You can freewrite answers to these questions, or you can have a conversation with someone about them. Alternatively, if you need more structure, try the following exercise (you can find a printable version online at www.write-yourself-in.com). It's powerful!

EXTERNAL TO INTERNAL WORKSHEET

WHAT HAPPENED	HOW I FELT ABOUT IT AT THE TIME	WHAT I BELIEVED AND CARED ABOUT (VALUED) AT THE TIME
1.		
2.		
3.		
4.		
5.		

Though simple, this exercise is designed to help you go deep.

First, pick five events from your draft and list them in the first column.

For example, a student trying to sort through her summer in a Spanish-language immersion program might write:

1. The day I decided to do an overseas summer program
2. The morning I arrived in Spain
3. The horrible moment I realized that I couldn't communicate with anyone around me
4. The evenings I spent getting extra tutoring and practicing with friends
5. The day I had a meaningful conversation with my host mother in fluent Spanish.

In the second column, list the feelings you felt at each of these events. For the girl in Spain, these would be:

1. Excitement
2. Joy mixed with trepidation
3. Despair
4. Exhaustion, but felt I was growing
5. Both pride and humility

Finally, in the third column, list any beliefs or values that you had at the time. Though we're often tuned in to our feelings, we're usually less aware of how our beliefs/values change over time.

In this example, when this student decided to study abroad, she might have initially believed that she could do anything she set her mind to. But as her beliefs and values evolved, her table ultimately looked like this:

WHAT HAPPENED	HOW I FELT ABOUT IT AT THE TIME	WHAT I BELIEVED AND CARED ABOUT (VALUED) AT THE TIME
1. The day I decided to do an overseas summer program	Excitement	I believed in taking risks. I thought I could do anything I put my mind to.
2. The morning I arrived in Spain	Joy mixed with trepidation	
3. The horrible moment I realized that I couldn't communicate with anyone around me	Despair	I cared about connection, but I also valued my independence. I believed that asking for help was a sign of weakness.
4. The evenings I spent getting extra tutoring and practicing with friends	Exhaustion, but felt I was growing	
5. The day I had a meaningful conversation with my host mother in fluent Spanish.	Both pride and humility	With hard work, I can achieve great things. And asking for help is a sign of strength, not weakness.

Note that not every event in the first column has a corresponding entry in the third column. That's to be expected. Not everything that happens in your life will cause your beliefs or values to change. We're looking for the events that do cause those big shifts, because they are the turning points in your internal story.

Red Flag 2: Not Enough Description

In an effort to get to the finish line, many writers skimp on description. When there aren't enough descriptive details, especially in the first few paragraphs of the essay, the reader won't have enough context to understand or "see" the story you're telling.

For example, in a story about a transformative experience on a wilderness adventure, the writer might tell us that she "loved the outdoors" but forget to show us why. Maybe it's the majestic, awe-inspiring mountains, the crystal-clear streams that give her a feeling of serenity, or the sense of warmth and camaraderie around the campfire at night.

You, however, may not notice missing description in your own writing. You have vivid memories of the events you're describing, because you were there! So rely on your committee to tell you where description is missing. When a reader says something such as "I didn't really care about this moment" or "I didn't understand why Mr. Jones's class was important to you," that may be a flag that description is missing.

The solution is to slow down and give the reader specific details that allow them to place themself in the setting, whether it's a national park, a football field, or a library. Or, as your English teacher has, hopefully, taught you: **show, don't tell.**

Use your senses: What did you see, hear, smell, taste, and touch in this particular place? Like an establishing shot in a movie, concrete details pull the reader into your world and cause them to invest in your story—and in you!

Red Flag 3: An Unclear Opening

Most of us have been taught to start an essay with background material, perhaps a big-picture idea or historical context that frames the topic. In a 650-word essay, however, there's no room for philosophical musings. **The best approach is usually to dive right in.**

If you find your opening isn't working, here are two strategies you can use to fix it.

The first is to trim the fat. Ask yourself: How much could I cut from the beginning of the essay and still have my story make sense? Omit as many needless words as you can. Start with the actual story you're telling, not with another story that gives context to the "real" story.

The second involves looking at the structure of your essay. Start by reviewing the three structural options on page 86: starting at the beginning, the middle, or the end.

Sometimes, a writer's first choice for how to start their story isn't where they end up. If you started at the beginning in the first draft, try starting at the end and rewind—or vice versa. Though the vast majority of finished essays start at the beginning, starting at the end can be useful when you want to draw a big contrast between where you started and where you ended up.

Red Flag 4: Not Enough Struggle

It's an odd thing, but we often downplay the challenges we face. I once had a student write an essay about editing her high school yearbook. Her first draft was boring, largely because it omitted the obstacles she had faced in getting it published. But when she started adding details about the challenges—an unhelpful administration, no support from peers because yearbook wasn't "cool," lack of a faculty sponsor—suddenly the essay got interesting.

Then, in her next round of edits, she added the actions she had taken to overcome these obstacles: meeting with the principal on multiple occasions, finding a faculty sponsor, visiting English classes during her free periods to talk up yearbook, and recruiting more students to her cause. It ended up being quite a thrilling story, all the more so because she was someone who had struggled with social anxiety. And it worked; she was admitted to the University of Michigan's competitive undergraduate business program in the Early Action round.[*]

If this is an issue for you, look back at Body Strategy 2 (page 100). Reread that section, review your essay, then ask yourself:

1. What was my goal? What did I want to do or accomplish and why?
2. What were the challenges? What were the specific roadblocks and obstacles that came up—whether from other people or institutions or my own self-doubts/lack of skills?
3. What did I do to overcome those challenges? What specific concrete steps did I take to meet them? What led me to succeed?

[*]Intrigued? You can read the essay in appendix V, page 287.

Red Flag 5: Not Enough Vulnerability

If you've read this far, you probably understand why showing your vulnerability is so important. I mention it again here because often we need a reminder at this point to "check in" on the essay's vulnerability.

If your essay still isn't quite landing with your readers, go back and reread the section on vulnerability (page 100). Pay particular attention to the examples and how they show vulnerability in different ways. Ask yourself: Am I being honest about my low points? This does not mean overdramatizing or exaggerating them, simply being honest about when you doubted yourself, thought about giving up, or realized you'd made a mistake.

Clichés

Stop worrying if your vision is new . . .
Anything you do, let it come from you.
Then it will be new.

—Stephen Sondheim, "Move On," from
Sunday in the Park with George

Very often in this process, a student will come up with an interesting idea or turn of phrase but immediately delete it, telling themselves, "That's a cliché."

We all know that clichés make for bad writing. English teachers rail about them. A cliché—"a phrase or opinion that is overused and betrays a lack of original thought"—is problematic because it is bland. The goal of your essays, after all, is to communicate something personal. Parroting someone else's words rarely accomplishes that.

Yet when you're immersed in the process of writing a personal essay, the impulse to omit every cliché will get in the way of your writing. Especially if you are a conscientious writer, it's a sneaky way for the Censor to slip in the back door and trip you up.

When you find yourself using a cliché, see it as a window into

something deeper. **Instead of reflexively deleting clichés, leave them in your first draft . . . then revise.**

Maybe you wrote "Suddenly I realized that the grass is always greener." Can you come up with a more pointed, personal way of expressing that truth? How, for you, is the grass specifically greener in your unique situation, and why? "I realized that I wanted those things only because other people had them" is one way you might express that idea more personally.

Finally, keep this in mind: William Shakespeare wrote more than 150 sonnets. Nearly all of them are about romantic love. Such a cliché, right? Yet he found 150 different things to say about it, and he said many more in his plays. Even perennial topics become clichés only if you let them.

Wrapping Up: Your Conclusion

Once the body of your essay starts to take shape, it's time to start workshopping your conclusion.

The best approach to writing a conclusion is to give it time to come to you. A strong conclusion isn't typically written until the third or fourth (or even fifth) draft of the personal essay. Any attempt to manufacture one too early in the process will feel forced. That's because the strongest conclusions wrap up the story while taking things to the next level. They introduce an idea, insight, or perspective that wasn't present in the rest of the essay yet feels like a natural outgrowth of the story that precedes it. It's hard to do that when you're still figuring out the body of the essay.

Wait until your story is coming together; then ask yourself: So what? Why should anyone care about this story? Freewrite an answer to that. If that answer doesn't feel right for your conclusion, pick a couple of the following questions and freewrite responses to them.

- What's next? Because of what just happened in the story, what do I see now in the future? (This could be your own future or the future of a community, an idea, or something else.)

- Why is this important? Is there a deeper meaning to all of this that I haven't addressed yet? If so, what is it?
- Why am I telling this story? (If you haven't yet communicated why the story seems so important to you personally, a conclusion can be a great place to tell that.)
- Why should anyone else care? (A conclusion can be a good place to put a stake into the ground and say, "This is what I believe. This is who I am and what I stand for." Essays that end with conviction are often strong.)

Writing Is Rewriting—And It Ends

My sister's dog, Pearl, loves to shuffle balls of paper around on the floor. At first glance it looks as though she's organizing them, pushing them around with her little nose. She approaches it with a great deal of intensity, which is why I call it her "paperwork."

Pearl's paperwork, however, is just a game. There is no goal. She's not actually trying to organize the paper; she just enjoys pushing it around.

Don't let your revision process turn into paperwork. If you keep tinkering too long, you will only be moving pieces of the essay around. Not only is that unproductive, but eventually it will make the essay worse.

How do you know when to stop? On average, a personal essay will take five or six "turns" of revision before it's done. Usually, the first few revisions will be large-scale rewrites, with the last few getting smaller. Some take more, some take less.

Stop revising when the essay feels whole and feels done. More specifically, stop when you and your committee agree that the essay says what you want to say, honestly reflects your voice and values, and shows personal qualities that are relevant to the admissions process.

Personal Essay Revision Checklist

How do you know when your essay is done? As you revise, here are some questions to help answer that question. Feel free to use this list yourself, or you can share it with someone who is reviewing your essay.

- ❑ Does the essay sound like you?
- ❑ Is the story complete, i.e., is there a beginning, a middle, and an end?
- ❑ Are there enough specific, descriptive details (sights, sounds, smells, names, etc.) that the reader can imagine the story coming to life?
- ❑ Does the essay show some of the Top Ten personal characteristics *in action*? That could include your learning what leadership, community, resilience, and other things mean to you and/or putting those qualities to work in your life.
- ❑ Have you been honest and vulnerable about your weaknesses and challenges, as well as your strengths?
- ❑ Does the essay give the reader a sense of what you might contribute to a college community?
- ❑ If you focused on events from your childhood (i.e., before high school), is it clear how those events impacted the person you are today?
- ❑ By the end of the story, have you changed, grown, learned an important lesson, or come to see the world differently in some way? In other words, is there an internal story?
- ❑ Does the conclusion add some new idea, insight, perspective, or sense of meaning—as opposed to just repeating things you've said elsewhere in the essay?

Proofreading: The Final Stage

Once you feel your essay is solid, the last step is to proofread it for errors: grammar, punctuation, and vocabulary. You probably caught many of these errors as you revised. If so, great! However, it's still important to do a final proof before submitting. You can proofread now or do it at the end of the process as you prepare to upload your work to the admissions websites.

Proofread the essay once or twice, then ask a trusted friend or adult to proofread it for you. English teachers are great at this, if they have time—so ask them in advance! Remember that it's an editor's job to point out mistakes, and it's your job to fix them.

Moving On

Congratulations! You have just finished the heaviest lift in your college application process. You've also built skills that will help you with your other essays. Everything will be much easier from here on out. Which is good news, because it's time to move on to the next stage of the process: your supplemental essays.

CHAPTER 5

Supplemental Essays, Part I

The Why Our School Essay

The Supplemental Essays: Bird by Bird

> Thirty years ago my older brother, who was ten years old at the time,
> was trying to get a report written on birds that he'd had three months
> to write, which was due the next day. We were out at our family cabin
> in Bolinas, and he was at the kitchen table close to tears, surrounded
> by binder paper and pencils and unopened books about birds, immobi-
> lized by the hugeness of the task ahead.
>
> Then my father sat down beside him, put his arm around my broth-
> er's shoulder, and said, "Bird by bird, buddy. Just take it bird by bird."
>
> —Anne Lamott, *Bird by Bird: Some Instructions on Writing and Life*

Now that your personal essay is in good shape, it's time to move on to
the final chunk of your portfolio: the supplemental essays.

Supplemental essays are, as the name suggests, supplements to your
application. In them you'll respond to questions from a school's admissions committee that aren't covered in the Common App. Colleges take
a variety of approaches to the supplemental essays. Some may ask you to
write several essays, some may require just one long or short essay, and

some may require none at all. Before we dive in, here are two important pieces of advice.

First, **write your supplemental essays one school at a time**. Or, as Anne Lamott put it, take it bird by bird.

There are a couple of reasons to use this approach. One is about saving time. Because schools ask similar questions, you will be able to recycle material you write for your first few schools in subsequent applications. It's much more efficient to get your first school essay into good shape, then adapt that material for other schools.

The other has to do with keeping your head on straight. If you start working on supplemental essays for multiple schools at the same time, it's very easy to lose track of what you wrote for one school versus what you wrote for another. This can be especially problematic for students applying to ten or more schools, who may end up writing dozens of supplemental essays. In the Why Our School essays, which are detail oriented, I've seen even the cleverest students mix up which school offers a particular class, program, or activity.

Second, **approach each school's supplemental essays as a group**. Since your entire college application is a portfolio, you want to make sure that every essay shows the committee a new side of you. Each essay should tell a different story and say something unique about what you might contribute to the school's community. You don't want to repeat material from your personal essay in your supplemental essays, and you don't want to repeat material in multiple supplemental essays, either.

That's why I have my students approach each college by first brainstorming ideas for *all* of that school's supplemental essays and then picking topics so that each essay highlights something different about them, whether it's a particular activity, academic pursuit, or simply another side of their personality.

Although the next two chapters are organized by genre—i.e., type of essay—keep in mind that you will want to organize your work by school. The University of Michigan, for example, typically asks for a long-form Why Our School essay and a Community essay. If you're applying to Michigan, brainstorm, outline, and write both of those essays. Take time to polish them. Then use that material as a starting point for the next school on your list.

Finally, which school should you start with? **Start with the schools you're considering for Early Action or Early Decision. Among those schools, start with the one you're most excited about.** The first supplemental essays will be the hardest to write, and you're more likely to do your best writing when you're excited about your topic. The good news: these essays get easier as you go along, and you'll find that you can often repurpose material from your early essays for subsequent schools.

Pro Tip: Watch Out for "Bonus Essays"

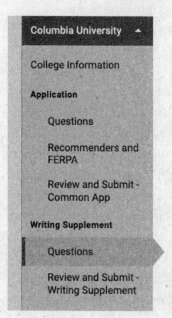

Figuring out exactly what supplemental essays a college requires can be surprisingly difficult. When you start adding schools to your Common App account, you might notice a little tab called "Writing Supplement" that pops up under some schools (pictured to the left).

In a perfect world, all the supplemental essay prompts would be right there. But in reality, supplemental essays can appear anywhere in a college's application—sometimes in the "Academics" or "Other Information" sections or, in the case of a recent "Why Wake Forest?" essay, in the "Contacts" section.

To make things even more confusing, in my opinion, the Common App software is written in such a way that some essay prompts don't materialize until *after* you've answered a school's introductory questions, such as the specific college or division you're applying to (College of Arts and Sciences, School of Engineering, and so on).

One of my students recently gave these sneaky prompts a wry name: her "bonus essays." **To make sure you don't miss any of these hidden gems, fill out all of the school-specific information in the Common App *before* you start writing that school's supplemental essays.** Be sure to answer all questions in that school's "General" and "Academics" sections, particularly the questions about which school, major, or programs you're applying to.

After answering those questions, scan through the rest of the sections to see what essay prompts pop up.

Understanding Essay Genres

> **genre** (noun): a category of artistic composition, as in music or literature, characterized by similarities in form, style, or subject matter.

If you've started reading the various supplemental essay prompts for schools on your list, you've probably noticed that a lot of them sound similar. There are prompts about communities you've joined, conversations you've had, life events you've experienced, and more. I call these different categories of essays "genres," and until a few years ago there were only a few of them: Why Our School, Community, and Activity essays. Recently, however, a number of new genres have appeared as schools respond to changes in their applicant pool, shifts in the political climate, and most recently, the 2023 Supreme Court affirmative action ruling.

In this chapter and the one that follows, I'll be addressing the six most important essay genres in selective college admissions today. Much like TV and film genres, each comes with different expectations and conventions.*

---

*Confession: I am a genre geek. Genre is the "secret sauce" to good storytelling, whether you're writing a college essay, a movie, or a Broadway musical. For more on how genre works and why it's so important, two great books are *Story: Style, Structure, Substance, and the Principles of Screenwriting* by the Hollywood screenwriting guru Robert McKee (he's controversial; some people love him, others hate him) and—if you *really* want to geek out—*The Story Grid* by New York publishing veteran Shawn Coyne. Full details on both in appendix IV.

I'll break down each genre to help you understand what the prompts mean and what admissions officers are looking for, so you can pick the most appropriate stories from your life and tell them in ways that will resonate with the committee.

The good news is that once you start seeing the different essay genres, you can start adapting the same essay for different schools. Some students find it helpful to make a spreadsheet or Google Doc with every prompt for every school they're applying to, so they can map out the overlaps. Others just start with their first school and repurpose their essays as they go along. Both approaches can work—it all depends on your personality—as long as you're actually *writing* the essays one school at a time.

Here are the six genres I'll cover in this and the following chapters:

1. **Why Our School**: Make a case for why a particular school is a good fit for you.
2. **Contributions/Lived Experience**: Explain how your experiences have helped you develop qualities or skills that you would contribute to a college community (this is the "post–affirmative action" question, a direct response to the 2023 Supreme Court ruling).
3. **Intellectual Engagement**: Demonstrate your intellectual curiosity and show how you've pursued it.
4. **Activity**: Discuss an extracurricular activity or work experience that has been meaningful to you.
5. **Community**: Describe a community that matters to you and your role in it, how it's changed you, the impact you've had on the community, and so on.
6. **Diverse Perspectives**: Write about a time when you engaged with a person or group whose views differed from yours.

The following pages will give you concrete guidance on how to approach each kind of supplemental essay, along with information on what admissions committees are looking for and how each contributes to your overall portfolio. We'll start by looking at one of the most common: the Why Our School essay.

The Why Our School Essay

If you struggled with the narrative style of the personal essay, take heart! In the Why Our School essay—also known as the Why Us or Why This College essay—you'll make use of the writing skills you've painstakingly developed in high school: crafting a thesis, supporting it with evidence, and connecting the dots with analysis.

Although these essays require some research, they're much easier to write than the personal essay. In fact, they're my favorite type of supplemental essay. Why? **Because writing these essays forces you to learn more about each college you're applying to.**

To write a good Why Our School essay, you need to learn more about a school, then make a case for why it's a good fit for you. I can't tell you how many students have changed their ED/EA college because, in writing this essay, they realized that their "dream school" actually wasn't right for them. Conversely, each year I see kids become excited about a school they initially thought was boring because, in researching this essay, they discovered that it had exactly what they were looking for.

Let's start by exploring the form, audience, topic, and purpose of this essay.

Unpacking the Why Our School Essay

Form: 100–650-word argumentative essay

Audience: One specific school's admissions committee

Topic: How a college's offerings intersect with your interests

Purposes: (1) To make a compelling argument that this particular school is a good fit for you and that you are a good fit for the school; (2) to show the committee that you've done your research and understand their school

Form: Unlike the personal essay, which is a personal narrative, I recommend structuring the Why Our School essay as an argumentative essay. In it, you make a claim—usually some variation of "This school is a good fit for me"—and support that claim with evidence.

The length of these essays varies from school to school; 250 to 550 words is typical. The shortest I've seen is 100 words (Dartmouth), and the longest these days is 650 words (Cornell and UW-Madison).

Audience: As with the personal essay, your audience is college admissions officers. However, while you wrote the personal essay for admissions officers in general, your audience for this essay is narrower: the AdCom at one particular school.

Topic: Whereas the personal essay allowed you to choose almost any topic, your topic here is clear, straightforward, and set by the school's prompt. It's usually some version of "What draws you to our school, and how would you pursue your interests here?" Different schools have different variations of this prompt, so pay attention to exactly what each school asks.

Note: If you're applying to engineering programs, your Why Our School essay will have a slightly different focus. Turn to page 144 for an in-depth discussion of Why Our School essays for engineering. For other specialized programs, such as business, you can follow the process described here; just be sure to include any relevant experiences (e.g., internships, starting your own business) and how they led you to choose that particular program.

Purpose: Your purpose is twofold. First, you want to persuade your reader that their college is a good fit for you. Second, you want to show them that you've done your research: that you understand what their school is about and what it has to offer.

Several years ago, Northwestern University served up some fantastic insight into the first purpose. Although their supplemental essay has since changed, this now-retired prompt is a remarkably clear distillation of what this genre of essay is all about.

Northwestern's 2021–2022 Prompt

Prompt: Do you plan to complete the "Why Northwestern" Statement? We strongly encourage a response, as *your answer will help us connect the dots across your application to imagine what kind of college student you might become*. (Emphasis mine.)

I love this language, because the admissions office is telling you *exactly* how they're going to read your essay. Since they'll likely never meet you in person, they want to imagine you as a student on their campus. As they read your essay, the readers would be asking themselves: "Is this person a good fit for Northwestern?" And "How will they take advantage of our unique resources and community?"

Try looking at the exchange from the admissions officer's perspective. You won't persuade them that you'd be a good fit at their school by waxing poetic about how prestigious it is and how beautiful the campus is. Every admissions officer already knows these things. Instead, make your case by showing them some concrete details: what you'd major in, what classes you'd take, how you'd get involved in student life, and so on.

As for the second purpose—showing that you've done your research—this is a case where your willingness to put in some effort can have a very positive impact on your candidacy! Details matter. You'd be surprised how many seniors shoot themselves in the foot by failing to do thorough research, even when applying to top schools.

The Secret to Writing a Good Why Our School Essay

When a typical student sits down to write a Why Our School essay, their process usually looks something like this: browse the school's admissions website, find some things that look interesting, and drop them into an essay.

Ten years ago, when I started coaching kids on college essays, I'd let them take this approach if they wanted to. But it always turned out to be a massive waste of time—both my time and theirs—because it never resulted in a compelling essay. Usually it led to a jumbled mess, which they then had to spend many hours revising and rewriting. After a few years, I finally discovered the secret, which I now insist that my students follow:

Make an outline.

This is one of those cases where a little extra work now will save you hours of time, energy, and frustration later. Outlines are particularly useful here because, in the words of a former Yale admissions officer, "There's no formula for these essays, but they *are* formulaic." Lucky for you, you won't be starting from scratch. I've given you examples of outlines below, and my website has Google Docs templates for you, which happen to be the same templates I use with my students.

The Three-Step Process for Writing a Why Our School Essay

Because there's less introspection than in personal essays, the writing process for these essays is shorter. I recommend just three steps:

1. Research
2. Write
3. Revise

Step 1: Research

The first step in writing a Why Our School essay is to do your research.

Why is research so important? Check out the first three paragraphs from a Why Our School essay that worked—the author was accepted Early Action to the University of Michigan. (I'll be using Michigan as an example throughout this section, because it has required a standard, long-form Why Our School essay for many years. You can read this student's entire essay in appendix V.)

Sample Why Our School Opening Paragraphs (University of Michigan)

The first time I visited Michigan's campus, I felt at home. The students I met were enthusiastic, engaged, and shared a sense of intellectual curiosity that resonated strongly with me. I would love to be a student at the University of Michigan's College of Literature, Science, and the Arts. At LSA, not only could I pursue my interests, I could pursue interdisciplinary studies that explore how they intersect.

First and foremost, I am a science geek. I love biology and genetics, and after last summer at Columbia University, I'm passionate about psychology. I want to go to Michigan because it has one of the best psychology programs on the planet, and I'm particularly drawn to the Biopsychology, Cognition, and Neuroscience major. This unique program would allow me to explore my fascination with how humans think, process, and remember information. I can't wait to take classes like "Psychology of Thinking," which would give me a foundation for understanding the complex pathways of the mind.

When I think about college, I'm especially excited to do research, and there is no better place for scientific research than Michigan. I would love to work with Professor Brenda Proudfoot and help expand our understanding of the biological mechanisms that humans use to store memories. I would also love to participate in research at the Brain, Cognition, and Action Laboratory, perhaps as part of a UROP. Professor Bolger's research on how we multitask, process information, and remember images is fascinating, and would allow me to deepen my understanding of both cognitive psychology and neurobiology.

Now write down two specific facts that this applicant mentioned about Michigan and what she likes about them.

Specific UMich fact 1: _____

Why this appeals to the applicant: _____

Specific UMich fact 2: _____

Why this appeals to the applicant: _____

What did you come up with? Here are some of the facts you could have listed:

- The Biopsychology, Cognition, and Neuroscience major
- The class "Psychology of Thinking"
- Professor Brenda Proudfoot
- The Brain, Cognition, and Action Laboratory
- UROP (an undergraduate research program at UMich—google it to learn more)
- Professor Bolger's research

It's a lot of information, right? And it's pretty densely packed into a few short paragraphs. Note that all of these specifics add to the general color she includes about Michigan, such as the "sense of intellectual curiosity" she felt on campus and the fact that it has "one of the best psychology programs on the planet," which is true.

Just as important, notice how for each of these very specific facts, the student told us exactly what she liked about it. The "Psychology of Thinking" class appeals to her because it offers "a foundation for understanding the complex pathways of the mind." Similarly, she is drawn to Professor Bolger's research because she wants to "deepen my understanding of both cognitive psychology and neurobiology."

This explanatory material is analogous to analysis in a history or English essay—the stuff that teachers are always telling you to include after every quote or piece of evidence. **Analysis is the key to making your Why Our School essay stand out, because most applicants just list facts.** They don't do the work of explaining why and how those facts make the school a good fit for them.

Make your essay stand out. Find specific offerings at the school that appeal to you, organize them into an outline, and explain why each offering appeals to you personally. That's the magic formula for a good Why Our School essay.

CREATING THE OUTLINE

I recommend you start your research phase by using an outline template, such as the following. It will give you a sense of what you're looking for. Although it's customized to the University of Michigan's long-form essay, it can easily be adapted to any school. You can find digital versions of these outlines on my website, www.write-yourself-in.com.

"Why Michigan" Outline (Based on 2023–2024 Prompt)

Prompt: Describe the unique qualities that attract you to the specific undergraduate College or School (including preferred admission and dual degree programs) to which you are applying at the University of Michigan. How would that curriculum support your interests? (550 words max)

1. Introduction
   a. Start personal: an anecdote or story of your attraction to the school.
   b. Be sure to specifically address the college/school (see prompt).
2. Academics—primary
   a. Briefly describe what interests you about [your main academic interest].
   b. Do research: Find two to three majors and minors that would interest you.
   [Helpful link: https://admissions.umich.edu/academics-majors/majors-degrees]
   i. _____
   ii. _____
   c. Do research: Find two classes, one to two professors, one to two programs and institutes that interest you.

[Helpful link for institutes: https://provost.umich.edu/resources
-policies/academic-program-center-planning/centers-institutes/list
-of-institutes-centers/]

   i. _____

   ii. _____

   iii. _____

   iv. _____

   v. _____

3. Academics—secondary

  a. Briefly describe what interests you about [your secondary/other interest(s)].

  b. Do research: two to three programs, institutes, professors, and classes that interest you.

   i. _____

   ii. _____

   iii. _____

4. Community and extracurriculars

  a. Do research: three to four clubs and programs *and* one to two aspects of the Michigan community that appeal to you.

   i. _____

   ii. _____

   iii. _____

   iv. _____

   v. _____

This outline reflects the overall structure of these essays: an introductory paragraph, followed by two-thirds on academics and one-third on community and extracurriculars. Note that when schools ask for shorter essays, your outline will be much shorter. For example, you won't have room for a secondary academic section.

Here's a sample outline for a shorter essay, "Why Duke?," which as of 2023–2024 was 250 words.

"Why Duke" Outline (Based on 2023–2024 Prompt)

Prompt: What is your sense of Duke as a university and a community, and why do you consider it a good match for you? If there's something in particular about our offerings that attracts you, feel free to share that as well. (250 words)

1. Introduction
   a. Start personal: an anecdote or story of your attraction to the school as you see it.
2. Academics
   a. Majors: Briefly describe what interests you about [your main academic interest].
      i. Do research: Find one to two majors/minors that interest you. [Helpful link: https://trinity.duke.edu/undergraduate/majors-minors]
      ii. _____
      iii. _____
   b. Do research: Find two classes, one professor, one program/institute that interest you.
      i. _____
      ii. _____
      iii. _____
      iv. _____
3. Community and extracurriculars
   a. Do research: Find two clubs and programs *and* one aspect of the Duke community that appeal to you. [Helpful links: https://servicelearning.duke.edu/; https://dukegroups.com/club_signup]
      i. _____
      ii. _____
      iii. _____

Not only are these templates road maps for your research process, they will also serve as the outline for your essay.

PRO TIPS FOR AWESOME RESEARCH

Where can you find these facts? On the internet, of course! The school websites are full of information about classes, professors, extracurricular activities, research and volunteer opportunities, and more. Here are some tips to find details that will lead to an awesome essay.

Tip 1: Look beyond the admissions website

Most schools have an undergraduate admissions website that will serve as your first point of contact with the school. It often has the word "apply" or "admissions" in the URL. At Michigan it's https://admissions.umich.edu/. These websites are intended for you: the prospective student. They are a good place to start your research, but **the best Why Our School essays go beyond the admissions websites and include information from the school's "real" website; i.e., the pages intended for current students, faculty, and staff.** That's where you'll find the gold: a list of every club and volunteer activity, explanations of how the different majors work, what classes are offered, and what the professors are researching.

Tip 2: Use Google

Each college website is different, and they range from well organized to incredibly confusing. Most of the time, I find that a Google search will get you what you want faster than trying to click through a school's various menus and submenus. Be specific. For example, google terms such as "University of Michigan physics major," "Duke English department faculty list," or "Georgetown undergraduate course catalog."

Tip 3: Read the course descriptions

Most universities provide a one-paragraph course description for each class they offer. Read them! Rarely will the course title alone give you enough information to comment intelligently on it in your essays.

Tip 4: Take your time

In researching these essays, you're being asked to become a mini-expert on each college. Because you're a high school student and haven't yet attended college, this will take some time. When you're first starting out, I would give yourself at least an hour or two per school to do your research. It will take time to familiarize yourself with college websites, as well as the particulars of each school. The good news: once you've written one or two of these essays, it gets much easier—and faster—to research and write the remaining schools!

Step 2: Write

If you did your research using the templates suggested above, you are now in great shape to begin writing, because you already have an outline. Though it's certainly possible to write a Why Our School essay using a narrative structure, I advise my students to keep it simple and write a persuasive essay in three parts: introduction, body, conclusion. We'll take those parts one at a time.

I. INTRODUCTION

In the longer-form essays (more than 400 words), you'll want to start with an introductory paragraph. As with the personal essay, you don't need a flashy hook, so don't get stuck trying to come up with the perfect opening. Instead, your goal in the introduction is twofold:

1. Establish a personal connection to the school
2. Make your thesis claim

The best way to accomplish the first goal is through a brief story or vignette. For example: How did you first hear about this college? Do you have a friend or family member who's been there? When did you first become excited about this school or get the feeling that it's *the* school for you?

In the second half of the introductory paragraph, you want to move toward your thesis statement, which needs to be some version of "X University is the right school for me, because Y."

Let's look at two examples.* The first is an introduction that you read a few pages back for a Why Michigan essay:

Long Why Our School Introduction 1 (University of Michigan)

The first time I visited Michigan's campus, I felt at home. The students I met were enthusiastic and engaged, and shared a sense of intellectual curiosity that resonated strongly with me. I would love to be a student at the University of Michigan's College of Literature, Science, and the Arts. At LSA, not only could I pursue my interests, I could pursue interdisciplinary studies that explore how they intersect.

Note how the writer opens with the story of a campus visit but doesn't say just "I love the beautiful campus." Instead, she explains *why* she loved it: the fact that the students she met "were enthusiastic and engaged and shared a sense of intellectual curiosity."

Afterward, she immediately moves on to her thesis statement, which is spread over the last two sentences. She argues that Michigan would be a great place for her to "pursue my interests" and to "pursue interdisciplinary studies that explore how they intersect." Because Michigan offers lots of opportunities for interdisciplinary study, this is a great pitch to make at this school.

Here's another example, for the University of Chicago.

Long Why Our School Introduction 2 (University of Chicago)

When I was fifteen, my biology teacher told me I had a "Rubik's Complex." He was right. I love science because I love the puzzles, the complexities, the possibility of discovery. But I also love the humanities, especially history, art, poetry, and jazz. The University of Chicago is the perfect school for me because it is an incredible place to study science and is also one of the best places in the world to engage with the liberal arts tradition.

*You can read the full versions of all sample essays in appendix V.

This student took a different approach to the opening: he hadn't visited the campus, so instead of starting with the school, he started with a vignette about himself. But he didn't pick just any vignette. By self-deprecatingly describing his "Rubik's Complex," he's immediately making a connection to UChicago's nerdy, intellectually curious culture.

The paragraph ends with a one-sentence thesis statement: "The University of Chicago is the perfect school for me because it is an incredible place to study science and is also one of the best places in the world to engage with the liberal arts tradition." This sentence contains two accurate facts about UChicago—the school has strong sciences *and* it emphasizes a classical liberal arts education—and sets up the rest of the essay, in which he'll use evidence to show the committee what he might look like as a UChicago student.

For shorter essays, you still need an introduction, but it will only be one to two sentences long. In this first example, from a 150-word "Why Duke?" essay, the introduction is just one sentence.[*]

Short Why Our School Introduction 1 (Duke University)

Duke's strength in the sciences, incredible interdisciplinary opportunities, and groundbreaking AI research make it the ideal school for me.

Here the student gets right down to business, opening with his thesis statement. This can be a great approach in shorter essays.

In the next example, also for Duke, the writer takes a two-sentence approach:

Short Why Our School Introduction 2 (Duke University)

Throughout high school, I've been inspired by opportunities to develop my skills, think big, and solve global problems. Duke is the perfect

---

[*]Although "Why Duke?" was slightly longer in the 2023–2024 admissions cycle (250 words), these older essays are excellent examples of short Why Our School essays. They're pithy, and they pack a punch.

fit because it's a world leader in the health sciences that also offers a uniquely global perspective.

Like the "Rubik's Complex" writer, this applicant opens with personal color that's directly connected to her thesis: Duke is right for her "because it's a world leader in the health sciences that also offers a uniquely global perspective."

II. BODY

The body of the essay, like the body of most English or history essays you've written, will consist of your argument: evidence and analysis showing why this school is a great fit for you. Since you already have an outline, your biggest task in writing the body will be to explain why each fact you mention about the school appeals to you personally.

You first saw how that might work back on page 130, where we broke down part of a "Why Michigan?" essay. Following is the entire body of that essay, so you can see how the student's argument unfolds over several paragraphs. As you read this essay, keep in mind two things. First, notice how much space the author devotes to academics versus extracurriculars. Second, notice how she consistently makes arguments about why the University of Michigan is a great fit for her.

Why Our School Body (University of Michigan)

First and foremost, I am a science geek. I love biology and genetics, and after last summer at Columbia University, I'm passionate about psychology. I want to go to Michigan because it has one of the best psychology programs on the planet, and I'm particularly drawn to the Biopsychology, Cognition, and Neuroscience major. This unique program would allow me to explore my fascination with how humans think, process, and remember information. I can't wait to take classes like "Psychology of Thinking," which would give me a foundation for understanding the complex pathways of the mind.

When I think about college, I'm especially excited to do research, and there is no better place for scientific research than Michigan. I would love to work with Professor Brenda Proudfoot and help expand our understanding of the biological mechanisms that humans use to store memories. I would also love to participate in research at the Brain, Cognition, and Action Laboratory, perhaps as part of a UROP. Professor Bolger's research on how we multitask, process information, and remember images is fascinating, and would allow me to deepen my understanding of both cognitive psychology and neurobiology.

Michigan is also a place where I could learn broadly. This year I'm taking a microeconomics class and have become fascinated by economics. Through LSA, I could take classes that explore how economic principles play out in the real world, such as "International Economics" and "Industrial Organization and Performance." I'm also intrigued by the relationship between science and society. I would love to participate in the Science, Technology, and Society program, which offers a uniquely interdisciplinary approach, and even to minor in STS.

Beyond the classroom, Michigan is a place that I want to call home. My work as president of my school's HIV/AIDS Awareness Club has taught me the importance of taking a stand on issues I care about. I was excited to learn that Michigan has a GlobeMed Organization that focuses on both local and international improvements in health. I would love to get involved with GlobeMed, as well as service groups such as University Students Acting Against Cancer. Working on my school's newspaper and as editor of the yearbook has been extremely rewarding, and I would be thrilled to write for *Blueprint Literary Magazine*, where my passion for literature could shine. In my free time, I know that I would often be found jogging around Ann Arbor, hopefully with members of the MRun running club. Michigan has everything I could want from a college and more, and I can't imagine a better place to spend the next four years.

You probably remember from our earlier discussion of this essay how specific this writer is in tying each class, professor, and program directly to her interests. Note how she took the same approach in her activity paragraph, making direct connections between her high school activities and clubs at Michigan. She uses her experience in the HIV/AIDS Awareness

Club to set up an interest in Michigan's GlobeMed organization, and she ties her work on the yearbook to a literary magazine. This one-two punch highlights her extracurricular engagement to date while strengthening the case for her candidacy at Michigan.

III. CONCLUSION

The conclusion of a Why Our School essay should be short and sweet. In the longest essays—more than 500 words—you may want to include a brief concluding paragraph of two to three sentences. But for the vast majority, wrap it up with one or two sentences. In the shortest essays (less than 150 words), you may not even need a conclusion.

Why so short? Simple: you want to devote most of your "real estate" to making your case in the body. For example, in the "Why Michigan?" sample above, note that the conclusion is a single sentence appended to the extracurricular/community paragraph: "Michigan has everything I could want from a college and more, and I can't imagine a better place to spend the next four years."

If you want a *slightly* meatier conclusion, here's an example from a different "Why Michigan?" essay, which ended with a two-sentence concluding paragraph.

Why Our School Conclusion (University of Michigan)
With its incredible spirit, world-class academics, and unbelievable community, the University of Michigan is the perfect place to spend my college years. I would be honored and thrilled to call it my home.

Overall takeaway: keep that conclusion short!

Step 3: Revise

Happily, revising these essays is usually a much simpler process than revising a personal essay. Once you've written your first draft, put it away for a day or two, then take another look at it, clean it up, and share it with your committee.

In addition to looking for clarity, grammar, and flow, here are five common problems to watch out for in Why Our School essays.

RED FLAG 1: TOO VAGUE

Good news: if you followed the steps described above, you have almost certainly avoided this common problem! Many Why Our School essays are vague and general, which is why I suggest that you do substantial research before you start writing.

If you skipped or rushed through the research stage, however, your essay may be lacking on particulars. If that's a problem, simply go back to Step 1 and do some more research. Every four-year college in the United States has more than enough information on its website to fill dozens of essays with unique, specific particulars.

RED FLAG 2: DISORGANIZED

Yet more good news: if you followed the steps above, you will also have avoided this common trap. Especially at schools that ask for longer essays, many applicants submit essays that ramble back and forth between topics.

As with any argumentative essay, you want to be sure that each paragraph has a coherent topic *and* that ideas flow within each paragraph. The outline templates I've provided should ensure that your paragraphs are coherent. If the individual paragraphs feel choppy, try reordering the evidence within them or ask your committee how you might improve the flow—outside eyes can be very helpful here.

RED FLAG 3: READS LIKE A LIST

Perhaps the most common problem I see in essays that are well researched and well organized: they read like a list of facts about the school.

The solution to this problem is analysis: ensuring that for each class, professor, activity, or other fact about the school you *explain why that specific feature appeals to you*. I can't emphasize enough how this connective tissue, though it takes effort to write, will make the difference between an acceptable essay and an essay that rises to the top of the pile!

RED FLAG 4: READS LIKE AN ADMISSIONS BROCHURE

A common mistake, especially when applying to name-brand schools, is to emphasize prestige over personal connection. For example, I once had a student write something like this in an early draft of a "Why Columbia?" essay:

> I would love to be a student in Columbia's prestigious Classics Department. Professor Carmela Vircillo Franklin has achieved worldwide renown for her research on Latin manuscripts, while the distinguished Professor Gareth Williams, holder of the Anthon Professorship of Latin Language and Literature . . .

This student clearly did her research. Everything she says is factually correct. In fact, it would be great marketing copy for the Columbia Department of Classics website. **However, it doesn't work as a Why Our School essay because it says nothing about *her*.**

In revising this essay, I urged the student to remove flowery words such as "distinguished" and "prestigious." Instead of telling us what's so great about Columbia's professors, she needs to show us *why* each professor's research is so interesting to her, personally. What does she like, for example, about Latin manuscripts? What does Professor Williams actually study, and how is that interesting to her? Once she wove in her own voice, this generic, unwieldy passage became strong and persuasive.

RED FLAG 5: WRONG SCHOOL

Yup, you read that right! You'd be surprised how often people refer to the wrong school in an essay. Perhaps they mention the sports mascot of a rival school, a class offered at a different university, or wax on about "Brown's diverse community" in an essay for Columbia. Sometimes, students will even upload an entirely wrong essay to a particular school!

The reality is that it's very easy to make mistakes like this. Applying to college is stressful, and if you're applying to ten to fifteen schools, as many people do, you'll inevitably make mistakes at some point.

This is another reason I strongly urge students to write the supplemental essays one school at a time; it minimizes this kind of error. The other key to avoiding this mistake is to proofread. Be sure to have someone else review each essay, and proofread one last time before you submit each application online.

Engineering School Essays
Show 'Em What You've Done

So you're interested in engineering? Fantastic! Undergraduate engineering schools are a tremendous opportunity for students with a clear sense of their passions and direction. These programs tend to be more focused and specialized than liberal arts schools. But if their curriculum aligns with your interests, you can look forward to four years of hard work and incredible fun.

When writing the Why Our School essay for an engineering school, keep in mind that most selective universities are looking for students who know what they're getting into. At the top programs, competitive applicants have usually spent time doing engineering in high school, whether in a computer science course, a robotics summer camp, or by developing iPhone apps in their spare time.

Unlike in liberal arts programs, where you can often change your major on a whim, enrolling in engineering school is a commitment. At some schools, you'll be applying to a specific track, such as Civil or Mechanical Engineering. Once you get there, changes of major are usually possible, but they often involve a lot of work. It may not always be possible to transfer into highly competitive majors such as Computer Science.

Engineering essays thus need to highlight your past experience in more detail than liberal arts essays. They also need to give the reader a very clear sense of the path you want to take, showing how it springs from everything related to science and engineering you've done up until now.

Here's an excerpt from the body of a "Why Cornell?" essay by a student who was admitted Early Decision to Cornell's highly competitive College of Engineering; you can read the entire essay in appendix V.

> I've spent much of the last six years building robots, and I want to major in Mechanical Engineering with a focus on robotics. Robots fascinate me because they are physical, combining logic with the power of mechanics. I have also seen firsthand the positive impact they can have on people, especially children. Last summer I began working in UVA's Mechatronics Lab, researching human-robot interaction alongside a team of graduate students. I worked to design and build DAMEON, a robot that displays emotions and can teach social skills to autistic children. I also worked on a multirobot swarm that educates children about robotics. In the process I've learned ROS (Robot Operating System) and MATLAB; I've also learned how to contribute in a professional environment and participate in high level discussions. Our lab uses technology every day to improve lives, and this sense of purpose drives me to continue this work.
>
> In college, I can't wait to take classes that will deepen my understanding of robotics. Through Cornell courses like "Human-Robot Interaction—Research and Design," I could continue the work I began at UVA this summer, exploring how robots communicate and interpret their user's needs. I would enjoy taking Professor Petersen's "Bio-Inspired Coordination of Multi-Agent Systems" and, with any luck, work in her Collective Embodied Intelligence Lab. There, I could contribute to the control of advanced robotic swarms as they coordinate in completing complicated tasks.

Notice how in the first paragraph the student doesn't simply say that he's interested in robotics; he explains why. "Robots fascinate me because they are physical, combining logic with the power of mechanics. I have also seen firsthand the positive impact robots can have on people, especially children." He then goes on to give specific examples of how he explored his interests through an internship at a Mechatronics lab.

When describing your own experiences, don't be afraid to geek out! Engineering is a proudly nerdy world. Admissions committees are looking for people who know something about the field and can articulate why they want to focus on mechanical engineering instead of, say, electrical engineering.

In this essay, the student strengthens his argument by mentioning specific tools, languages, and systems such as ROS and MATLAB. You can do the same; just make sure that your essay doesn't end up reading like a technical manual or a list of every language you've ever coded in (that belongs in your résumé).

In the second paragraph, this essay goes in a more traditional Why Our School direction, tying the writer's interests to academic offerings at Cornell. Note how both classes he mentions relate directly to activities discussed in the previous paragraph, as does the Collective Embodied Intelligence Lab. The second paragraph lands because he's already given the reader concrete details about his past engineering experiences.

The Why Our School Essay Is Not a Contract

As you get into the weeds with these essays, you may find yourself worrying about the level of specificity required. "But wait, do I *really* want to major in Citrus Science with a minor in Egyptology?" you might ask yourself. "Will a course in Advanced Puppet Art still look interesting in three years?" Or (more likely) "What if I change my mind and decide not to major in biology?"

It's entirely normal to ask these questions. In fact, it indicates maturity on your part, because the reality is that a class or major that looks interesting to you now may not appeal to you at all next September. Don't let this stop you from writing a compelling essay! Keep in mind that unless you're applying to a preprofessional program like engineering, you are not making a commitment about what you're going to do over the next four years. In fact, once you are admitted to or rejected by a school, no one is ever going to read your essays again.

Instead, remember the quote from Northwestern. The purpose of this essay is to help an AdCom "connect the dots across your application to imagine what kind of college student you might become." **Your essay is a guide that allows the reader to make that imaginary journey, *not* a cast-in-stone road map of your next four years.**

And it shouldn't be. A liberal arts education is designed to give you the opportunity to try new things, changing your mind when necessary. That's how you become a mature, educated adult. Use this essay to talk about what interests you *now*. When you get to college, you'll have the freedom to pursue whatever you want.

You'll also have the freedom to get involved in your school's community, which will be an important theme in the next set of supplemental essays you'll write: the Contributions/Lived Experience, Intellectual Engagement, Activity, Community, and Diverse Perspectives essays.

CHAPTER 6

Supplemental Essays, Part II

The Contributions/Lived Experience, Intellectual Engagement, Activity, Community, and Diverse Perspectives Essays

This chapter deals with five remaining genres of supplemental essays: the Contributions/Lived Experience, Intellectual Engagement, Activity, Community, and Diverse Perspectives essays. Although I'll discuss each of these genres separately, keep in mind the big picture: your application is a portfolio. You'll want to use each supplemental essay to show a different side of you, giving the admissions committee more opportunities to see who you are as a person.

The Contributions/Lived Experience Essay

Form: 50–400-word narrative essay

Audience: The admissions committee

Topic: An experience in your life that led you to develop personal qualities or skills

Purpose: To show the committee how you would contribute to their college community, and to give you an opportunity to discuss aspects of your identity, particularly race and ethnicity, that aren't addressed elsewhere in the application

Although schools have been asking about diversity, identity, and personal experiences for years, the summer of 2023 gave birth to an entirely new supplemental essay genre: the Contributions/Lived Experience essay.

This section, more than any other part of this book, comes with the caveat that the information here is subject to change. The Contributions/Lived Experience essay was created as a response to the Supreme Court affirmative action ruling, so it is very, very new. Admissions officers will be tweaking, or even overhauling, these prompts in the coming years; visit www.write-yourself-in.com for updated info and tips.

Unpacking the Contributions/Lived Experience Essay

The basic **form** of this essay is a narrative essay, typically medium length, that connects your past experiences to personal qualities, skills, perspectives, or other ways you would contribute to a college community. Here are some examples of the new prompt.

Sample Contributions/Lived Experience Essay Prompts

(From the 2023–2024 admissions cycle)

Harvard University

Harvard has long recognized the importance of enrolling a diverse student body. How will the life experiences that shape who you are today enable you to contribute to Harvard? (200 words)

Yale University

Reflect on an element of your personal experience that you feel will enrich your college. How has it shaped you? (400 words)

Johns Hopkins University

Tell us about an aspect of your identity (e.g., race, gender, sexuality, religion, community, etc.) or a life experience that has shaped you as an individual and how that influenced what you'd like to pursue in college at Hopkins? (This can be a future goal or experience that is either academic, extracurricular, or social.) (300 words)

Stanford University

Please describe what aspects of your life experiences, interests, and character would help you make a distinctive contribution as an undergraduate to Stanford University. (250 words)

Lehigh University

What factors have most shaped who you are and what you believe today? You might discuss an obstacle that you have overcome or an experience that has inspired you. (300 words)

Your **audience** is the admissions committee, and the **topic** looks pretty straightforward, at least on the surface: experiences that have shaped you. The **purpose** of this essay, however, is not what it immediately seems, and it's important to understand it if you want to write a good essay.

Why Are So Many Schools Suddenly Asking This Question?

This new genre of essay is all about diversity.

Some background: in the 2023 affirmative action ruling, the Supreme Court struck down the use of race as an independent factor in college admissions. Practically speaking, that means that admissions officers will no longer see your responses to those race/ethnicity checkboxes that have been a part of college applications for decades.[*]

---

[*] The checkboxes are still there, but the Common App allows colleges to ensure that their admissions officers never see your responses. Instead, that data will be used *after* you're admitted in order to understand what the admitted class looks like and to help the school comply with various federal regulations. Is this confusing for students? Yes!

Those checkboxes were one of the tools schools used to put together diverse classes (alongside recruiting efforts, access programs for first-generation students, and more). Though the Supreme Court made that particular tool illegal, it did leave the door open for schools to take race into consideration—as long as they take into account not simply your race or ethnicity itself but *how experiences connected to race shaped you into the person you are today and how you might contribute to a campus community.*

Does that sound technical and convoluted? That's because it is! As Johns Hopkins University explained on their website:

> In this essay question, we are looking for how an aspect of your identity or background has contributed to your personal story—your character, values, perspectives, or skills—and how you think it may shape your approach to college as a scholar, leader, or community member.
>
> Please note that the U.S. Supreme Court recently limited the consideration of race in college admissions decisions but specifically permitted consideration of "an applicant's discussion of how race affected his or her life" so long as the student is "treated based on his or her experiences as an individual—not on the basis of race." Therefore, any part of your background, including but not limited to your race, may be discussed in your response to this essay if you so choose, but will be considered by the university based solely on how it has affected your life and your experiences as an individual.

In other words, what colleges are trying to do in the Contributions/Lived Experience essay is give you an opportunity to talk about how some aspect of your identity, including race, has helped you developed qualities you could contribute to their university.

Why is this so complicated? Partly because the Supreme Court decision was so weird—the majority bent over backward to argue that getting rid of race/ethnicity checkboxes was *good* for people of color, rather than the other way around—and partly because of the legal nightmare that it

---

*For a more complete discussion of the affirmative action ruling and its implications, see the section on Diversity that starts on page 42.

created for colleges. If schools consider your race without making it about your individual experiences, they risk breaking the law (and big lawsuits). But colleges still want diverse classes. The upshot is that they're asking you, the applicant, to thread a very tight needle.

So what exactly is a "contribution"?

As you learned in chapter 2, admissions officers have long been asking "What will this person contribute?" The twist with this new essay is that there's more of an onus on you—the applicant—to show them what those contributions might look like.

For a Contributions/Lived Experience essay, it's helpful to consider three different ways you could contribute to a college community.

1. **Character traits.** Think back to the qualities in the Top Ten list (see page 25): achievement, leadership, community engagement, etc. Any of these traits—all of which are "race-neutral" in that they exist independent of race or ethnicity—could help you contribute to a vibrant campus community. So if you've been reading this book, you are ahead of the curve!

2. **Skills and abilities.** Can you design a website, take beautiful photographs, program in Python, play the trumpet, strike out a batter, write short stories, organize a potluck, or bring people together around a common cause? All of these are skills and abilities you could contribute on campus.

3. **Point of view.** Do you have a particular perspective on chemistry, current events, race, ethnicity, gender, sexual orientation, the Romantic poets, cinematography, or any other topic? A unique point of view that's been shaped by your life experiences will add richness to a college community, both inside and outside the classroom.

To understand how you might contribute as a college student (which can be hard when you haven't yet gone to college), a good starting point is to identify how you are *already* contributing. The "How Do I

Contribute?" worksheet at www.write-yourself-in.com is an exercise that will help you do exactly that.*

In addition to those three categories, you can also discuss any particular way of contributing that can be **directly tied to the college's mission statement**. For example, the mission statement of Lehigh University (google "Lehigh mission statement") is "to advance learning through the integration of teaching, research, and service to others." If in a Lehigh essay you tie your contributions directly to ideas like "serving others" or "advancing learning through research," that will further strengthen your case.

As you're writing a Contributions/Lived Experience essay, the trick—as the name suggests—will be to tell a story that connects your potential contributions to your actual life experiences. The strongest essays won't just say "I'd contribute a passion for biology and a unique point of view on sub-Saharan African politics." They'll also *show* the reader how you developed those qualities.

The Process for Writing a Contributions/Lived Experience Essay

Because these essays are so particular, writing a good one takes some thought. Here's how I would approach it:

1. Pick a topic
2. Narrow your focus
3. Identify the impact
4. Outline
5. Write and revise

Step 1: Pick a topic

To select your topic, start by **thinking about aspects of your lived experience that you want to highlight**. The obvious candidates are social

*Visit http://www.write-yourself-in.com/contributions-worksheet.

identities such as race, ethnicity, gender, sexual orientation, and socioeconomic status.*

But there are others, too. Maybe you experienced some adverse events in childhood that deeply affected you. Maybe your community has had a strong impact on you, by nurturing you or by putting obstacles in your way (or both). Growing up neurodivergent could also be a powerful topic, if you're able to write about it in a way that doesn't raise red flags.†

As you're planning your essay, be sure to pick a topic that doesn't repeat what's already in your personal essay. If that essay is about race, there's no need to discuss it again here, unless you have something important to add. Use this essay to write about something you haven't covered elsewhere.

What if there's no aspect of your identity that you want to highlight? What if you're, say, a white, cisgendered, straight, middle-class male? Or an Asian American female who doesn't want to write about her race?

If you don't want to write about social identity, simply pick an experience in your life that had a big impact on the person you are today. Your task will be the same: to show how it helped you develop qualities and skills you would contribute on a college campus. Just as when you chose a topic for your personal essay, if you feel in your gut that something is important to you, it's probably worth writing about.

Step 2: Narrow your focus

If you've already picked a specific event in your life to highlight, great! You can move on to step 3.

If you want to work with a broader aspect of identity such as race or gender, however, you'll need to get more specific. Ask yourself: What are one or two relevant stories or moments that you want to share? Remember that this essay *cannot* simply be about race, sexual orientation, or

---

*For our purposes, "socioeconomic status" refers to your parents' or guardians' income level and how much education they have (middle school, high school, college, graduate school, etc.).
†For more on writing about mental health challenges, see the section "Should I Write About Mental Health Struggles in My Essays?" on pages 81–85.

gender in general; it needs to be about your individual experiences that relate to this aspect of your background.

It does not, however, have to be about hardship! I'll be honest: when these prompts were first released, I assumed that colleges wanted stories of struggle and strife. Since then, I've heard admissions officers at top schools emphasize that, while these essays can certainly address adversity, they can also be a celebration of your race, of your gender, of anything that's shaped you as a person. You get to choose the message and emotional tone for your story.

Step 3: Identify the impact

Since these essays are ultimately about the impact this experience had on you, the next step is to describe what that impact was. That "impact" is ultimately the key to what you'll contribute on campus.

For example, one possibility is that the experience shaped your character or personality in certain ways. Look back at the Top Ten list (page 25); did this experience help you develop any of those qualities? Maybe it pushed you to build resilience or empathy or take on new leadership roles. Perhaps it inspired you to engage in your community in new ways or develop new intellectual interests. Those are all qualities colleges look for, so discussing them here is great.

Another possibility is that the experience helped you develop new skills that you could put to use in a college setting, inside or outside the classroom. In past years, I've seen students write about challenging experiences that helped them learn how to articulate their views more clearly and with conviction—even when others disagreed with them. That kind of story could be great for a Contributions/Lived Experience essay.

Or perhaps the experience inspired you or helped you develop new perspectives that, as a college student, you could contribute in class discussions. All of those could be great "impacts."

Step 4: Outline

If you've gone through all the steps in developing your strategy, the good news is that it will be relatively easy to outline your essay. The simplest approach is to structure your essay in three parts:

1. Your lived experience
2. How it impacted you
3. Potential contributions

The first part, which will form the majority of the essay, should tell the story of the lived experience you've chosen to discuss. If that experience is related to a broader aspect of your identity, open with a sentence or two describing it, then dive into the story. You could narrate a specific event, or you could relate a more general experience of growing up in a certain community, as a member of a certain race, with a certain sexual orientation, and so on.

In the second part you'll explain the impacts of the story you just told: lesson learned, personal qualities the experience helped you develop, new skills or insights gained. Be specific; language such as "Because of _____, I learned how to _____" or "Although _____ was challenging, it gave me a new understanding of [empathy/resilience/whatever], which I was able to use to _____" can be helpful.

Finally, in the third part you'll close the essay by connecting what you wrote about in the second part to how you might contribute to a college community. For example, if the experience helped you find your voice as a leader, how do you see yourself leading on campus? If it helped you develop resilience, how might that contribute not only to your own success in college but to the experiences of those around you?

Step 5: Write and revise

Once you have your outline, it's time to write! Here's a sample Lived Experience essay in response to the 400-word Yale prompt "Reflect on an element of your personal experience that you feel will enrich your college. How has it shaped you?"

In seventh grade I began playing the bassoon in band, and a dream quickly developed in my mind: to play in an orchestra. Having listened to classical music from a young age, I knew that I loved the orchestral sound, and I believed strongly (if inaccurately) that all the "serious" music was written for orchestras. There was just one problem: I live in rural Virginia, and there is no orchestra in my town.

So I started asking every adult I met—at church, at school, while doing volunteer work—how I could play in an orchestra. Eventually I learned about a small youth orchestra on the campus of Eastern Mennonite University, about 30 miles north of my town. As soon as I got my driver's license (my parents work nights and weekends, and they can't afford to take time off to shuttle me around), I called the orchestra's conductor, auditioned, and was accepted.

As a gay teen, I was nervous about being on the campus of a conservative, Christian school, but people there turned out to be very open and welcoming. The experience was incredible, and the following year, it led to an offer to play in the campus orchestra of Washington & Lee University, which is 40 miles *south* of my town (more driving!). Playing the exposed second bassoon part in Mozart's A-major piano concerto was terrifying, especially because all of the other players were college students or professors. But the feeling of being totally surrounded—literally and figuratively—by such beautiful music was one of the most thrilling experiences of my life.

Reaching beyond my local community has not only made me a better musician, it's transformed me as a person. It's meant less time for friends, schoolwork, and other activities, so I've had to get much better at managing my time. I've also become more resilient, learning to trust my inner voice, persist in the face of challenges, and to keep asking questions even when I don't know the way forward. In college, I can't wait to continue playing orchestral music. I also want to bring the spirit of this experience to the Yale community, not only for myself but to support my classmates in following their dreams and creating meaningful experiences that enrich their lives.

You'll notice that this essay mentions sexual orientation ("As a gay teen" in paragraph three), but it's not actually *about* the writer being gay—or about race or gender. Instead, it's about challenges he faced due to geography and socioeconomic status.

The essay is effective because it shows the writer overcoming obstacles and making sacrifices in pursuit of a goal and then explains how that experience impacted him as a person. He developed character traits such as resilience, persistence, maturity, and self-confidence, while also building time management skills (and presumably becoming a better musician, too). Finally, the essay directly connects those traits to ways he might contribute to the college community: not only as a musician but also by supporting his classmates in following their own dreams.

The Intellectual Engagement Essay

Form: Medium length (typically 150–350-word) narrative essay
Audience: The admissions committee
Topic: Your engagement in a project or activity that engaged your intellectual curiosity
Purpose: To demonstrate intellectual curiosity and show how you might express it on campus

Intellectual curiosity has been long been prized by college admissions officers, and this essay, which is appearing in more supplements each year, gives you the opportunity to write about it. Although the prompts take different shapes, they typically ask you to describe a topic, idea, intellectual, or creative experience that was meaningful to you.

Note that I call this the "intellectual engagement" prompt, not the "intellectual curiosity" prompt. That's because admissions committees don't want you to wax poetic about a topic that you're interested in. Instead, they want to see you actually engaging with it!

Unpacking the Intellectual Engagement Essay

The **form** of this essay is a (typically medium-length) narrative essay in which you demonstrate your intellectual curiosity by describing one or more experiences that engaged it. Here are some sample prompts.

Sample Intellectual Engagement Essay Prompts
(From the 2023–2024 admissions cycle)

Swarthmore College

Tell us about a topic that has fascinated you recently—either inside or outside of the classroom. What made you curious about this? Has this topic connected across other areas of your interests? How has this experience shaped you and what encourages you to keep exploring? (250 words)

Amherst College

Tell us about an intellectual or creative passion you have pursued; what did you learn about yourself through that pursuit? (350 words)

Stanford University

The Stanford community is deeply curious and driven to learn in and out of the classroom. Reflect on an idea or experience that makes you genuinely excited about learning. (250 words)

University of California

Think about an academic subject that inspires you. Describe how you have furthered this interest inside and/or outside of the classroom. (350 words)

Yale University

Tell us about a topic or idea that excites you and is related to one or more academic areas you selected above. Why are you drawn to it? (200 words)

Harvard University

Briefly describe an intellectual experience that was important to you. (200 words)

Your **audience** is the admissions committee, your **topic** is an idea, subject or experience that makes you excited about learning, and your **purpose** is twofold. First, it's to give the committee a sense of your intellectual curiosity, and second—as always—it's to help them imagine how you'll express that curiosity on campus. Will you be researching basic science in the lab, editing work by other students in the office of the literary magazine, exploring some arcane topic deep in the library stacks? Any of these (and these are just a few examples) would be very interesting to a committee.

Note that some of these prompts (Swarthmore, Amherst, Stanford, Harvard) ask about intellectual interests in general, whereas others (University of California, Yale) ask you to discuss your interests in the context of a major or academic area. Either way, you'll want to take the same basic approach to the essay.

The Three-Step Process for Writing an Intellectual Engagement Essay

As with most supplemental essays, I recommend a three-step approach:

1. Brainstorm
2. Outline
3. Write and revise

Step 1: Brainstorm

If your college list includes a lot of selective schools, you'll probably be writing a lot of these essays. In the long run, it will save you time to find a topic you can repurpose for multiple schools.

Start by thinking about an academic subject or two that you might major in. If you're stumped, go to the websites of a few of your top-choice schools and see what majors they have on offer. Then ask yourself:

- Why am I interested in this major?
- What got me interested in this topic?
- What it is about this specific topic that makes my eyes light up?

And perhaps most important . . .

- What are some specific ways I've *already* pursued my interest in this topic?

This last question is key, because ideally, a story about your pursuit of this interest will become the core of this essay. The phrase "learning in action," which admissions officers at the University of Michigan's undergraduate business program often use, quite nicely captures the energy of what you're going for. The readers don't want to see you sitting in a classroom, passively receiving information about this topic. Instead, they want to see you engaging in an active process of learning.

What could that look like? The possibilities are endless, but here are some examples.

Brainstorming an Intellectual Engagement Essay

Here are five kinds of experiences that could show your intellectual curiosity and engagement.

- Doing an academic, in-school research project that truly engaged you (especially if you went above and beyond the basic requirements)
- Learning about something that excites you outside of class, simply for the fun of it (could be a "passion project")
- Teaching yourself a new intellectual skill (e.g., computer programming, a foreign language, economics)
- Applying knowledge or skills you've learned in school to another context (such as developing statistics-based strategies to help your football team win more games, or bringing psychological principles to your activism)
- Learning about or researching a topic as part of an internship, job, or summer course

Since some of these prompts require you to write in the context of a potential major, ideally you're looking for an experience or two that's connected to an area you want to major in. But keep in mind that the connection doesn't have to be precise. A math project may have ignited your interest in physics or economics, while a history research paper may have helped you realize that what you truly care about is psychology (or health care or gender equality or international relations or . . .).

In fact, sometimes the story of "I started out studying X but realized I was actually interested in Y" can make for a powerful essay. Not only does it clearly show learning in action, it also reflects how academic inquiry often works in the real world: you start out looking for one thing but end up discovering something new and completely unexpected.

Step 2: Outline

Keep in mind that the structure of this essay will be determined in part by each particular prompt. A school might ask you to connect your passion to a major or academic field, to explain what you learned about yourself through the experience, or to dive in on the "why" of what engages your curiosity.

Regardless of the prompt, you can approach this essay with a simple three-part structure, then tweak it to fit each school's requirements. In longer essays, each section can be a separate paragraph. In shorter ones, you'll need to combine them.

1. Introduction
2. Body: Your experience of learning in action
3. Conclusion

Let's break these down.

1. INTRODUCTION

The introduction of this essay should briefly give the reader some background for the story you're about to tell. For example, how did you first get interested in this topic? Is it a relatively recent interest, or is it something that's been bubbling inside you for a long time?

The introduction will also need to respond directly to the prompt, which means that it should be customized for each school. In a shorter essay (200 words or less), the introduction could be just a sentence or two.

2. BODY

The body of the essay will, not surprisingly, tell a story in which you engage with this topic. Here is where you want to be sure to show, not tell. You also want to give the reader a clear sense of what you are doing *and* thinking throughout, which can be harder than it sounds.

To help you get to the heart of showing your intellectual engagement, here some questions you might ask and address.

Story Questions for Intellectual Engagement Essays

- What got you started on this specific project?
- What did you set out to do, learn about, or discover?
- What happened that was unexpected and maybe sent you in a different direction?
- What challenges and obstacles did you run into? How did you overcome them?
- What specific actions did you take? (For example: going to the library, researching on JSTOR, asking your teacher for help, reading three books, watching instructional YouTube videos.)
- What were your inspiration and motivation? When things got tough, what kept you going?
- What kinds of questions did you ask yourself along the way?
- What new ideas and insights occurred over the course of the project?
- When did you find that your initial beliefs or assumptions were wrong or needed revising? (If it happened, this is gold!)

Do you have to answer all of these questions? No, and you certainly won't have room to do so in a 200-word essay. Instead, focus on the ones that seem most meaningful and relevant, and be sure that you're telling a clear story.

3. CONCLUSION

As with every essay, your conclusion is the place to pull up and reflect. An Intellectual Engagement conclusion will vary depending on the prompt; important questions to ask yourself are:

- What did you learn from this experience?
- Why was it meaningful to you?
- How did you grow? How has this experience shaped you as a person?
- What will you take from this experience to future pursuits?

- What's next? Based on this experience, what do you want to keep exploring, whether around this topic or something else entirely?

Your goal: after reading your essay, you want the admissions officer to have a clear sense of what you did, why you did it, what you got out of it, and ideally, a glimpse into how your mind works.

Step 3: Write and Revise

After your outline, of course, comes the writing. To give you a sense of where you're headed, here is an Intellectual Engagement essay in response to Amherst's prompt, "Tell us about an intellectual or creative passion you have pursued; what did you learn about yourself through that pursuit?"

For as long as I can remember, American history has fascinated me. When I was in elementary school, I loved visiting Washington, DC, with my family and driving past the massive limestone buildings where democracy actually happened. As I've grown older, I've been inspired by the multiple generations of women in my family who have served in the Navy.

So last year, when I had the opportunity to do an extended research project for AP US History, the obvious choice was my favorite president: Franklin Delano Roosevelt. Although I didn't know much about him at the start, his fireside chats and leadership through World War II had always intrigued me. As I started to learn more about him by reading biographies, analyzing primary sources, and watching interviews with scholars, what began to captivate me were the inherent contradictions in his character. Roosevelt projected strength and boldness, yet he was crippled and often went about in a wheelchair. He was a passionate advocate for the common man, yet he came from a wealthy, aristocratic background. And while he was a staunch defender of democracy, some of his political maneuvering—say, the court-packing plan or his promise in the 1940 election to keep America out of war despite his intention to do the opposite—seemed frankly undemocratic, almost authoritarian.

While this project taught me a lot about our 32nd president, it taught me something much more important about myself: I'm passionate about psychology. My high school doesn't offer a psychology class, but after finishing the paper I found myself checking out books on psychology from the library, watching YouTube videos on personality and character traits, and reading articles on new psychological discoveries when they appeared in the *New York Times* and my local newspaper. Looking forward, I can't wait to take psychology and sociology classes in college, or perhaps even major in the social sciences. History will always be a source of fascination, but I now know that my true interest is in people: how they see the world, why they do what they do, and what makes them tick.

This essay opens with background and context about the author's long-standing interest in US history. She supports her story with specific details about her family's military ties and early trips to the nation's capital.

In the body paragraph, the writer wisely chooses to focus on one specific research project involving Franklin D. Roosevelt. The story "shows" (instead of telling) by highlighting specific actions the writer took, including "reading biographies, analyzing primary sources, and watching interviews with scholars." It then shows the writer's intellectual curiosity in the following sentences, where she describes how certain aspects of FDR's biography intrigued her.

In the final paragraph, the writer directly ties her story back to the question in the prompt, which is "what did you learn about yourself through that pursuit?" She explains how the project led her to develop an interest in psychology, adding some specifics about how she is now pursuing that interest. The essay ends on a forward-looking note that reaffirms her interest in history while also expressing excitement about her newfound "interest in people."

On the whole, this essay succeeds because it is specific, passionate, and directly related to the prompt. Note that it isn't only about history, although it certainly could have been. Instead, it tells the story of how diving deep into one academic subject led her to discover an entirely new interest. In other words, it shows a student clearly engaged in learning in action.

The Activity Essay

Form: 50–250-word narrative essay

Audience: The admissions committee

Topic: One extracurricular activity or work experience

Purposes: (1) To show how you engage with your community; (2) to give the reader a sense of how you pursue your passions outside the classroom

Activity essays used to be very common at selective schools, but in recent years they've largely been replaced by the other genres in this chapter. However, there are still enough out there, including at powerhouses such as Stanford and Harvard, that they're worth discussing.

When you do see an Activity essay requirement, take heart: they can be fun to write! Although they're often short—between 50 and 200 words—this genre gives you a chance to talk about something that you genuinely enjoy.

These essays can also be an opportunity to let your hair down a bit and show a more playful side, while continuing to highlight personal qualities such as leadership, passion, and engagement.

Unpacking the Activity Essay

The **form** of these essays is straightforward: a narrative essay about your engagement with a particular activity, work experience, or family obligation. The form doesn't vary much from school to school; here are three sample prompts.

Sample Activity Essay Prompts

(From the 2023–2024 admissions cycle)

Stanford University

Briefly elaborate on one of your extracurricular activities, a job you hold, or responsibilities you have for your family. (50 words)

Harvard University

Briefly describe any of your extracurricular activities, employment experience, travel, or family responsibilities that have shaped who you are. (200 words)

Brown University

What is your most meaningful extracurricular commitment, and what would you like us to know about it? (100 words)

Vanderbilt University

Vanderbilt offers a community where students find balance between their academic and social experiences. Please briefly elaborate on how one of your extracurricular activities or work experiences has influenced you. (250 words)

Most of these essays are short, à la Brown's and Stanford's. A few, such as Harvard's, are longer. These require more legwork but also give you more of an opportunity to talk about something cool that you've done.

Your **audience** is, of course, an admissions committee. You'll likely write one Activity essay and then adapt it for multiple schools. The core of the essay, just like your personal essay, won't be particular to any school. Your **topic** will be one activity or work experience. Finally, I suggest that you think of a primary **purpose** here as to **show the admissions committee something that isn't highlighted elsewhere in the application.** Maybe there's an important part of your life that didn't make it into your personal essay. Or maybe there's a line on your résumé that deserves to be expanded into a paragraph or two. This is your chance to tell that story.

In doing so, you'll accomplish two things. First, you'll show the reader how you engage with the world around you. Second, you'll show them how you pursue your passions outside the classroom. Like the Why Our School essay, this information will help the committee imagine the kind of student you might be at their college.

The Three-Step Process for Writing Activity Essays

I recommend this three-step process for the Activity essay:

1. Pick a topic
2. Brainstorm and outline
3. Write and revise

Step 1: Pick a Topic

Remember those brainstorming lists you created for the personal essay? Now is a great time to pull them out again. Those unused essay topics will be great fodder for this and other supplemental essays.

When selecting a topic, first and foremost you're looking for **a story that shows a different side of you than what you showed in your personal essay.** As you get deeper into the supplemental essays, remember the image of your entire application as a portfolio, much like an artist or designer's portfolio. Each piece of the portfolio should show a different side of you; you don't want to waste your limited space saying the same thing over and over! If your personal essay was about your love of science, use the Activity essay to talk about running cross-country or doing theater. If your personal essay focused on sports, you might use this essay to talk about a service experience.

Second, as in the rest of your application portfolio, **pick a topic that allows you to highlight qualities admissions officers are looking for.** Though it can be useful to highlight any of the qualities from the Top Ten list, three lend themselves most naturally to Activity essays: leadership, passion, and community engagement.

LEADERSHIP

If you hold an official leadership role—president, vice president, captain, or some other—the Activity essay is a great place to show the committee why and how you lead. If you've founded a club or organization, which in and of itself shows leadership, this is a great place to tell that story.

Keep in mind, however, that there are many ways to show leadership. Maybe you don't have a formal title in your favorite club but you took charge of a project or led an initiative that positively affected your community or helped you see the world differently. An essay about that kind of leadership experience can be just as powerful as one that involves official titles and roles.

PASSION

Nearly every good Activity essay describes a pursuit that the writer truly cares about. Admissions officers know that you didn't choose to take chemistry or US history. They also know that you *do* have choices about how you spend your time outside the classroom. Readers want to get to know young people who are genuinely engaged with groups and causes they care about, because those people are likely to create a thriving campus community.

If you're writing about a work experience, note that passion functions slightly differently. If you're passionate about the work you're doing, great! Write about that. But don't pretend that you're passionate about a job you might not enjoy but have taken on because you or your family need the money. Instead, write about the impact the job is having on your life (or your family's life) and how you've learned and grown from the experience.

COMMUNITY ENGAGEMENT

Whenever possible, write about an activity that you were engaged with over multiple years. For an admissions officer, it's much more interesting to read a story of your engagement with something you truly care about over time versus something that you just joined—even if you think the new thing sounds more prestigious or interesting.

For example, at first glance it might not sound impressive that you joined the anime club as a freshman, stayed involved, and became president your senior year. But if that club is something you're genuinely passionate about *and* put a lot of time, energy, and creativity into, consider writing about it. That story is going to make a much more compelling essay than a story about someone who was just elected president of the National Honor Society but hasn't actually done much in that role.

If you don't have any long-term commitments, don't worry. It can be perfectly fine to write about an activity you've done for only one or two years, especially if it's something you're truly passionate about. Just be sure to show the reader how you were committed and engaged.

Now that you know what to highlight, review your résumé and brainstorming from the personal essay, and pick an activity that will show you at your best!

Step 2: Brainstorm and Outline

Once you've settled on a topic, a little bit of brainstorming will help you create a strong outline. **As with the personal essay, it's important to include both internal and external story elements in your Activity essay.** The basic story structure you've already learned—beginning, middle, end—is a good jumping-off point for these essays. Start your process by doing the following activity.

Brainstorming and Outlining an Activity Essay

Briefly answer the following questions. Bullet points or sentences are fine.

1. Beginning:
   a. How, why, and when did I first get involved with this activity?
   b. What motivated me to sign up for it (or start this club, or . . .)?
2. Middle:
   a. What did I actually *do* for this activity?
   b. Did that change over time? If so, how?

c. What do I *enjoy* about this activity, and why? (Why do I keep doing this?)

3. End:

   a. Where am I now with this activity? (I.e., have I taken on a leadership role?)

   b. Why is it important to me?

   c. How have I learned and grown from it?

   d. How do I see myself continuing it in the future? (This could include continuing to do this activity and/or using its skills in a different context.)

Did you notice how the questions are designed to bring out both the external story (what you actually did) and the internal story (why you did it and how it affected you)? I bet you did. By now, you're becoming an expert on these things!

Once you've completed this exercise, you have two options. Very often, your responses will suggest a clear story structure with a beginning, middle, and end. If you're seeing that, great! This is your outline. Move on to the next step and start writing a draft of that essay.

Alternatively, answering these questions may inspire you to pursue a different take on this essay. You might want to highlight a specific aspect of the activity that's especially meaningful to you, or to focus the essay on one particular part of the story.

If that's the case, sketch out a brief outline for how you might structure the essay—no more than two or three bullet points—and then get writing! If you're confused by the second option, take a look at the examples that follow.

Step 3: Write and Revise

As with the personal essay, it works best to overwrite a bit, then cut back. For a 150-word essay, aim for 200 to 225 words in your first draft. If you try to keep it below 150, you are inviting your Censor to come in and derail your process.

Here are two examples of Activity essays that were successful. I've also included mini-outlines for the first two, so you can see how the outlines led to the final product.

SAMPLE ACTIVITY ESSAY 1

Mini-outline

1. Beginning:
   a. Done yearbook since freshman year
   b. Love writing, design, being organized
   c. It's a break from classes and homework
2. Middle:
   a. Was editor this year
   b. I like the responsibility and seeing all the different pieces
3. End:
   a. Future: Train the juniors
   b. Do something similar in college (not necessarily yearbook)

Essay (100 words)

For the past three years I've constantly looked forward to sitting down, grabbing my mug of coffee, and diving in on the yearbook. I love yearbook because it ties together three of my favorite activities: writing, graphic design, and organization. This year, as editor, I'm especially excited because I'm responsible for everything from the overall theme to cover design. After we publish this spring, I look forward to passing on my experience to the rising class of editors. Next year, I can't wait to join another student publication where I can channel my inner writer, designer, and manager.

Even though it's only 100 words, this essay follows the classic story structure of beginning, middle, and end. The student opens by telling us what she loves about doing yearbook. We see her hard at work on "writing, graphic design, and organization," while her description of the coffee mug adds a bit of warmth and character.

In the brief "middle" section, she describes being an editor, highlighting her leadership role and responsibilities. In the "end," she looks toward the future in two ways: passing on her experience to others—another kind of leadership!—and getting involved in student publications in college.

Pretty neat how she managed to fit so much into 100 words, right? Many students don't realize they can fit that much content into a 100-word essay until they see it done.

Here's another example that makes use of a different structure.

SAMPLE ACTIVITY ESSAY 2

Mini-outline
1. Part 1: What I love about ultimate Frisbee
   a. Community and friendships
   b. Not a "normal" sport
   c. Spirit of the Game—balances competition, friendliness, fair play
2. Part 2: My relationship to ultimate Frisbee
   a. Friendships, exercise, time outdoors
   b. Will definitely keep playing in college. Will be looking for ultimate in the first week

Essay (150 words)

I love ultimate Frisbee. Not only is the sport physically challenging, but it also forms incredible relationships, requires quick decision making, and brings out the best in people. Since ultimate is self-officiated, anyone can call a foul at any time, with obvious potential for abuse. However, ultimate players also follow an unwritten code known as "Spirit of the Game." This code promotes respect and sportsmanship, from honesty in foul calls to complimenting opponents on a nice play. Thanks to this honor system, ultimate can be fiercely competitive while also creating an ethos of community and inclusivity.

Ultimate has enriched my life immensely, and I hope to keep playing in college. At Michigan, joining the MagnUM ultimate team would give me an instant community of new friends, help me stay in shape, and—given that I'll spending most of my time at North Campus— offer regular opportunities to enjoy the outdoors and nature.

Unlike the first essay you read, this one is written in a two-part structure. This student cared deeply about the community he'd found through ultimate Frisbee, and he held strong beliefs about the "Spirit of the Game" ethic. He also felt strongly that he wanted to keep playing in college.

So instead of a classic beginning-middle-end story structure, this student tried something different. In the first paragraph, he made a claim about something he believed in: how the Spirit of the Game ethic creates a unique kind of community. I call this "putting a stake in the ground," i.e., staking out a claim about something he believes in. The second paragraph goes in a more narrative direction: he briefly mentions that ultimate has "enriched my life immensely," then shows the reader what his engagement with this activity might look like in college.

Writing About Sports: Focus on the Internal Story

Sports often come up as a potential topic for supplemental essays, and with good reason. Athletics can make for fantastic Activity essays (and Community essays), but they also introduce a challenge: What to talk about? After all, the outward experiences of many players of lacrosse, hockey, football, basketball, and other sports are often quite similar.

The solution here is simple: **focus on the internal story**. Think about the sports stories that you love. In any article, book, or movie about an athlete, the most compelling material isn't who won or lost; it's what went on inside the player's head and heart. The same is true in your college essays.

With that in mind, here are three strategies for moving from the external to the internal story in sports.

1. One approach is to identify what you, personally, love about the sport. For example, do you love the camaraderie? The sense of team spirit? Or is it the game itself, perhaps the scoring of points or the way time melts away when

you're on the field? There are as many different reasons to like a sport as there are people who play them. If nothing immediately comes to mind, do some freewriting about this. Describing what you love and why you love it will quickly draw the reader into your story.

2. A second option is to reflect on what you've learned from playing the sport over the years and how you've grown. You'll want go beyond surface-level claims such as "I've learned leadership" or "I've learned about being a team player." Instead, dig deeper and ask yourself questions such as: What have I learned *about* leadership from playing this sport, and how did I learn that? How has this sport taught me what being a team player looks like? What have I learned about *why* being a team player is important?

3. Finally, a third possibility is to go for the classic sports genre angle: focus on the challenges. Every successful athlete has to overcome obstacles. What were yours, how did you overcome them, and—very important for college essays—how did the process of overcoming them help you become the person you are today?

Keep in mind that none of these three options is better than any other. They're not mutually exclusive, either. Feel free to mix and match from multiple pathways until you find the story that works for you.

Finishing the Activity Essay

Some good news: unlike the personal essay, an Activity essay often takes only one or two rounds of revision to get into tip-top shape. Even better, it can easily be repurposed for multiple schools. In the examples you read above, the first and third essays could be used verbatim in different applications, while the second essay could be quickly adapted to different schools by changing the details in the last paragraph.

Because Activity essays are so versatile, it's worth investing the time in writing a strong one. If you're applying to the University of California (which includes UCLA, UC-Berkeley, UC Santa Barbara, and others), a solid Activity essay can even be expanded into one of the four required UC essays (see chapter 7 for more on the UC process).

This is also true, by the way, for a good Community essay, which is the next type of supplemental essay we'll explore.

The Community Essay

Form: 100–400-word narrative essay

Audience: The admissions committee

Topic: Your relationship to a community that's important to your life

Purposes: (1) To show the reader what you value; (2) to give the reader a sense of who you are in a community

The Community essay is another classic supplemental essay genre. Although some schools are phasing it out in favor of the Lived Experience essay, it's still worth examining because others are still asking for it. Similarly to the Activity essay, you'll be talking about a group that you are a member of, inside or outside school. The difference is in your focus. Instead of primarily emphasizing your own actions and efforts, you'll be highlighting the community itself, why it matters to you, and how it's shaped you.

Unpacking the Community Essay

Much as with the Activity essay, the **form** is a narrative essay about your engagement with a particular community. The prompts are often similar; here are three examples.

Sample Community Essay Prompts

(From the 2023–2024 admissions cycle)

University of Michigan

Everyone belongs to many different communities and/or groups defined by (among other things) shared geography, religion, ethnicity, income, cuisine, interest, race, ideology, or intellectual heritage. Choose one of the communities to which you belong, and describe that community and your place within it. (300 words)

Yale University

Reflect on your membership in a community. Why is your involvement important to you? How has it shaped you? You may define community however you like. (400 words)

William & Mary

Are there any particular communities that are important to you, and how do you see yourself being a part of our community? (300 words)

Your **audience** for these essays is, of course, the admissions committee. Keep in mind that part of an admissions officer's job is to put together a class that will function as a community. They will be reading these essays with an eye to how you might become a part of their campus community.

The **topic** of this essay will be one community that is meaningful to you. Note how in each of the prompts above, you're given pretty wide latitude in how you define "community." The Michigan prompt gives you examples, while the Yale prompt comes right out and says it: "You may define community however you like." I'll talk more below about how to pick a community that shows you at your best.

Finally, the **purpose** of this essay is to give the reader a sense of who you are in community. What are the roles you tend to play? What do you contribute to a community, what have you gotten out of it, and what might you look like as a member of this school's campus community?

On the whole, the best Community essays do three things:

1. They identify your community and show your place in it.
2. They tell a brief story that shows you as active, engaged, and involved.
3. They make some sort of statement about the kind of community you value.

This essay is also a way to explicitly or implicitly talk about your values. By "values," I simply mean the things you care about and believe are important; they could be religious or spiritual, but they could be completely secular as well. Social justice, the environment, peace, diversity, compassion, showing up for others, integrity, good sportsmanship, and family relationships are all things that you might value.

Values, of course, show up in all of the college essays, but since colleges are communities, this essay highlights your values in a way that's especially relevant to the admissions process. Whether your school, a church, synagogue, or other house of worship, or your family, the communities you care about say something profound about who you are. This essay is a chance to share that with the reader.

Finally, as with all the supplemental essays, remember that your application is a portfolio. This essay is an opportunity to tell the admissions committee something that you haven't yet talked about in your personal essay or other supplemental essays, so you can give the admissions committee more insight into how interesting you are.

The Three-Step Process for Writing a Community Essay

I recommend the same three-step process as for the Activity essay:

1. Pick a topic
2. Brainstorm and outline
3. Write and revise

Step 1: Pick a Topic

Most prompts allow you to define "community" in almost any way you like. Your community could be your school, an activity you participate in, or a sports team you're part of. It could be your church, synagogue, mosque, or other religious community. Your family and any ethnic/racial group that's part of your heritage are all communities. If you identify as a person of color or as LGBTQIA+, this can be a great place to highlight how community has shaped you.

Since you have so much latitude, it's important to pick a community that you genuinely care about; that passion will show in your writing. Ideally, you also want to select a community in which you have been involved for a substantial period of time, either over the years or by investing many hours each week in it.

If a community immediately comes to mind, great! Move on to the next step.

If not, take five minutes to brainstorm all the communities you are part of. Start by looking at your résumé and listing every community that is represented on it. Then add any communities that aren't on your résumé. As the examples above show, there are nearly limitless types of communities, both in person and virtual.

Step 2: Brainstorm and Outline

Once you have a potential topic, your next step is to brainstorm and outline your ideas. As with the Activity essay, it can be useful to highlight leadership, engagement, and passion. In addition, the Community essay can be a great place to show your empathy. How do you relate to the people around you? Have you become invested in causes and people that you genuinely care about? Do you take the time to understand others' concerns and points of view? The following questions are designed to help you flesh out your story in a way that will make it shine.

Brainstorming a Community Essay

Briefly answer the following questions. Bullet points or sentences are fine.

1. The Why:
   a. What is the specific community I have chosen?
   b. What matters to me about this community?
   c. Who are the other people in the community, and why do I care about them?
   d. Why is this community meaningful to me?
   e. Why do I want to be part of this community? Put differently, why have I decided to invest my time, energy, and heart into it?

2. The What:
   a. How, when, and why did I become a part of this community?
   b. As a member of this community, what have I done? How have I participated in it?
   c. Have I taken on any leadership roles in this community, either formally or informally?
   d. How have I learned and grown through my engagement with this community?
   e. Where am I now in relationship to this community?
   f. What's next? For example, do I want to stay engaged with this community, or other communities like it, in the future? If so, why and how?

Once you've done this brainstorming, make a mini-outline. Keep it simple. Using your answers from the "What" section—which, you may have noticed, pertain mostly to your external story—make a mini-outline as follows:

1. Beginning:
   a. How I first got involved with this community
2. Middle:
   a. Some specifics about my involvement with the community
3. End:
   a. Where I stand today with the community, and/or what's next

As far as the "Why" questions go, there are various ways of integrating them into your essay. In the next section, we'll look at some possibilities.

Step 3: Write and Revise

Successful Community essays can take different forms. Here's one that helped the writer get admitted to the University of Michigan.

SAMPLE COMMUNITY ESSAY 1

Prompt: Everyone belongs to many different communities and/or groups defined by (among other things) shared geography, religion, ethnicity, income, cuisine, interest, race, ideology, or intellectual heritage. Choose one of the communities to which you belong, and describe that community and your place within it. (250 words)

Essay

Judaism is at the core of my identity. I was raised in a Jewish household, and at age thirteen I officially joined my synagogue as an adult. While I'm only seventeen, I take my "adult" responsibilities seriously. Two Jewish concepts in particular are central to how I approach the world. One is *mitzvah*, which literally means "good deed" and also translates to "commandment." The other is *tzedakah*, or charitable giving.

Through Torah study and service work at temple, my community has given me a hands-on understanding of both terms. *Tzedakah*, I've learned, comes in many forms: donations of time, knowledge, and passion. *Mitzvah*, as well, is a social obligation to alleviate suffering and pain. These concepts inform everything I do. For example, I see my work as president of the AIDS Awareness Club at my school as *tzedakah*, whether we're organizing fundraisers to support AIDS research or raising awareness around the disease. In another club I lead, Helping Out People Everywhere (HOPE), the principle of *mitzvah* inspired me to expand the scope of our volunteer work to nursing homes, community centers, and other places where we can directly relieve suffering.

One of the many things I love about Judaism is that it immerses me in multiple communities. Locally, I'm part of my synagogue and the Jewish Community Center, yet I'm also a member of the global Jewish community. Giving back, through both *mitzvah* and *tzedakah*, connects me to all of these communities and to the human community at large.

This essay does a fantastic job of illustrating the student's values, then backing them up with specific evidence of how she's put them into action. The essay as a whole is structured around her lifelong experience with Judaism, from being raised in a Jewish household to her leadership roles in clubs today.

She also had the marvelous idea of using two Jewish theological principles—*mitzvah* and *tzedakah*—to talk about her values (the "Why"), and then gives us examples of how she's put them into practice both at school and at her synagogue. Structurally, she front-loads the "Why" values in the first paragraph, then develops them throughout. This essay has the additional bonus of highlighting her leadership roles in various service organizations.

SAMPLE COMMUNITY ESSAY 2

Prompt: Everyone belongs to many different communities and/or groups defined by (among other things) shared geography, religion, ethnicity, income, cuisine, interest, race, ideology, or intellectual heritage. Choose one of the communities to which you belong, and describe that community and your place within it. (300 words)

Essay

Last fall, I never would have imagined that a group of juniors, who at first glance have little in common, would become so important to me. The Teen Prevention Education Program (Teen PEP) is a peer-to-peer sexual education program that equips students with knowledge and skills for sexual health. Through interactive workshops that include skits, talks, and group discussions, we create safe environments to educate students about topics like gender and homophobia, while teaching skills to make healthy decisions and resist peer pressure.

The work I've done for Teen PEP has been incredibly meaningful, and I'm proud to have had a positive impact on the next generation of Westlake High students. What surprised me, however, was how close I became to the other peer educators in my cohort, and how we became a community.

Our cohort contains students from a variety of social, ethnic, and economic backgrounds. We practice different religions and come from different cultures, but through the hours of honest and personal discussions that PEP demanded, we found that we shared a deep desire to help others and to bring more justice into the world. Often, we would stay late at night after our Teen PEP meetings, discussing current events, world politics, and social change.

This community, with its diversity of thought and opinion, has changed me. It has exposed me to new ideas and led me to broaden my circle of friends. Over time, I even surprised myself with how vocal I became about my own ideas and passions, especially around gender and equity.

Although we will soon split up to follow our own paths, I'm grateful for what my Teen PEP community has given me, and I know I will find similarly inclusive and engaging communities at the University of Michigan.

At first glance, this essay reads more like an Activity essay. The topic is a school activity, and the essay starts with a solid focus on the "what." At the end of the second paragraph, however, the student makes a pivot toward community with the sentence "What surprised me, however, was how close I became to the other peer educators in my cohort, and how we became a community." Then, in the second half of the essay, she focuses on the "Why." We see that she values diversity, both "a variety of social, ethnic, and economic backgrounds" and a "diversity of thought and opinion." This nuanced understanding shows maturity and suggests that, for her, "diversity" is more than a buzzword. She was admitted Early Action to Michigan, and I have no doubt that this essay played a role.

Finishing the Community Essay

Like the Activity essay, your Community essay can be used in multiple applications and even repurposed as a University of California personal insight question. Because a strong Community essay requires more depth and nuance than an Activity essay does, it can take a bit more time to revise, but not too much. Do two or three drafts, run it by your committee, and you will be good to go!

The Diverse Perspectives Essay

Form: 50–400-word narrative essay

Audience: The admissions committee

Topic: A moment in your life when you engaged with someone with a different point of view

Purpose: To show the committee that you have the ability to hear, understand, and respond with empathy to people you disagree with

The Diverse Perspectives essay is a relatively new genre that's popping up in more and more supplements. As you're probably aware, discussions about free speech have in recent years become more prominent—and heated—on college campuses. Unlike the other short essays, this essay is specifically focused on assessing how you engage with different viewpoints.

Unpacking the Diverse Perspectives Essay

Though the precise requirements vary from school to school, the overall **form** of these essays is a first-person reflection on a time when you encountered someone whose viewpoint differed from yours.

Here are a few examples.

Sample Diverse Perspectives Essay Prompts
(From the 2023–2024 admissions cycle)

Yale University

Reflect on a time you discussed an issue important to you with someone holding an opposing view. Why did you find the experience meaningful? (400 words)

Vanderbilt University

Vanderbilt University values learning through contrasting points of view. We understand that our differences, and our respect for alternative views and voices, are our greatest source of strength. Please reflect on conversations you've had with people who have expressed viewpoints different from your own. How did these conversations/experiences influence you? (250 words)

Boston College

At Boston College, we draw upon the Jesuit tradition of finding worthwhile conversation partners. Some support our viewpoints while others challenge them. Who fulfills this role in your life? Please cite a specific conversation you had where this conversation partner challenged your perspective or you challenged theirs. (400 words)

Your **audience** is, of course, an admissions committee, and your **topic** will be a time when your views were challenged. Note that in this essay you should *not* simply discuss your beliefs about empathy, dialogue, or diversity in general; the prompts ask you to write about a particular moment in your life. As far as the **purpose** of this essay is concerned, it's a bit different from that of the other supplemental essays in that it's focused on spotlighting the trait of intellectual empathy: understanding and responding to ideas that are different from your own.

In a world filled with echo chambers, this prompt is a chance to show an admissions committee that you are able to engage respectfully and productively with people who have different views—the kind of dialogue that is at the heart of a liberal arts education.

Writing the Diverse Perspectives Essay

To write an effective Diverse Perspectives essay, at the minimum, you need to:

1. Describe the situation
2. Explain the other person's viewpoint and how it differed from yours
3. Show how you responded

The best essays, however, will also contain a fourth element: a reflection, perhaps on how this situation relates to a broader idea or principle, or on how you learned and grew from this experience.

I recommend this three-step process for writing a Diverse Perspectives essay:

1. Brainstorm
2. Outline
3. Write and revise

Step 1: Brainstorm

Start your work on this essay by brainstorming: **What were some times when you encountered someone who held different views from yours?** Come up with at least three or four possible ideas. Conversations about hot topics such as race, gender, and sexual orientation can certainly work, but so can less political conversations that may have taken place in the context of class projects, team sports, or even just hanging out with friends.

As you're evaluating these various encounters, you'll also want to be thinking about how you responded to the other person. Your response will be the centerpiece of the essay, and many Diverse Perspectives essay prompts ask you to talk about responding with some kind of empathy or understanding. In past years, schools have even hinted at the kinds of responses they're looking for in their prompts, whether it's being an "empathetic speaker or generous listener" (University of Virginia), "gaining insight" (Princeton), or being led to "change your opinion or to sharpen your reasons for holding on to it" (Yale).

As you look at your list of options, ask yourself: In which situations did I respond with empathy? That could look like:

- Changing your beliefs or perspective in response to the other person's views
- Disagreeing with the other person but leaving the conversation with a better understanding of their viewpoint
- Learning something new and unexpected
- Gaining a better understanding of your biases and limitations
- And more . . .

Ultimately, you want to find a story from your life where the other person's perspective impacted how you thought or acted. That impact is what will show—not just tell—the committee that you possess intellectual empathy.

Step 2: Outline

Here's a basic two-part structure that I recommend you start with:

Part 1: The story of what happened (50 to 80% of the essay)
Part 2: Your reflection on that story (20 to 50% of the essay)

Whatever the prompt is, you'll want to structure part 1 like any three-part story: make sure that it has a beginning, a middle, and an end. For example, you might describe the situation in the beginning, show the other person expressing their view (as well as your initial reaction to it) in the middle, and then explain your response in the end.

Part 2 will vary more from school to school, depending on the length and the prompt itself. For longer prompts, I would look to the last sentence of Vanderbilt's prompt as a starting point because it gives a good sense of what admissions committees are looking for. That sentence is "How did these conversations/experiences influence you?"

The strongest responses will show how the discussion impacted the writer in a meaningful way. Maybe you gained an insight into this specific issue that will influence how you approach it in the future. Or—even better—maybe you realized the importance of questioning your own assumptions or discovered a new approach to how you might navigate differences.

Step 3: Write and Revise

Once you have a basic outline, it's time to start writing your essay.

Although it's easy to talk about these essays, I've found that for many students, these stories can be surprisingly difficult to nail down. So don't worry too much about word count in your first draft. Aim to get the entire story down on paper, and just try to keep the length to no more than 200% of the final word count.

As with the personal essay, it can be a good idea to write a first draft of this essay, put it away for a day or two, then come back to it and revise. You're writing about a moment that may have been emotionally intense, and the more perspective you can bring to it, the better the essay will be.

Once you're ready to start revising, definitely make use of your committee. Show your readers this chapter and ask them if it's clear in your essay how the other person's point of view impacted you and how you responded. A common issue in Diverse Perspectives essays is that while you may feel strongly that you showed intellectual empathy in a given situation, it is not at all clear to the reader.

Finally, here's a sample essay to give you an idea of what a strong response might look like.

Sample Diverse Perspectives Essay

Prompt: At Princeton, we value diverse perspectives and the ability to have respectful dialogue about difficult issues. Share a time when you had a conversation with a person or a group of people about a difficult topic. What insight did you gain, and how would you incorporate that knowledge into your thinking in the future? (250 words)

Essay

Last year, while hiking near my home, I ran into a man who wanted to talk about COVID. Despite the fact that he worked in health care, he wasn't getting vaccinated. In fact, he believed there was a conspiracy and that vaccines caused COVID.

My initial reaction was anger. I knew he was wrong, and I had statistics to challenge his unscientific views. Yet as he spoke, I began to notice something else: he was afraid. Thinking back to my own vaccination the previous month, I remembered that when the National Guard medic stuck that needle in my arm, I, too, had an irrational fear that it might give me COVID.

So instead of reiterating the facts, I listened. When he was done, I told him about my vaccination, how scared I had been. Sure, I felt sick for a few days afterwards, but I got better. Today, I had just hiked a mountain!

He nodded, and I think he heard me. While I'd like to think that my empathy helped persuade him to get the vaccine, I do know that I learned a valuable lesson: there is power in simply listening to someone's story and sharing your own.

I love science, and I'll always believe in the power of truth and reason. Yet I now know that facts are not the only way to persuade. If I truly want to have an impact, I need to continue listening to others' stories and finding the courage to share my own.

From Genres to Schools

Since you'll be writing your supplemental essays one school at a time, in the next chapter we'll examine how to approach essays for several individual schools. Because the prompts and length requirements can change each year, you'll find up-to-date guidance at www.write-yourself-in.com.

CHAPTER 7

Supplemental Essays at Highly Selective Schools

The Ivies and Ivy Adjacents

In the previous two chapters, we explored how to approach each of the six most important genres of supplemental essays you're most likely to run into: Why Our School, Lived Experience, Intellectual Engagement, Activity, Community, and Diverse Perspectives. In this chapter, we'll pull back a bit and look at how you can use that information to put together a powerful supplemental essay for any highly selective school on your list.

To make things manageable, I've broken the chapter down into five clusters of schools that are in the back of most people's minds when they start applying to selective colleges. Even if you don't know all the names yet, you're probably already thinking about them, because these schools form the background of how nearly everyone in the United States thinks about prestige and selectivity in higher education. They are:

1. The Ivy League
2. The Ivy Plus Schools
3. The Little Ivies
4. The Public Ivies
5. Hidden Gems

Even if you're not applying to any Ivies, I still recommend reading this chapter, because the advice will help you tailor your essays to particular schools. The only wild card here is the fifth category—which you will find only in this book, because I made it up—which contains schools that have higher acceptance rates but are still fantastic schools. To quote the greatest movie of all time (Disney's *Aladdin*), these schools are "diamonds in the rough."

One thing this section *doesn't* include is specific guidance on how to write each supplemental essay at every school. That's because the prompts for those essays often change from year to year and are typically announced the summer before applications open, so much of that information would be out of date before this book is published.

Instead, I'll include general guidance on applying to each category of selective school. I'll also break down the most recent questions from a few key schools in each category, so you get a concrete sense of how to approach these kinds of supplemental essays. For more specific guidance on this year's prompts, you can visit my website at www.write-yourself-in .com.

General Principles for Selective Supplemental Essays

- Do your research
- Tell your story and be true to yourself
- Approach each school's application like a portfolio

The good news is that the same general principles apply to all of your supplemental essays, whether you're applying to Harvard, Haverford, Harvey Mudd, or Hampshire.

The first is to **do your research**. I emphasize this point throughout the book, of course, but nowhere is it more important than in your supplemental essays, and especially at the most selective schools. Make sure that you understand what your school is offering, which you can do by spending some time on its website at minimum and taking a tour—real or virtual—if you have more time. The Why Our School essay you write for a big university with lots of research opportunities should be different from the one you write for a small liberal arts college that emphasizes tutorial-style learning.

That said, however, it's equally important to follow the second principle—another theme of this book—which is to **tell your story and be true to yourself.** Though your essays might be different for a big university and a small liberal arts college, both need to sound like you. They're simply reflections of how you personally might show up in two different kinds of communities.

If writing a particular school's supplemental essays feels really wrong to you—you feel as though you have to "fake it" to seem as though you will fit in—pay attention! That's very useful information, because it may well mean that the school is not a good fit for you. When that happens, thank the prompt for giving you that insight, then take the school off your list and find one that fits you better.

Last, as discussed in chapters 5 and 6, **approach each school's application like a portfolio.** Begin working on one school (remember that you'll be doing the essays one school at a time, bird by bird, right?) by brainstorming topics you might write about for *all* of that school's essays. Then pick topics that will highlight different sides of your personality, different ways you might show up in the school's community. Be sure you're not repeating yourself in different essays and that none of them is repeating the core messages of your personal essay.

Any questions? Great! Let's move on to the first set of schools that comes to mind when most people think about selective colleges: the Ivy League.

The Ivy League

There's a river of power that flows through this country . . . And that river flows from the Ivy League.

—President Joe Biden[*]

The Ivies run on mystique.

—Yale professor

For better or for worse, the eight Ivy League schools represent the pinnacle of American higher education. All of them are private research universities located in the Northeast, and all but one were founded before the American Revolution. While the term "Ivy League" may conjure up images of, as the comedian Tom Lehrer put it, "Ivy-covered professors in ivy-covered halls," many folks are surprised to learn that the Ivy League is not actually an academic organization; it's an NCAA-affiliated athletic conference.

For aspiring college students, the Ivies have a lot to offer. They have vast resources (at $50 billion, Harvard's endowment is larger than the GDP of many countries), which translate into generous financial aid and seemingly limitless on-campus opportunities. You'll be surrounded by the best and brightest, and for many students the Ivies also hit a sweet spot in terms of size. They're big enough to give you the wide range of options found at a large university but small enough that you feel as though you're part of a community.

As you'll see throughout this chapter, the Ivies are important not only

---

[*]Fun fact: Joe Biden is the first US president since Ronald Reagan who did *not* attend an Ivy League school. Both Bushes went to Yale (W. also has an MBA from Harvard Business School), Bill Clinton went to Yale Law School, Barack Obama attended both Columbia and Harvard, and Donald Trump has a degree from the University of Pennsylvania. Biden, however, graduated from the University of Delaware and Syracuse Law. For more on Biden's tortuous relationship with the Ivies, see this fantastic piece in the *Economist*: "Joe Biden Should Run Against the Ivy League," June 12, 2023, https://www.economist.com/united-states/2023/07/12/joe-biden-should-run-against-the-ivy-league.

in and of themselves but also because other selective colleges tend to define themselves in relation to the Ivy League. I first became aware of this as a high school junior when, at a marching band competition at James Madison University (an excellent state school in the Shenandoah Valley of Virginia), I heard the announcer describe JMU as "Ivy League education in the South." It may have a been a bit of a stretch, but it was effective; I immediately started to take JMU more seriously!

Writing Ivy League Supplemental Essays

When you sit down to write essays for Ivy League schools, it's not uncommon to have the same reaction as when you're invited to a fancy dinner party: you tense up, start acting formal, and forget to be yourself. The prestige of these schools can be so immense that it's easy to get caught up in our often misguided ideas about what an admissions officer at Harvard, Princeton, or Yale wants to read.

Successful applicants do the opposite: instead of pretending to be someone else, they let their personality shine through. Yes, the Ivies have Big Names, and yes, the bar is high, but in the end, they are just colleges. Their admissions officers are looking for essentially the same things as admissions officers at every other selective school.

One general principle to keep in mind as you're applying to Ivies: highlight your intellectual curiosity. Though these schools are looking for a range of people who embody the various characteristics on the Top Ten list, they are also global centers of scholarship. Ivies value the life of the mind, and you want to be sure that side of you comes through in your essays.

For example, if your personal essay was about a research project that you fell in love with and that changed your life, great! You may already have that base covered. But if your personal essay highlighted "softer" skills such as community engagement and empathy, use a supplemental essay to highlight your intellectual curiosity by writing about something that excited your mind, inside or outside the classroom.

In the pages that follow, you'll get a sense of the individual flavor of several schools. Just be sure to keep the big picture in mind; in the end, these schools are much more alike than different. Each offers a challenging, rewarding four-year liberal arts education. Don't try to paint yourself as a different person for each school you apply to; admissions officers are highly trained at sniffing that out. Be yourself in your essays, because the committee is reading them to get a sense of the real you.

Here are some tips on applying to the three Ivies that I get the most questions about from students, parents, and teachers.

Harvard University

A Harvard admissions officer once told me that what he looked for in applications was "distinguishing excellence." The admissions committee wants young people who excel. They're looking for intelligence, and they also want kids who've done exciting things outside the classroom.

Yet "distinguishing excellence" can take different forms. It could be an award or honor—preferably at the national or state level—but it could also be something less traditional that you highlight in your essays: maybe a creative approach to a problem or to unusually challenging circumstances in your life. As another Harvard admissions officer said, "Every year we could put together a class of high-testing valedictorians. But we don't, because it would be a disaster."

When filling out a Harvard supplement, pay special attention to qualities that highlight your achievement, intellectual curiosity, and passion.

The 2023–2024 Harvard Essays

After many years of a virtually unchanged supplement, in 2023 Harvard switched things up. Instead of two short essays and an optional, longer essay, the application now requires you to write five medium-length essays, each with a 200-word limit.

As with every school, brainstorm a few options for *each* prompt before you dive in. Especially when there are five essays, you want to be sure that (a) you're not repeating yourself and (b) you're highlighting everything you want the committee to know about you, because they're giving you an opportunity to do just that.

1. Harvard has long recognized the importance of enrolling a diverse student body. How will the life experiences that shape who you are today enable you to contribute to Harvard?

This is a standard Contributions/Lived Experience essay. See page 149 for guidelines on writing it.

2. Briefly describe an intellectual experience that was important to you.

If you think this looks like an Intellectual Engagement essay, you're right! See page 159 for instructions.

3. Briefly describe any of your extracurricular activities, employment experience, travel, or family responsibilities that have shaped who you are.

This is a standard Activity essay with options to also discuss work, travel, or family. See page 168 for guidance.

4. How do you hope to use your Harvard education in the future?

At its core, this is a question about impact. Think about it from an admissions officer's perspective: if you get into Harvard (or Yale or Princeton or any other school in this section), you get a chance to swim in that "river of power" that Joe Biden referred to. What are you going to do with that opportunity? What do you care about, and what kind of impact do you want to have?

As with all essays, specificity helps. Saying "I want to use my Harvard education so I can become a doctor who helps people and gives back" is unlikely to make much of an impression on your reader. But explaining how you want to use your education to help cure a disease that has impacted your family or how you want to solve pressing public health problems in a community you care about is something that might really land.

Finally, you could approach this question by looking up Harvard's mission statement, which reads "The mission of Harvard College is to educate the citizens and citizen-leaders for our society." Imagine yourself ten or twenty years from now: What kind of citizen or citizen-leader do you want to be? What kind of impact do you want to be having on society?

5. Top 3 things your roommates might like to know about you.

This is a fun question that's designed to give the admissions committee a bit of "color" about you beyond the other prompts, which are more serious. Stanford has asked a similar question for years. But because you have some latitude, it's also a "grab bag" opportunity to show the committee anything else you really want them to know.

Start by thinking about this question in the context of the rest of your application. If your other four essays were about heavy topics such as climate change or human trafficking, maybe you will want to use this response to lighten up a bit and show your more playful side. Alternatively, this could be a chance to share something more meaningful that didn't make it into any of the other essays. Either way, don't sweat this question too much. Be real, and think of it as the icing on the cake for your Harvard supplement.

Yale University

Like Harvard, Yale is looking for students who are intellectually curious, mature, and driven. Having spent several years at both schools, I can tell you that their undergraduate experiences are very similar. Both schools organize campus life around a residential college system based on Oxford and Cambridge universities, and both are filled with very smart, very ambitious students. There are some differences: my impression was that Yale undergrads tend to be a bit more community-oriented than Harvard kids, and the Yale colleges are more tight-knit communities than the Harvard houses.

When working on a Yale supplement, highlighting attributes such as achievement, passion, and intellectual curiosity is crucial; so are community and empathy. (Note that Yale has a Community essay; Harvard currently doesn't!) In the past, I've seen Yale admissions officers take risks on applicants who may not have had perfect grades and test scores but who did say something strong, clear, and personal in their essays.

The 2023–2024 Yale Essays

Yale has historically asked a range of questions, with essay lengths varying from short to medium. I recommend that you approach the Yale supplemental essays in three chunks. Note that this *not* the order in which the essays appear in the Common App; rather, it's a process I've developed over time that will help you end up with coherent, powerful results.

1. WHY YALE?

Start by focusing on what I call the "Why Yale?" prompts. They appear in both the "Academics" and "Short Takes and Essays" sections of the Common App Yale Supplement. They are:

1. Academic Interests: As of this moment, what academic areas seem to fit your interests or goals most comfortably? (Pick up to three potential majors from a list.)
2. Tell us about a topic or idea that excites you and is related to one or more academic areas you selected above. Why are you drawn to it? (200 words, after picking up to three potential majors)
3. What is it about Yale that has led you to apply? (125 words)

Before you write a word for either of these essays, think carefully about question 1: the academic areas you will choose. Take the time to do some research on what Yale majors actually look like, and pick the ones that give a genuine sense of where you are today. Yale admissions officers will look carefully at your selections and may use them not only to classify you (Is this a STEM kid? A potential English major?) but as a lens through which they'll read your other essays.

Also keep in mind, as the prompt makes clear, that it doesn't matter whether you're certain or uncertain about your potential major; this is *not* a commitment but rather a snapshot of where your head and heart are today.

After picking your major(s), approach these two "Why Yale?" questions as a unit. The "Tell us about a topic or idea that excites you" question is an intellectual curiosity prompt, which is very similar to Harvard's "Briefly describe an intellectual experience" question. In fact, because both prompts call for answers of 200 words, you can adapt a single essay for both! Read the Harvard advice on page 159 for more guidance on approaching this question, and be sure that in your Yale version, you specifically address one or more of the academic areas you chose. Finally, you might also feel free to throw in a few "Why Yale?" tidbits about how you might pursue these interests at Yale—but given that the prompt doesn't explicitly ask for it, it should be only an extra flourish at the end, not the core of the essay.

The final essay in this group, "What is it about Yale that has led you to apply?" is a simple, short Why Our School essay. Refer to chapter 5 for guidance, keeping in mind that even in an essay this short it's critical to do your research and briefly outline your thoughts before writing.

2. YALE ESSAYS

Next, move on to the "Yale Essays" section (the university's name, not mine), which consists of one 400-word essay. You'll have a choice of prompts for this essay, which tend to change slightly from year to year. Luckily, the 2023–2024 prompts were all standard essay genres, meaning that you can easily repurpose your essays for other schools.

1. Reflect on a time you discussed an issue important to you with someone holding an opposing view. Why did you find the experience meaningful?

This is a straightforward Diverse Perspectives essay. (See page 186 for guidance.)

2. Reflect on your membership in a community to which you feel connected. Why is this community meaningful to you? You may define community however you like.

This is a standard Community essay (see page 178).

3. Reflect on an element of your personal experience that you feel will enrich your college. How has it shaped you?

This is a standard Contributions/ Lived Experience essay (see page 149).

3. SHORT TAKES

Finish your Yale application with the "Short Takes" section, which has very short responses (200 characters max, around 35 words). In some admissions circles, these are known as "popcorn" questions; your answers will be short, but you want them to pop.

Why should you do this section last? Most students start with it, because it's the easiest. But the smart approach is to wait until you know what you're writing in the other sections; that way you can use it as a "grab bag" for ideas and passions that weren't reflected in the "Why Yale?" or "Yale Essay" sections.

Here are the most recent "Short Takes" prompts; usually the Yale Admissions Office changes one or two of them each cycle.

1. What inspires you?
2. If you could teach any college course, write a book, or create an original piece of art of any kind, what would it be?
3. Other than a family member, who is someone who has had a significant influence on you? What has been the impact of their influence?
4. What is something about you that is not included anywhere else in your application?

Useful guidelines for approaching the "popcorn" questions:

1. **Stick to one idea per question.** With only 200 characters (that's about 25 words, or one to two sentences) per prompt, you have to be brief. Pick one thing to focus on, get to the point quickly, and then finish. (If you have a particularly clever idea for a list in response to one of the prompts, feel free to use it. Just be warned that unless it really "pops," a list tends to have less impact than a well-written, focused response.)

2. **Have fun and be creative.** As you may have noticed, these prompts tend to focus on two qualities: passion and intellectual curiosity. Within that realm, the committee truly wants to get a flavor for who you are as a person from these questions. Attempts by applicants to sound "sophisticated" and "Ivy League" usually fall flat. Instead, find a creative, smart way to talk about something that you're truly interested in, whether it's the accordion, baseball, Geoffrey Chaucer, or Dr. Dre.

Princeton University

Princeton has always struck me as fully embodying the contradictions at the heart of elite education in the United States. On the one hand, it can seem like the most "old boys' network" of the Ivies, with its leafy suburban setting and culture of exclusive eating clubs. Yet in 2001, it was the first Ivy to guarantee full scholarship support to every student who needed it, which opened the doors to students from all economic backgrounds and prodded the other Ivies to quickly follow suit. It's also been the proud home of BIPOC luminaries such as Toni Morrison, who taught there for nearly twenty years, and Supreme Court justice Sonia Sotomayor, who is an alumna.

Princeton is looking for students who will bring something unique to a community where the informal motto is "In the nation's service and in the service of humanity." Throughout your essays, be clear and direct about who you are and the impact you hope to have on the world.

The 2023–2024 Princeton Essays

Princeton asks for several medium-length essays plus a few short "popcorn"-style responses, and it also requires you to submit a graded written paper from the last three years of your high school career.

1. WHY PRINCETON?

Start by working on your 250-word "Why Princeton?" essay. Though all applicants are required to write one of these, the prompts are slightly different for those applying to the arts and sciences program and those applying to the engineering school.

For students applying to arts and sciences (and those who are undecided):

> As a research institution that also prides itself on its liberal arts curriculum, Princeton allows students to explore areas across the humanities and the arts, the natural sciences, and the social sciences. What academic areas most pique your curiosity, and how do the programs offered at Princeton suit your particular interests?

This is a standard Why Our School essay. See chapter 5 for guidance, and keep in mind that since Princeton (unlike Harvard and Yale) does not have a separate Intellectual Engagement prompt, be sure to highlight your intellectual curiosity in this essay.

For students applying to engineering:

> Please describe why you are interested in studying engineering at Princeton. Include any of your experiences in, or exposure to engineering, and how you think the programs offered at the University suit your particular interests. (Please respond in about 250 words)

This is a standard Why Engineering essay (see page 144).

2. YOUR VOICE

Princeton also asks two medium-length essay questions:

1. Princeton values community and encourages students, faculty, staff and leadership to engage in respectful conversations that can expand their perspectives and challenge their ideas and beliefs. As a prospective member of this community, reflect on how your lived experiences will impact the conversations you will have in the classroom, the dining hall or other campus spaces. What lessons have you learned in life thus far? What will your classmates learn from you? In short, how has your lived experience shaped you? (500 words)

This prompt, which was new to the 2023–2024 admissions cycle, reads like a mash-up of a Diverse Perspectives question (Princeton used to have one of those in this slot) and a Contributions/Lived Experience prompt. It provides you space to talk about the kinds of conversations you want to have, to show admissions officers how you'll show up on campus, and—perhaps most important—to talk about your background and how it's shaped you.

That lack of focus presents a challenge, as does the length; 500 words is a lot of room to write. As such, I would start your process by narrowing your focus. At its core this is a Contributions/Lived Experience question, so review the guide on page 149 and approach the essay accordingly. It's certainly possible to include a Diverse Perspectives–type story; just be sure that you're directly addressing how the experience shaped you and what you would contribute to Princeton's community.

2. Princeton has a longstanding commitment to understanding our responsibility to society through service and civic engagement. How does your own story intersect with these ideals? (250 words)

Service is a core part of Princeton's culture. As you read a couple of pages back, the school's informal motto is "In the nation's service and in the service of humanity." Think of this prompt as a Community essay, with an emphasis on impact that overlaps with Harvard's "How do you hope to use your Harvard education in the future?" essay (which means that if you're smart, you can repurpose one essay for both prompts!).

Follow the same guidelines you would for any Community essay (see page 178); just make sure that you emphasize how you were of service to your community or to a broader cause.

If you want to take a different approach to this essay, you could also make it more forward looking. You could use it as a place to talk about your goals for service and civic engagement, ideally tying into things you've already done.

An even better approach could be to do both. Because you have 250 words, you have enough space to tell a short story about a way you've already been of service, then to talk about your goals and dreams, with a sentence or two on how a Princeton education would help you achieve them.

3. MORE ABOUT YOU

Finally, Princeton asks three "popcorn"-style questions, each with a 50-word max:

1. What is a new skill you would like to learn in college?
2. What brings you joy?
3. What song represents the soundtrack of your life at this moment?

The same principles apply here as to the Yale "popcorn" questions. The admissions committee wants to get a sense of your personality. With that in mind, you want to:

1. **Stick to one idea per question.** For each prompt, you want to pick one topic to focus on, elaborate a bit, and then finish. You have one or two sentences to elaborate on your answers, so make them count. If you're stuck, approach each of these questions as a mini-story, with a beginning, a middle, and an end.
2. **Have fun and be creative.** Whereas the longer essays aim to

uncover your more serious, reflective side, these essays are looking for a sense of your personality. Attempts to sound "sophisticated" and "Ivy League" usually fall flat. Instead, find a creative,
smart way to talk about something that you're truly interested in,
whether it's Beethoven or the *Euphoria* soundtrack. If your response can bring a smile to the admissions officer's face, it's probably helping you.

Lightning Round: The Rest of the Best

Since the remaining Ivies mostly have short to medium-length essays,
you can and should apply the same principles I've just discussed for Harvard, Yale, and Princeton. Just be sure to do your research and understand
what each school is offering; don't make the common mistake of applying
to multiple Ivies and assuming that they're all the same!

Here are a few tips for the remaining schools.

Columbia University: Keep in mind two things that make Columbia
distinctive: the Core Curriculum (google it) and the fact that it's in New
York City. Your essays don't need to revolve around these things, but it
can be helpful to reflect on how each could support your educational
journey.

Brown University: Take some time to make sure you understand
Brown's Open Curriculum and to think creatively about how you might
make use of it.*

Cornell University: Unlike the other Ivies, Cornell is made up of nine
undergraduate schools and colleges that range from Business to Engineering to Agriculture and Life Sciences. Do your research (some of the
schools have better acceptance rates than the others), choose the school
that seems best for you, and make sure your Why Our School essays are
clear and specific.

University of Pennsylvania: Note that the Penn Community essay

---

*Brown has several web pages describing its Open Curriculum. Here's my favorite:
https://college.brown.edu/design-your-education/explore-open-curriculum.

asks you to discuss how you will explore community *at Penn*, not just describe a community you're already part of. The "Thank You Note" essay should be fun to write, and it tends to work best when it's from the heart. Instead of trying to figure out the "right" person to thank, ask yourself: Who's someone I genuinely feel a lot of gratitude for?

Dartmouth College: It may be the smallest of the Ivies, but Dartmouth has some unique and really cool academic opportunities (try googling "Dartmouth D-Plan"). The "Why Dartmouth?" essay is short, but it's still important to do your research and understand what the school has to offer!

The Ivy Plus Schools

While the Ivy League is a formal organization, "Ivy Plus" is a colloquial term with a looser definition. It refers to a small set of wealthy, highly prestigious, private research universities that look and feel a lot like the Ivies but aren't technically part of the Ivy League. At a minimum, most lists of Ivy Plus schools would include MIT, Stanford University, and the University of Chicago. Some would add Duke University, Johns Hopkins University, and UC-Berkeley to the list.* Personally, I include Duke and Johns Hopkins but move Berkeley to the "Public Ivies" list, which will be covered later.

Because the Ivy Plus schools are similar to the Ivies, everything in the previous section also applies to Stanford, the University of Chicago, Duke, and Johns Hopkins. Below are some brief tips on those schools, followed by more detailed advice on MIT.

Stanford University: If you're applying to Stanford, start early! Its supplemental essays may look simple on the admissions website, but when you actually open up the Common App, you'll find five short-answer questions (50 words each) and three medium-length essays (250 words each). One bit of good news: one is an Engagement essay much like those of Harvard and Yale, another is a Contributions/Lived Experience essay,

---

*The Ivy Plus Libraries Confederation, a club of university libraries (imagine what their parties are like!) does exactly that.

and the third is a Letter to Your Roommate, which overlaps with one of the new Harvard prompts.

Perhaps more than any other school, the key to a successful Stanford application is to put some thought into brainstorming and picking topics for the essays *before* you start writing. These eight prompts give you the opportunity to show the committee many different sides of yourself. Take advantage of it!

University of Chicago: University of Chicago is an academic power-house that has long valued creativity, quirkiness, and free speech. Its essays include a standard Why Chicago essay, as well as a one- to two-page "Extended Essay" (no precise word count), which is legendary in college admissions.

According to University of Chicago College Admissions, the Extended Essay "can be approached with utter seriousness, complete fancy, or something in between." Each year Chicago provides a completely new set of prompts, all of which have been inspired by submissions from current University of Chicago undergrads. Past questions have included: "'Where have all the flowers gone?'—Pete Seeger. Pick a question from a song title or lyric and give it your best answer," and "Find x" (yup, that's the entire prompt!). There's also the option to respond to a prompt from the past years or to even create a question of your own.

Start by reading through all of this year's prompts, then find the list of prompts from previous years on the university's website and check it out. What you'll find is that all of the questions combine a sense of intellectual curiosity with a spirit of playfulness. And that's the key to writing a great UChicago Extended Essay: finding a topic that engages both your right and left brains.

Because you need your intellectual, creative voice to come through in this essay, take some time to pick a topic you really enjoy writing and thinking about. If you're stuck, freewrite a few ideas and see what lands.

One caveat: make sure your final essay has a structure. Though creativity is highly encouraged, you don't want to submit a rant or diatribe that will cause the admissions officer to tilt their head to the side and go "Huh?" Inventive structures will get bonus points (if they work), but a simple Introduction + 3 points + Conclusion can also be your friend here, as long as your ideas are fun, interesting, and persuasive.

Duke University: Historically, the Duke supplemental essay has been mercifully short. In 2023–2024, however, the school mixed things up a bit by combining a 250-word "Why Duke?" essay with a list of five optional prompts. You can pick up to two of the prompts and respond in a 250-word essay, but you don't have to respond to any of them if you don't want to.

In general, I *always* recommend that you answer optional questions. If you're serious about the school, why not give the committee another chance to learn something interesting about you? The good news here is that many of the optional Duke questions line up closely with topics for other selective schools, so you'll be able to adapt material you've already written.

Johns Hopkins University: In 2023–2024, Johns Hopkins had a single supplemental essay combining the Contributions/Lived Experience and Why Our School essay genres into one. To write it, focus first on your Contributions/Lived Experience story (see page 149), and then use the last 20% or so of the essay to show some forward-looking, "Why Hopkins?"–type ideas.

MIT: MIT is a bit of an outlier in that it doesn't use the Common App (neither do the University of California system and Georgetown University), which means the admissions office won't see your personal essay. Instead, they will be reading five shorter essays on a range of topics. As with any school that has multiple essays, start by brainstorming the topics you might write about for each, then pick topics that will show multiple sides of your personality.

The 2023–2024 MIT Prompts

1. What field of study appeals to you the most right now? (Note: Applicants select from a drop-down list.) Tell us more about why this field of study at MIT appeals to you. (100 words)

This straightforward prompt is all about highlighting your intellectual curiosity: Why are you so excited about this particular field that you want to spend the next four years immersed in it? It's only 100 words, so you won't have room to say much, but you could choose to use the space by highlighting an episode from your past that shows why the field appeals to you, or (à la "Why Our School") mentioning one or two specific ways you might pursue it at MIT.

2. What do you do for fun? We know you lead a busy life, full of activities, many of which are required of you. Tell us about something you do simply for the pleasure of it. (150 words)

MIT may have a serious, STEM-heavy application, but here it wants to see a different side of you. So don't overthink this one. Just be honest; if you build computer mainframes for fun, say that. If you windsurf or play D&D or hike for fun, it's absolutely fine to talk about those things, too. Whatever you choose, show them *what you enjoy about it*, so that the admissions officer can understand your personality beyond your academic focus.

3. How has the world you come from—including your opportunities, experiences, and challenges—shaped your dreams and aspirations? (225 words)

This is an intentionally broad question. You could use it to talk about your community, your identity, your family, your heritage—whatever is important to you. You could even approach this as a Contributions/Lived Experience essay, possibly adapting something you've already written for another school. Feel free to dream big ("I want to start the next Google") or small ("I want to spend my life playing with circuit boards"); just be honest and clear about what your dreams and aspirations are right now.

4. MIT brings people with diverse backgrounds together to collaborate, from tackling the world's biggest challenges to lending a helping hand. Describe one way you have collaborated with others to learn from them, with them, or contribute to your community together. (225 words)

This question appears often in engineering school supplements, and the key to a strong response is specificity. Note that it says "Describe *one way* you have collaborated with others." You want to pick one specific story to tell here that shows you in action—possibly, but not necessarily, in an engineering context—learning from, learning with, and/or contributing. This is definitely an essay in which you want to show, not tell.

5. How did you manage a situation or challenge that you didn't expect? What did you learn from it? (225 words)

To find a situation for this essay, you might recall some challenging moments where you really *feel* something in your gut as you remember what happened. Or think back to some of the biggest lessons you've learned in the last three years and ask yourself: How did you learn them? Once you've found a topic, the easiest way to approach it is in three parts:

a. Describe the situation or challenge
b. Show how you responded to/managed it
c. Explain how you learned and grew from the experience

The Little Ivies

As with the Ivy Plus schools, the group of schools known as the Little Ivies is unofficial and amorphous. What makes them "Little" is that most of them are liberal arts colleges with around two thousand or fewer students.

Most admissions officers would consider Williams, Amherst, Middlebury, Swarthmore, Hamilton, Bates, Bowdoin, Colby, Trinity, and Vassar to be Little Ivies; the list might also include Tufts and Wesleyan, which are technically universities. Like the Ivies, these schools are all located in the Northeast, and they overlap heavily with NESCAC (the New England Small Collegiate Athletic Conference), an NCAA Division III conference that's the liberal arts college equivalent of the Division I Ivy League.

Some people think of the Little Ivies as inferior to the "real" Ivies. I've heard them called "backup schools" for kids gunning for Ivies, and I'll be honest: as a teen in rural Virginia (where almost no one, certainly not my parents, had gone to an Ivy League school), I was convinced that these small colleges were inferior to places like Yale, Stanford, and Cornell.

But nothing could be further from the truth. Liberal arts colleges aren't inferior to research universities; they're just different. Though a Little Ivy might not give you the same global brand recognition, super-star professors, or cutting-edge research opportunities as an Ivy League or Ivy Plus school does, what you gain instead is a tight-knit community, the chance to really get to know your professors, and smaller classes—in short, a more "collegial" experience overall.

You also end up with an excellent degree. As a Harvard undergradu-ate, I was surprised to discover how many of the graduate students in Harvard's ultracompetitive PhD programs and professional schools (Har-vard Law, Harvard Medical School, etc.) had attended not Harvard, Yale, or Princeton but the Little Ivies—the same schools I'd looked down on as a teen. Oops!

Writing Little Ivy Supplemental Essays

The good news about Little Ivy supplemental essays is that there aren't that many of them. Some schools, including Williams, Middlebury, and Wesleyan, don't require supplemental essays at all.* Those that do tend to require just one or two essays.

When you run across a Little Ivy supplemental essay, you'll often find that it's framed in a distinctive, even quirky way, such as asking you to reflect on a text that's an important part of the school's culture. So read the prompts carefully, do your research (especially at schools like Hamilton that ask for a Why Our School essay), be creative, and tell your story.

Here are tips for a few schools with more robust supplemental essays.

Amherst College: Though Amherst does require a supplemental

---

*Williams gives you the option to submit a sample of your academic writing, but there's no supplemental essay.

essay, it gives you a wide range of choices in how to approach it. For some students, deciding which supplemental essay to write (or submit) can be the hardest part of the application!

Here's how it works: Amherst gives you the option of writing one 250-word essay or submitting a graded paper from junior or senior year. Students who apply to Access to Amherst, a diversity outreach program, have the additional option of using their Access to Amherst application essay for their supplemental essay.

If you choose to write an essay, you can choose from three prompts. The first asks about leadership and service, the second is a kind of Contributions/Lived Experience essay, and the third gives you the chance to talk about an intellectual or creative pursuit. There are lots of choices—and you can pick only one! So how to choose? There's no "right" answer, except that you should pick the option that you think will present you in the best light.

For example, is there something important about your background that you want the admissions committee to know about but isn't reflected in your personal essay? Do you have very strong beliefs about leadership, service, and community? If so, pick one of the prompts and write a short essay, or adapt one you've already written.

On the other hand, you might have a fantastic paper from junior or senior year that you really want to share. If you feel as though your personal essay says everything you want to say, submit the paper!

Swarthmore College: Swarthmore asks for two 250-word essays: a Contributions/Lived Experience essay and an Intellectual Experience essay. Feel free to repurpose essays from other schools, and consider adding a sentence or two to make them more specific to Swarthmore.

Bowdoin College: Bowdoin has two optional supplemental essays. The first gives you 250 words to reflect on "The Offer of the College," a lovely piece written by a Bowdoin president that sums up the best of what a liberal arts education can do. Bowdoin admissions officers have been reading essays on this piece for years, so your task is to make your response personal. How does some part of this "offer" resonate with you, and how will a liberal arts education help you bring it to life?

The second optional essay, also 250 words, is a Contributions/Lived Experience essay that emphasizes the theme of "navigating through differences"; see page 149 for guidance.

Finally, note that Bowdoin also gives you the option to submit a short video response. Read the instructions carefully before deciding whether to do it, as it's very much like an interview in that you'll respond to a prompt through the school's website and you can't delete your response. If you feel comfortable presenting yourself on camera, go for it!

The Public Ivies

The Public Ivies are another unofficial grouping of highly selective schools. Many of the Public Ivies are household names, including the University of California-Berkeley, University of Michigan, University of Virginia, University of North Carolina at Chapel Hill, and the University of Texas at Austin.

The term, which was first introduced in the 1980s, refers to the country's top public universities, i.e., schools that are owned or heavily funded by a state government. That state funding means that for many students, the cost of attending a public school can be much less than at a private school. According to data from *U.S. News & World Report*, in 2022 the average cost at a private school (tuition + fees) was $38,185, but at public schools that number was only $10,338 for in-state students and $22,698 for out-of-state kids.

In addition to being a bargain, Public Ivies tend to have higher admissions rates than their private peers. One possible downside, at least for some students, is that the Public Ivies tend to be larger than the other schools in this chapter (the University of Michigan has around 33,000 undergrads, whereas Princeton has close to 5,500). But for other students, bigger is better. With larger size often come a more dynamic campus, lots of school spirit, more sports and other extracurricular options, and a more robust Greek life.

Writing Public Ivy Supplemental Essays

Unlike the Little Ivies, the Public Ivies tend to require supplemental essays. In general, the guidelines for the Ivies and Ivy Pluses also apply: do your research, highlight your intellectual curiosity, and tell your own story rather than trying to fit into a mold.

Nearly all of the Public Ivies use the Common App; the one major exception is the University of California, which has a separate admissions platform and a unique approach to the essays. I'll start by breaking down the UC essays and how to approach them, followed by some customized tips for a few other schools.

University of California

The good news about the University of California is that it uses a single, unified application for all ten of its campuses (Berkeley, Davis, Irvine, Los Angeles, Merced, Riverside, San Diego, San Francisco, Santa Barbara, and Santa Cruz). If UC-Berkeley is your dream school but you also want to be considered at UCLA and UCSD, all you have to do is fill out your Berkeley app, check two additional boxes, and you're set.

The bad news is that UC takes a rather idiosyncratic approach to the essays. Instead of requiring one long personal essay and some supplemental essays, UC requires you to write four medium-length essays of 350 words each. UC will *not* see your Common App personal essay, which means you'll have to take a different approach to creating your "portfolio" than you do for other schools.

The good news is that while this takes some planning, it's actually less work than it might initially seem. I have my own students wait to start their UC essays until *after* they've finished the applications for several other schools. This is partly because of the UC deadline, which on November 30 comes one month after most Early Action/Early Decision deadlines, but also because it allows kids to repurpose essays they've already written for the UC application.

Tackling the Personal Insight Questions

For its essays, which UC calls "Personal Insight Questions" (PIQs), eight prompts are provided. You'll pick four of them—no more, no less—and write four essays in response.

If you haven't done so already, start by spending some time reading about the essays on the UC admissions website. It's a surprisingly thorough, friendly, and helpful site with useful advice on what UC is looking for and how to approach each prompt.

As with other schools that require multiple essays, your actual writing process should begin with brainstorming. Create a Google Doc, paste all eight prompts into it, and brainstorm a few topics that you might write about for each prompt.

As you brainstorm, think about your personal essay and how you might adapt it; most students are able to retool their personal essay to address one (and occasionally two) of the UC prompts. Also, think about supplemental essays you've already written; could you use any of them in response to the UC prompts?

Then look at the entire list and ask yourself: Which four topics are going to paint the most complete, compelling picture of who I am and the kind of student I would be on a UC campus? Those are the four that you want to pick for your essays. Note that there are no good or bad prompts; a range of options is provided so you can pick the ones that work best for you to tell your own story.

Here are the latest personal insight questions, as well as some thoughts on how to respond to them and how they relate to the genres of essays you're already familiar with.

The 2023–2024 University of California Personal Insight Questions

1. Describe an example of your leadership experience in which you have positively influenced others, helped resolve disputes or contributed to group efforts over time.

This question is obviously about leadership, and you want to respond to it by telling a story that shows you in action as a leader. If you have an Activity or Community essay you've already written that highlights a leadership role, you may be able to repurpose that essay for this prompt. Alternatively, if you've shown leadership in the classroom (or other academic settings), this essay can be a great place to talk about that.

Since most Activity and Community essays are under 350 words, how will you fill up the extra space? Keep in mind that the best essays not only tell a story but also show the committee what you learned from the experience and how you're taking it forward to other areas of your life. Consider using the extra words to do just that.

2. Every person has a creative side, and it can be expressed in many ways: problem solving, original and innovative thinking, and artistically, to name a few. Describe how you express your creative side.

Think back to our discussion of creativity in the Top Ten list (page 35). Remember that creativity isn't just about painting, making music, or writing a play (although it can be all of those things)—it can also be about creative problem solving in the classroom, in a club or activity, even on the athletic field.

In responding to this prompt, think broadly about creativity and the imagination. If you choose this PIQ, use it to tell a story that shows you putting your most creative self into action, ideally with some reflection on how it relates to other parts of your life (academics, future plans, goals and values, and so on).

3. What would you say is your greatest talent or skill? How have you developed and demonstrated that talent over time?

If you talk to admissions officers at schools across the country, one common theme you'll hear is that they want applicants to *share things about themselves that they're proud of.* This deliberately open-ended prompt is designed to help you do just that. You could describe a talent or skill that you use inside or outside the classroom; either way, it should be something you feel that you're good at and are proud of.

The only real pitfall to avoid in this PIQ is focusing on events that happened before high school. You may have done something in elementary or middle school that you're really proud of, but the committee is much more interested in hearing about events and situations from the last three years. It's fine to tell a story that starts in elementary or middle school; you just want to be sure that the bulk of the essay is focused on your high school years.

4. Describe how you have taken advantage of a significant educational opportunity or worked to overcome an educational barrier you have faced.

I like this prompt because it allows you to go in a couple of different directions. One would be to focus on an educational opportunity, in which case this becomes kind of an Intellectual Engagement essay (yes, you may be able to repurpose one you've written for another school!). The other would be to write about an educational barrier, in which case it becomes an opportunity for you to highlight your resilience, possibly even doing some Contributions/Lived Experience essay work and showing the admissions committee how your life experiences have shaped you into the person you are today.

Either way, these essays tend to work best when they are specific. You'll want to be very clear about the opportunity or challenge you faced and the specific actions you took to take advantage of it or overcome it. Be sure to emphasize what you learned or how you grew from this experience.

5. Describe the most significant challenge you have faced and the steps you have taken to overcome this challenge. How has this challenge affected your academic achievement?

This PIQ is kind of doing two things at once. On the one hand, it's a bit like a Contributions/Lived Experience essay in that gives you the opportunity to write about a challenge you faced and how it shaped you into the person you are today. On the other hand, it gives you the opportunity to talk about how some kind of adversity has affected your academic record. If your grades went down junior year because a family member died or because your parents moved, or if you were working two jobs to help support your family and didn't have enough time to study, this is the place to tell that story.

Whatever you choose to write about, note that this prompt specifically asks about *how the challenge affected your academic achievement*. I've seen students respond to this prompt with excellent essays about challenges, but then they forgot to tie those challenges back to their academic achievement. Don't make that mistake! If you pick this question, be sure that your essay addresses the impact on your academics.

6. Think about an academic subject that inspires you. Describe how you have furthered this interest inside and/or outside of the classroom.

This is a clear and simple Intellectual Engagement essay. It's very much like the ones you might be writing for Ivy League schools, with the caveat that it's not asking about one specific project or activity. You could certainly choose to focus on one, but you also have the option to write about how you pursued your love of an academic subject in different ways. However you approach it, make sure that you highlight your intellectual curiosity; that's what the admissions committee is looking for.

7. What have you done to make your school or your community a better place?

This is essentially a Community essay, and as with most Community essays, you're free to define "community" however you want. It's also asking about your impact, so you'll want to pick a community in which you've taken actions—by yourself or with others—that have changed things for the better.

8. Beyond what has already been shared in your application, what do you believe makes you a strong candidate for admission to the University of California?

This "grab bag" question is your opportunity to share some story or information about yourself that wasn't reflected in another essay but that you really want the committee to know. As you're brainstorming, approach this question last. Are there big stories or aspects of you—perhaps something from your personal essay—that weren't included in the other essays? If so, this is the place to write about them.

A final note: if you choose this essay, don't be afraid to flex a little. Though you don't want to appear arrogant, this prompt, like PIQ 3, can be a place to show off some quality or skill that you're genuinely proud of.

Other Public Ivies

University of Michigan: The University of Michigan has historically asked two supplemental essay questions. One is a long-form Why Our School essay, which this book unpacks in chapter 5, and the other is a Community essay (see page 178).

Applicants to the popular undergraduate BBA program at Ross School of Business (Michigan's B-School) will also write two additional essays. Ross is looking for creative problem solvers, and the prompts are designed to help you show off your skills. The first is a business case study, and the second is an essay in which you submit an "artifact" and explain how it shows learning in action. Be sure to research these essays carefully by exploring the Ross admissions website, where both essays are discussed in detail. Or—even better—watch an interview with Ross's director of undergraduate admissions in which she explains exactly what they're looking for!*

University of Virginia: For 2023–2024, all applicants were required to write one Contributions/Lived Experience essay (250 words, but you can write up to 300; see page 149). Applicants to the School of Nursing

---

*Check it out at https://bit.ly/ross-interview.

were also required to write an essay about an experience that prompted them to study nursing. In addition, UVA introduced an optional 100-word prompt about your "personal or historic connection with UVA," such as "being a child of someone who graduated from or works for UVA, a descendant of ancestors who labored at UVA, or a participant in UVA programs." Because it's open-ended, this essay is a fantastic place to talk about *any* connection you have to the school. For example, if you happen to have a relative or friend who's a current or former UVA student, call them, talk to them about the school, and write about it here!

UNC–Chapel Hill: Last year UNC required two 250-word essays. The first is a Community essay (see page 178) with a twist: you need to connect a personal quality of yours to a positive impact you had on a community. If you're lucky, you might be able to adapt a Community essay you've already written by exploring how a personal quality relates to the story you're telling. Or you could write a new essay about a skill or quality you want to highlight that doesn't play a big role in your personal essay.

The second essay is a straightforward Intellectual Engagement essay (see page 159).

University of Texas at Austin: UT Austin has an unusual approach to essays: it doesn't look at the Common App personal essay, instead requiring one long essay of 500 to 700 words as well as three medium-length essays (300 words each).

The prompt for the long essay is "Tell us your story. What unique opportunities or challenges have you experienced throughout your high school career that have shaped who you are today?" Many students are able to adapt their Common App personal essay to this topic; usually the trick is to do some very light editing to (a) clarify what your "opportunities or challenges" were and (b) make sure that it's clear in the conclusion how this experience shaped the person you are today.

If, for some reason, your Common App essay just doesn't seem related to this prompt at all, you can write a new one. Approach it as you would a Contributions/Lived Experience essay (see page 149).

Of the three shorter prompts, the first asks about your interest in your major; it's an Intellectual Engagement essay (see page 159). The second is a Community essay with a twist: it asks about the impact you will have "both in and out of the classroom" in the future at UT. You can start it like a normal Community essay, but be sure to include some forward-looking description to help the admissions officer imagine who'll you'll be on the UT campus.

The final short-answer question asks you to "Share how you believe your experience at UT Austin will prepare you to 'Change the World' after you graduate." This question is asking about your impact; as with the Harvard (see page 199) and Princeton (see page 206) impact questions, write about the impact you want to have and how specific offerings at UT will help you get there.

Finally, UT gives you the option to write up to 300 words about "events or special circumstances that you feel may have impacted your high school academic performance." This is *not* a required essay, and you should fill it out only if you have something in your academic record that you want to explain. It's UT's equivalent of the "Additional Information" section of the Common App.

Hidden Gems

Seek thee out the diamond in the rough.

—The Cave of Wonders in *Aladdin*

Since the bulk of this chapter focuses on name-brand schools, I want to balance things out by exploring some colleges where you can get a fantastic education, but you don't have to win the lottery to get in. This section also includes strategies to find target and safety schools for your college list. Among the thousands of colleges and universities in this country, there are quite a few diamonds in the rough.

Medium-Sized Universities

Many students find that Ivy League and Ivy Plus schools offer a sweet spot when it comes to size: larger than a liberal arts college, but smaller than a big state school. So many, in fact, that admissions rates have plummeted at many medium-sized universities, to the point where places such as Vanderbilt and Rice, which used to be targets for some kids, now have Ivy League–level acceptance rates.

If you're looking for good schools in this category, a quick-and-easy search tool is the *U.S. News & World Report* rankings website. To find some good midsized universities, you'll want to go to the "Best National University Rankings" page.* Scroll down the left-hand side to the "Enrollment" slider, adjust it so the range is around 0 to 8,000 (that will cut out the big state schools), then find the "Acceptance Rate" slider and adjust it to 20% or higher (that will get rid of the Ivies and Ivy Pluses).

When you scroll down the list that comes up, you'll find a range of schools, such as Case Western Reserve University and American University, that aren't household names but still offer an incredible education. Here are essay tips for a few of my favorites.

Lehigh and Bucknell Universities

Lehigh University (37% acceptance rate)† and Bucknell University (33% acceptance rate) are excellent small universities. Both are located in Pennsylvania, and both have competitive—but not crazy—admissions.

Lehigh asks you to write three essays. One asks about what's motivating you to apply to Lehigh (150 words; think of this as a big-picture Why Our School question), while the second is a more in-the-weeds Why Our School essay (200 words). For the third essay (300 words) you have a choice: an essay about equality and equity or two variations of the Lived Experience essay.

Bucknell requires just one essay, a 250-word "Why Bucknell?" Note that the prompt asks you describe your interest in your major, as well as explaining why Bucknell is good place to pursue it.

---

*https://www.usnews.com/best-colleges/rankings/national-universities.
†Acceptance rates in the section are from the *U.S. News Best Colleges Guide* at https://www.usnews.com/ as of December 2023.

Brandeis University

Boston is a city of incredible universities: Harvard and MIT, as well as Boston University, Boston College, Brandeis, Northeastern, and Tufts. All of those are highly selective (ranging from 4% acceptance at Harvard and MIT to 17% at Boston College)—except for Brandeis, which pairs stellar academics with an acceptance rate of 39%.

Brandeis asks for one 250-word essay on how your educational experience has shaped your perspective on inclusivity and social justice. Be specific: clarify (at the beginning or end) your core beliefs on these topics, tell one or two brief stories from your life that show how you came to believe those things, and end with a sentence or two on how you hope to learn and grow in this direction.

Liberal Arts Colleges

There are two great strategies for seeking out excellent, less selective liberal arts colleges.

The first is to use the *U.S. News & World Report* approach described above. You'll want to go to the "National Liberal Arts College Rankings" page instead of the university page.* Once again, adjust the "acceptance rate" slider to 20% or higher—there's no need to fiddle with "Enrollment" unless you have a certain size in mind—and start looking at the schools that come up.

Another fantastic resource is Colleges That Change Lives. It's a unique consortium of 44 small colleges that grew out of an influential book from the 1990s.† Many of the schools have admissions rate over 50%; all pride themselves on being student-centered. If the Little Ivies appeal to you, check out these schools as well. You'll find the list on the CTCL website.‡

---

*https://www.usnews.com/best-colleges/rankings/national-liberal-arts-colleges.
†*Colleges That Change Lives: 40 Schools That Will Change the Way You Think About College* by Loren Pope. More on this book in appendix IV.
‡https://ctcl.org/category/college-profiles/.

As with the Little Ivies, many of these colleges don't require supplemental essays. The ones that do tend to require essays on the shorter side, and there are usually only one or two of them.

Big State Schools

If you want to go big, the *U.S. News & World Report* search tool is once again your friend. As with medium-sized universities, you'll go to the "Best National University Rankings" page. This time slide the "Enrollment" slider as high as it will go (you want to get it to 15,000 if possible, although it currently won't go above 12,000 or so) and the "Acceptance Rate" slider to above 20 or 25%.

You'll find a range of excellent universities here, such as UC Davis, which has a 37% acceptance rate. One school I often suggest to students who want great academics combined with a big, exciting state school experience is the **University of Wisconsin–Madison**. Though UW–Madison is hardly a secret (its School of Journalism ranks among the best in the world), it qualifies as a diamond in the rough because it combines academic excellence with a relatively high acceptance rate. Compared to its sister Big Ten school University of Michigan, which is considered a Public Ivy and admits just 18% of applicants, UW–Madison has a much more favorable acceptance rate of 49%. UW also requires only one essay: a Why Our School of up to 600 words (it recommends 300 to 500). If you're applying to both UW and University of Michigan, you can easily take your "Why Michigan?" essay and adapt it to Wisconsin. Just be *absolutely sure* to have someone proofread it, so you don't accidentally tell Wisconsin how much you want to be a Wolverine (that's the Michigan mascot, and yes, it happens).

Regional Colleges and Universities

Although the big state schools are, by definition, public, many of the liberal arts colleges and medium-size universities are private. Unless you get a great financial aid package, that means they're out of reach for many people. However, if you look beyond the national rankings, you'll find hundreds of regional colleges and universities scattered across the country. Not all of them are stellar, but many provide an excellent education, and bargains can be found. Public regional schools can be a great value for in-state students, while some of the private schools offer strong financial aid packages for high-achieving applicants.

To cite an example on the West Coast: the **Cal Poly** campuses in San Luis Obispo and Pomona are fantastic schools with much higher acceptance rates (30 and 55%) than flagship California universities such as UC-Berkeley and UCLA. And there are no essays to write!

One particular type of school, the regional comprehensive university (RCU), is worth highlighting. An RCU is a hybrid between a college and a university. Though their primary focus is undergraduate education, RCUs also offer graduate degrees; they just don't have the extensive research facilities of a traditional university.

RCUs should be on your list if you want a medium-sized school but don't have the grades or financial resources to attend a competitive, mid-sized private university. I happen to live near one of them, **SUNY New Paltz**, which is an excellent school with a 46% acceptance rate and no supplemental essays. There's probably a similar school in your own back-yard.

As with the other categories here, a good place to start is the *U.S. News & World Report* website. Skip the national rankings and check out its lists of "Best Regional Colleges" and "Best Regional Universities."*
Since acceptance rates at regional schools tend to be much higher, you can just start reviewing the list before playing with the sliders.

*https://www.usnews.com/best-colleges/rankings/regional-colleges; https://www.usnews.com/best-colleges/rankings/regional-universities.

CHAPTER 8

Scholarship Essays

For most teens, getting into college is only half the battle: you also have to figure out how you're going to pay for it. If you apply for financial aid, a college may offer you a financial aid package, including student loans and possibly some scholarship funding, along with its offer of admission.

But that isn't always enough. External scholarships can be a huge help, and thanks to the internet, they're easier to find than ever before. Websites and apps abound to help you find scholarships that you're qualified for. (Unigo, Going Merry, and Scholly are good places to start; Unigo and Going Merry are free, whereas Scholly charges a monthly fee.)

Essays are a crucial part of the application process for most scholarships. Just as in college admissions, most scholarship decisions are made by committees. Each scholarship committee wants to get to know you, and they use essays to do that.

The good news is that if you've gotten this far in the book, you already know 90% of what it takes to write a great scholarship essay. For the most part, the same principles apply to scholarship essays as to college admissions essays, although there are a few differences.

This chapter will start by giving you a process for planning and writing your scholarship essays. Next, I'll review the key principles of good essay writing that apply to both scholarship and college essays.

Then we'll take a look at the ways in which scholarship essays differ from college essays. After unpacking some common scholarship essay questions, in the final part of the chapter, we'll explore how to approach a scholarship application with multiple essays by examining all four essay prompts for the NAACP Uplift Scholarship, a $10,000 scholarship for students of color.

How to Do It: The Process for Writing Scholarship Essays

1. Start early

Many students wait until they've already submitted their college applications to start applying for scholarships. This is a colossal mistake. Though some scholarships have spring deadlines, many deadlines come *before* your college applications are due. For example, the Gates Scholarship, which covers 100% of financial need for three hundred lucky seniors, is due in September, whereas the Posse Scholarship, which covers tuition and provides extensive social support, requires nominations the spring or summer before senior year. Start thinking about scholarships at the same time you start thinking about college applications: in the spring of junior year and the summer that follows.

2. Do your research and make a list

Scholarship applications take work, and you won't have time to apply for all scholarships. Instead, use online tools such as Unigo, Going Merry, and Scholly to research the ones that you'd be eligible and competitive for. Narrow it down to a manageable list—for most students, no more than ten.

To improve your chances, make your list broad. Whereas students with strong grades should definitely apply for the competitive national scholarships, most students will have a much better chance at winning local scholarships. With some research, you'll also find scholarships related to your specific interests, heritage, or identity. That research can pay off, because fewer people tend to apply for those than for big ones.

As you do your research, you'll quickly discover that scholarships vary widely in their essay requirements. Some, such as the Gates, don't even require essays in the first round. Others require a number of essays early on, and some require videos. Plan a workload that seems manageable, keeping in mind that you'll also be applying to colleges at the same time.

3. Make a calendar

Once you have your list of scholarships, the next step is to make a calendar or list of the deadlines. When you're applying to a bunch of them, it's very easy to get confused about what is due when. Having all the information in one place will keep you on track. Aim to start each application at least two to three weeks before it's due, so you have enough time to do your best writing.

4. Write one scholarship application at a time

As with colleges, I strongly recommend that you complete all the essays for one scholarship before moving on to the next. Because each scholarship-granting organization is different, you need to spend some time thinking about how your experiences and dreams relate to the goals and values associated with that particular scholarship. If you try to write all the applications at the same time, your writing will quickly get confused.

5. Research the organization and brainstorm essay/video topics

When you sit down to write a scholarship application, the first step is to research the organization that grants it. What are the organization's goals, values, and priorities? As you tell your own story in your essays and videos, you'll want to do so in a way that reflects what the organization is looking for in applicants.

The organization's website is the best place to find that out. You may find that it describes its goals and values in the application itself. If not, look for an "About Us" or "Our Mission" page on the website. Once you know its goals, brainstorm topics for each essay and video in the application. For an example of how to do this, refer to the sample scholarship essays for the NAACP Uplift Scholarship on page 250.

6. Outline, write, revise

Once you have your overall ideas in place, approach each essay with the same basic process you've been using in your college essays. Since you've already brainstormed your topics, begin by briefly outlining the essay; bullet points are fine. Write a first draft, revise, and then move on to the next essay for that scholarship.

7. Get feedback

After you've written all your essays for a particular scholarship, share them with an adult you trust. Your English teacher or counselor probably won't have time to look at all of your scholarship applications, but it's fine to ask them to review one or two, ideally for big scholarships that involve a lot of writing.

For the rest, go to your parent or guardian (if they're available) or a trusted friend or an older teen. Show your essays to this person and ask for their feedback. Don't ask "Do you like this?" Instead, ask "Are my essays engaging?" "Does this application show who I am as a person?" And additional questions such as "Does my writing make sense? Where do you get lost?" Those questions will elicit feedback that will help you revise.

8. Proofread

Once you've solicited feedback and revised accordingly, it's crucial to proofread everything one last time. Sloppiness does not make a good impression on scholarship committees!

9. Submit, rinse, and repeat!

Once you've followed all these steps, congratulate yourself! Submit the application and move on to the next one.

10. Reuse your essays and modify as needed

It's not only fine to recycle essays in multiple scholarship applications, it's smart. You want the process to be efficient; the less you have to write, the more scholarships you can apply for. Just be sure to revise your reused essays to address the specific goals of each scholarship, as well as the specific requirements of each prompt.

The Basics: Key Principles of Essay Writing

1. Show, don't tell

You've probably heard your English teacher say it. "Show, don't tell" is a central principle of narrative writing. In a poem or short story, for example, instead of telling the reader that daisies are pretty, you want to *show* them daisies by describing the flowers' soft yellow petals or their sweet, honeylike smell. Similarly, in scholarship essays, you don't want to simply tell the reader that you're hardworking and resilient. Instead, use stories to show the specific times when you worked your butt off and the moments when you rose to the challenge. That brings us to our next principle, which is . . .

2. Structure around your story

One of the best ways to get a reader on your side is by telling them a story. Whether they're long or short, effective scholarship essays make use of stories from the writer's life. Stories also give you a simple way to structure your essay. Make sure that each story has three parts: a beginning, a middle, and an end. For longer essays you may want to expand the middle section, but in general, you want to make sure that each essay includes these three parts.

3. Use both internal and external stories

The best stories don't just tell us about things that happen; they show the reader how those events affected the characters—what they thought and felt and how their perspective changed.

I call the difference between those two elements internal and external storytelling. External stories are the obvious bits: you moved across the country, you joined the track team, you made it (or didn't make it) into All-State Band. The internal story is how you felt and responded. Perhaps you felt lonely when you moved but ultimately developed a sense of independence. Track may have led to the most important friendships in your life, whereas not making All-State Band helped you learn to play the trombone for the joy of it, not to accumulate more achievements. All of those are internal story elements, and they are the key to effective essays. For a more in-depth refresher, you can turn back to page 64 and review the section on internal versus external storytelling.

4. Write about challenges and how you overcame them

In any story, whether it's a movie or a college essay, we identify with a protagonist through their antagonist and their struggles to defeat them. Think about it: without Voldemort, Harry Potter would be kind of a dull kid. Without Darth Vader, the Emperor, and Kylo Ren, the *Star Wars* saga simply wouldn't exist.

As you're telling the reader stories in your essay, you want to emphasize two things: the challenges you faced, and the actions you took to overcome them. This can take some reflection, because we often don't remember the challenges after the fact. Think back to what made things difficult, be honest about them, and then be sure to show the reader how you moved on. Showing your actions is important, because in scholarship essays you want to . . .

5. Stay positive

Even though you'll be talking about challenges, you want to leave the scholarship committee hopeful and optimistic about your future. After all, they want to give their money to people who are going to use it to better themselves and society. That's why it's important to follow challenges with solutions. In picking moments from your life, you can choose to show times where you succeeded and achieved your goals. Those stories naturally have a positive ending. Yet you don't need to shy away from failure. We've all experienced disappointment, and it's fine to talk about times when you failed—as long as you're able to show how you learned and grew from that setback.

6. Proofread

Finally, before you submit anything, proofread! Details matter. Although a misplaced comma or two won't kill you, an essay filled with spelling, grammatical, or punctuation errors may well disqualify you from a scholarship. Proofread everything yourself, and whenever possible, also ask another person to proofread for you. We're much more likely to catch mistakes in other people's writing than in our own. If you can't find someone to help you proofread, try printing out your essays or even changing the font and text size before proofing them. You want to help your brain see the essays differently, so you can catch mistakes you didn't notice before.

How Scholarship Essays Differ from College Essays

Now that you know the basics, let's move on to the more advanced material. Here are four ways in which scholarship essays differ from college essays and some strategies for how to approach them.

1. Different prompts

While there will probably be prompts that you recognize from your college applications—"Describe a time when you had a belief or idea challenged. How did you respond?" or some variation of that is common in both scholarship and college apps—many of the prompts will be different. Scholarship committees may ask for a miniature version of your life story or biography. When asking about your community, you may see more requests for how you've *impacted* your community, as opposed to why a particular community is meaningful to you. You'll also see direct questions such as "Why do you deserve our scholarship?" and "How will our scholarship help you achieve your goals?"

2. Organizational mission

Most selective colleges offer the same thing: a liberal arts education. Most also have a similar mission, which is to educate while advancing knowledge through research. Scholarships, however, are given by a wide range of organizations with varying goals. Some are seeking to redress social and economic disparities, some are aimed at helping specific ethnic, religious, and cultural groups, while others are devoted to concepts like leadership or civic values. Because of this, it pays to do your research. Be sure you understand exactly what each organization is looking for. You want to be yourself, *and* you want to show how your experiences and goals relate to the organization's mission.

3. Emphasis on goals and action

Whereas college admissions officers are charged with putting together a community, scholarship committees are looking for people who will make the best use of their money. Much more than in college essays, it's therefore important to emphasize your plan for action, both in college and beyond.

Start your scholarship process by thinking through your goals. Why do you want to go to college? What do you hope to achieve and learn while there, and what do you plan to do with that education? You don't need to have it all figured out, but you do want to have a plan. Arriving at clear, honest answers to those questions will help you write strong essays.

4. Resilience and community engagement are key

Remember the list of the Top Ten qualities college admissions officers look for? You learned about this back in chapter 2: things such as achievement, passion, leadership, and empathy. Scholarship committees are looking for a combination of these qualities, too. Different scholarships will emphasize different qualities; if a scholarship has the words "leader" or "leadership" in its title, for example, that's a dead giveaway!

However, in most scholarship essays you'll want to pay special attention to two qualities: resilience and community engagement. Think about it from the committee's perspective: they're potentially making an investment in you, and they want people who can bounce back from setbacks. Similarly, they're looking for people who are going to use their education to benefit others: their community, their country, maybe even the world.

5. Use of videos

As of 2024, many national scholarship committees are a few years ahead of the selective college committees in the use of media. It's not uncommon to see a scholarship that requires several essays and one or two videos. Think of your essays and videos as a package that, working together, paints a picture of you. If your scholarship application requires videos, plan out your topics in advance so that your videos don't repeat what's already in an essay. Ideally, you'll use the videos to say something different or to elaborate on what you wrote in the essays. Finally, when planning your calendar, make time to write, film, and edit the videos. Don't try to wing it! In the best videos, the student has usually outlined what they're going to say in advance.

Common Scholarship Essay Questions

In this section, I'll look at some commonly asked scholarship essay questions and offer tips on how to address them.

1. Tell us about yourself

Form: Narrative essay (length varies)

Audience: A scholarship committee

Topic: How you became the person you are today

Purposes: (1) To introduce yourself: tell the reader who you are and what you value; (2) to demonstrate personal qualities such as resilience and maturity

At first glance this commonly occurring question looks a lot like the personal essay. But it's actually quite different. Whereas personal essays focus on a slice of your high school years, this prompt is asking for a broader perspective on your entire life to date. Readers of this essay will also be looking specifically at the challenges you've faced, how you've overcome them, and how you've grown and matured as a person. Though this might seem overwhelming, the good news is that it can be a fun, rewarding chance to tell your own story. Here's a simple strategy for writing this essay.

1. Pick a few key moments or themes from your life

Good stories are built around turning points, so you want to include a few moments or forces that shaped you into who you are. They could be externally "big" moments, such as when you were accepted into a selective high school or when you broke your leg and had to sit out a season of basketball. Or they could be more private, internal moments that had a huge impact on you, such as reading a book, listening to a song, or having a conversation with a family member. They could also be broader themes that have shaped your identity.

2. Create a simple outline

Once you've chosen the topics, your goal is to weave them together *and* offer some insight into how those forces shaped you. Look at the word count for the essay to see how much space you have, then put together a simple outline. For example, if you have to write 600 words, you might start with the following.

a. Moment 1 (use this to hook your reader) (around 200 words)
b. Moment 2 (around 200 words)
c. Moment 3, including a conclusion/reflection (around 200 words)

One important point: don't wait until the end to start reflecting! Reflect on each moment as you go along, using your reflections to transition from one story to the next. Then use your concluding sentences to talk about who you are today, your goals for the future, and/or how the moments or events you have written about combined to turn you into the person you've become.

3. Write and revise the essay

Once you have an outline, sit down and start writing! Be bold. Be bright. Be brief. Here's a sample essay to get you started.

Sample Tell Us About Yourself Essay (450 words)

Although I was born in Meridian, Mississippi, I don't consider myself a Southerner. My father is a petty officer in the Navy, which means I grew up on a series of naval bases on the West and East coasts. Being a "Navy brat" has shaped my life in a number of ways. Moving to a new city and new school every few years has certainly presented challenges, such as having to repeatedly say goodbye to friends and teachers. But it's also provided me with lots of new beginnings. I've learned to make new friends quickly, and living in five different states has given me an appreciation for just how broad, diverse, and varied this country is.

Another factor that's greatly influenced me is the experience of growing up as a mixed-race person. My skin is not very melanated, so most people assume I'm white. But actually, my ethnic heritage is a mix of Spanish, Mexican, Irish, British, and Native American. Conversations at home constantly switch between Spanish and English, and our holidays are a mix of traditional, "All-American" celebrations like the Fourth of July and Thanksgiving alongside family traditions like Día de Muertos and Corpus Christi. Strangers are often surprised when I understand their spoken Spanish and reply in their language; this has led to many raised eyebrows, but also to making new friends and unexpected connections. Having so many assumptions constantly being made about me is difficult, but it's taught me an important lesson, which is not to make assumptions about others. I may think I know a person's race, ethnicity, or even their gender, but the reality is that I don't. I also don't know what kind of day they've had or what might be motivating them to act the way they do, so I try to keep an open mind and open heart.

More recently, my life and academic plans have been shaped by Mr. Reishad Richardson, my tenth-grade chemistry teacher. Not only did his class make me more excited about science (I've always been a STEM kid, but math had been my focus), Mr. Richardson sponsors the Kearny High Robotics Team, which I joined at his suggestion and is now my second home. Designing and building robots has become my favorite thing in the world. Robotics has also inspired me to take courses in computer science and AP Physics and to participate in the Engineering Possibilities in College summer program at Cal Poly San Luis Obispo. I'm excited to pursue an engineering degree in college, because I want to help create new robots that can perform backbreaking, repetitive tasks, so more people are free to use their minds and bodies to pursue things they truly care about.

2. How have you contributed to your community?

Form: Narrative essay (length varies)
Audience: A scholarship committee
Topic: Your engagement with one or more communities that you are a part of
Purpose: To show how you personally demonstrate qualities such as community engagement, leadership, and empathy

As you've been writing your college application essays, there's a good chance you've come across the Community essay (see page 178). Scholarship committees also like to ask about the communities you're part of, but unlike in admissions essays, the prompts tend to focus on your *contributions* to the community, as opposed to how the community has shaped you. Fortunately, it's often easy to adapt an application essay on community for scholarships. For many of us, the communities that shape us are also the communities to which we contribute the most. For this essay, I therefore recommend you take a similar approach to what's recommended in chapter 6. Here are the steps.

1. Pick a topic

Start by deciding what community or communities you're going to address. Ask yourself: Where have I contributed most? Is it your school? Your neighborhood? Your church, synagogue, mosque, or other house of worship? It's usually best to pick one community and focus on it, but for longer essays you may be able to include two or three.

2. Brainstorm and outline

Throughout this essay you'll want to highlight specific actions. Maybe you tutored peers or younger children, helped pick up trash in a neighborhood cleanup drive, or volunteered at a soup kitchen. In telling your story, you'll want to showcase not only your community engagement but also your leadership and empathy. Have you inspired others to get involved? If so, how? And why is contributing to the community important to you personally? What do you get back in return? Though many structures are possible, I recommend that you approach this essay in two parts. Use this outline as a guide.

1. What I've done (roughly one-half of the essay)
   a. Briefly tell us about your community(s).
   b. Tell us the story of how you got involved with this community. What, specifically, have you done to contribute? (This is a place to show, not tell!)
   c. Describe the impact of your actions. How, specifically, do you think your actions have helped others? Have they helped individuals? Your community as a whole?
2. Why this is important to me (roughly one-half of the essay)
   a. What's meaningful to me about helping people in this community?
   b. How has this experience affected me? Has it changed my perspective? How has it helped me to grow up or to appreciate others in a different way?
   c. Optional: Conclude with a sentence or two about how this work has inspired you or how you see yourself taking it forward in your life.

3. Write and revise

Once you have an outline, you're ready to start writing! It can be useful to start and end the essay with a short introduction and conclusion, but these aren't required; it all depends on the length and the prompt. Here's an example.

Although I've contributed to my high school community in a number of ways—through leadership roles in student government, the marching band, and the varsity tennis team—I'm most proud of the contributions I've made through service at my church.

I've been part of a church community for as long as I can remember. If I'm being honest, church was pretty boring at first; it wasn't until I joined the junior choir in fifth grade that I began to feel like I was part of a community. That sense of belonging deepened in middle school, when I joined the youth group and began getting involved in service. Since then I've participated in multiple Habitat for Humanity house-building events each year, working alongside other teens and adults to build new homes for local families. I also went on summer service trips to Cuba and the Dominican Republic, where we built houses and provided free, basic medical care to rural villagers. In addition, each year on Christmas Eve, I help host an annual church dinner where we prepare and serve meals for inpatient residents of a nearby psychiatric hospital.

Learning how to serve others through my church has transformed me as a person. Building new homes has exposed me to people in my town that I otherwise would never have met, and it's helped me get to know the adults at my church in new and different ways. Dr. Pendergrass is no longer just our family doctor; now he's the funny guy who taught me how to put up aluminum siding. My family may have modest means, but seeing rural poverty up close in Latin America has made me much more grateful for what we do have, as well as for the rights we all enjoy as Americans. Perhaps most importantly, the service we do on Christmas Eve has shown me the incredible value of having a home and family. The patients we serve have no families to spend the holidays with, and it's rare that they enjoy a home-cooked meal. Over the years I've realized that it's a privilege to serve them and an even greater privilege to go home afterwards to a warm bed in an apartment with people who love me.

Membership in my church community has strengthened my faith. It's also taught me an important lesson: that "faith without works is dead." In the future I want to keep giving back to the communities that matter most to me, because I know it's the only way I can continue to grow, learn, and stay grateful for everything I've been given.

3. What are your academic/professional goals, and how will this scholarship help you achieve them?

Form: Narrative essay (length varies)
Audience: A scholarship committee
Topic: Your goals and how they relate to the scholarship
Purposes: (1) To show the committee that you have goals, what those goals are, and why those goals are important to you; (2) to show that you've thought seriously about your future; (3) to convince the committee that this scholarship will help you achieve your goals

As you can imagine, scholarship committees are curious about how you're going to use their money. So it's not uncommon to see some version of this essay question, which is actually two questions in one: the first prompt asks about your goals, and the second is about how they relate to this specific scholarship.

This question can show up in different ways. You might be asked about your goals, or you might see one prompt asking about career goals and another asking about academic goals. Sometimes the question about how the scholarship will help you achieve them will show up in the same prompts; other times it'll be a separate essay. Regardless, you want to take the same overall approach in responding to this kind of question, which is to identify your goals, to explain *why* those goals are important to you, and then argue how the scholarship will help you achieve them. Let's break that down.

1. Identify your goals

Start working on this essay by putting your goals on paper. List your top four to five academic and professional goals. For example:

1. Graduate from college
2. Go to law school and graduate with honors
3. Become a prosecutor
4. Give back to my community
5. Start a family

Notice how the first three goals are specific: graduating from college, going to law school, and becoming a prosecutor. Those goals are ready to work for you in a scholarship essay.

The fourth goal, however—"Give back to my community"—is more vague. That is a fantastic goal, and it's something most scholarship committees love to see, but in order to use it in essay, you need to get more specific. How, exactly would you give back to your community? What matters to you, and what kind of impact would you like to have? Many of us want to give back to the next generation in the same way that we've been helped, so it can be helpful to think back on what you've been given by those around you.

The fifth goal—to start a family—is also wonderful, but it's not academic or career related; it's personal. If you want to mention a meaningful personal goal or two in your essay, that's fine, but do so briefly. Keep the focus on the topics the committee is asking about: academics and career.

A revised version of this list might look something like:

1. Graduate from college
2. Go to law school and graduate with honors
3. Become a prosecutor
4. Do pro bono legal work for single mothers in my community [*pro bono* means when a lawyer or other professional offers their services for free]

5. Start a nonprofit that helps elementary school children learn how to read

All five of those items are great for a scholarship essay, because they are clear, specific, and connected.

2. Explain the "why"

Once you have a list of goals, the next step is to clarify why you want to achieve each of them. You might know this already. If so, great! Move on to the next step. If you need to clarify them more, use a table like this to write them out.

GOAL	WHY IT'S IMPORTANT TO ME
Graduate from college	My parents raised me to value education, and a college education is necessary to become a lawyer.
Go to law school; graduate with honors	I've wanted to become a lawyer since I first saw *Law and Order: SVU* as a kid. I love history and social studies, I believe strongly in justice, and I believe our system can work only when principled people fight for what's right.
Become a prosecutor	After experiencing violence firsthand, both in my home and in my neighborhood, I want to be responsible for bringing criminals to justice and for making sure that innocent people aren't locked up.
Do pro bono legal work for single mothers in my community	I was raised by a single mother who worked two jobs to support her family. When she was falsely accused of stealing at work and fired, there was no one to defend her. I want to be able to defend other innocent women like her, who are doing everything to provide for their kids.
Start a nonprofit that helps elementary school children learn how to read	Though I did not attend a great elementary school, I learned to love books from the old ladies who volunteered at our local library. I would like to give back by helping the next generation learn how to read.

3. Outline your essay

Structure your essay in two parts. First, talk about your goals and why they're important to you. Then explain how this scholarship will help you achieve them. We've already addressed the first part. For the second part, it's important to do your research into exactly what the scholarship offers. Some offer money to help with tuition; some cover other costs such as books, housing, and food; and others connect you with mentors, peers, and other support networks.

As you plan this essay, go back and look at exactly what the particular scholarship offers and ask yourself: How will this help me achieve my goals? If your family does not have the money to support you in college, explain that and write about how the scholarship funds would help. Graduate school is also expensive, and although most scholarships you'll be applying for only cover undergraduate studies, not graduate school, it's fine to mention that you plan to go to graduate school (law school, medical school, dental school, social work school, whatever) and that having lots of debt would keep you from achieving your goals. If the scholarship offers peer or mentorship support, definitely talk about how that would help you both academically and professionally.

Outlining the "Goals" Essay

1. My goals
   a. Describe three to five top academic/career goals and reasons for desiring them.
   b. Whenever possible, organize them chronologically (as in the example above).
2. How the scholarship will help me
   a. Explain two or three specific ways the scholarship will help you. These could include:
      i. Paying for college tuition
      ii. Paying for other college expenses (books, room and board, travel costs)
      iii. Reducing the amount of time you have to work at a job in college (which means you will be able to spend more time on your studies)
      iv. Reducing your overall student debt (especially if you're planning for grad school or for a career that won't make a lot of money)

v. Connecting you with mentors, motivated peers, and other support networks

4. Write and revise

Once you've answered these questions and put together a brief outline, you are ready to write and revise!

4. Describe a time when you faced a failure or setback. How did you learn and grow from the experience?

Form: Narrative essay (length varies)
Audience: A scholarship committee
Topic: A time when you failed or disappointed and how you responded
Purpose: To demonstrate your maturity, humility, resilience, and the ability to self-reflect

Whenever I was filling out applications for scholarships, this was the question that frightened me the most. I hate talking about my failures, and who doesn't? It sucks to open up to strangers about the times when we've been disappointed, embarrassed, even humiliated. Yet essays about setbacks can often be compelling and humanizing, because we've all failed at some time or another. The secrets to writing a good setback essay are to keep a light touch and to be sure to pick an example where you truly learned something and grew from the experience.

For example, one of my own biggest failures happened after college, when I spent a year studying modern dance in Austria. It was difficult, and although I felt that I learned a lot, my teachers did not. At the end of the year, I failed. I literally got Fs in most of my dance classes, with comments like "Eric showed no improvement this semester." As someone who had recently graduated from Harvard with honors, that came as a shock!

It was also a wake-up call. Back home the next year, I thought about what had gone wrong. I realized that I hadn't thrown myself fully into the program I'd signed up for. I'd skipped weeks of class to spend time with relatives stationed in Italy, and basically treated the whole thing like a relaxing year abroad instead of the intensive, preprofessional dance program that it was.

What I learned from that is that if I'm going to do something, I need to give it 100 percent. I'm not a great dancer, and giving my full effort wouldn't have turned me into Mikhail Baryshnikov or Lil Nas X. But when I give my all, I make progress, and I can walk out of the room with self-respect, knowing I've done my best.

Here's another secret: these essays can also be a time to talk about a success. Let's say you were placed into Honors English freshman year but quickly discovered that you were in over your head. You fell behind the other kids, your teacher hated your writing, and you ended up getting a D. For you, that was a failure—but after you got over the disappointment, you realized that you'd made a huge mistake: you hadn't wanted to admit that you were struggling, so you had never asked for help.

Realizing that mistake, when sophomore year began, you found a tutor through a neighborhood after-school center. You also started coming in during lunch to ask your English teacher for help on the assignments. By the end of sophomore year, your writing had improved, and you got an A. Your failure in freshman year led to an important lesson, which then led to success.

Not everyone has a story like that, of course. But I use it to remind you that although you do have to write about a failure or setback in the essay, it shouldn't end with failure. You want to end the essay on a positive note, whether that's the learning and growth that resulted or a success that came later because of a lesson you learned through the failure.

How to Approach a Set of Scholarship Essays: The NAACP Uplift Scholarship

The NAACP Uplift Scholarship, one of many scholarships run by the NAACP, is a $10,000 award given to thirty people per year. The requirements are that you must be a US citizen, Black or a person of color, enrolled in or accepted to college, have a 3.0 GPA or higher, and be able to demonstrate financial need.*

I chose this scholarship as an example because it's a solid "middle of the pack" scholarship. Though it's nationally competitive and generous ($10,000 is nothing to sneeze at), it's not a full-ride, superprestigious scholarship like the Gates. Because it's lesser known, it's therefore the kind of award that savvy scholarship hunters look for. Fewer people are likely to apply, so you'll have a better chance of winning.

The application for this scholarship requires you to write four short to medium-length essays and upload two videos of two to five minutes each. Here are the prompts.

Essays

1. What is the end goal of your education/career journey and how do you plan to get there? (100 words)

2. What ignites or uplifts you to make the world a better place? (250 words)

3. How would you use your education to improve the world? (250 words)

4. What is the importance of equity in education? What does a fair chance and equitable access to education mean to you? (250 words)

Videos

1. What dreams would you like to follow that this scholarship would help you attain? (2 to 5 minutes)

*You can learn more about the scholarship here: https://naacp.org/find-resources/scholarships-awards-internships/scholarships/uplift-scholarship.

2. Tell us about a personal achievement that has empowered you. (2 to 5 minutes)

The Process

1. Research the organization

Before writing a single word of an essay, you want to be sure you understand what the scholarship and the organization granting it are about. In this case, one clue comes on the web page for the scholarship: it tells us that at the NAACP, "we advance efforts to ensure equity in educational opportunity that prepares students for success in school, work, and life." The word "equity" is key here: it tells us that this is a scholarship focused on giving more people access to education, especially those who might not otherwise have the opportunity to go to college.

Let's look a little deeper and find out what the NAACP is all about. If you're not already familiar with the organization, look at its Wikipedia page, where you'll discover that it's one of the oldest civil rights groups in the country. Moving back to the NAACP's website and its "Mission & Vision" page, you can see that it envisions:

> . . . an inclusive community rooted in liberation where all persons can exercise their civil and human rights without discrimination.

You can also see its mission statement, which is:

> Our mission is to achieve equity, political rights, and social inclusion by advancing policies and practices that expand human and civil rights, eliminate discrimination, and accelerate the well-being, education, and economic security of Black people and all persons of color.

Why do we care? All of this is important, because it gives you lots of topics you could potentially bring up in your essays. You could talk about inclusion ("an inclusive community"), civil and human rights, the elimination of discrimination, and equity. You don't have to talk about all of these things, of course. Instead, pick the ones that are most relevant to your own story and reference them in your essays or videos.

2. Brainstorm the topics

Now that you know what the organization is about, the next step is to start thinking about what you might write about in each essay. The sample student filling out this application is a seventeen-year-old Black male-identifying boy living in Washington, DC, who's been raised by an aunt ever since his mother passed away. He's interested in soccer, skateboarding, and English (he loves to read), and wants to become an architect. Here's what his brainstorming looked like.

Essays

1. **What is the end goal of your education/career journey and how do you plan to get there? (100 words)**

    Becoming an architect who designs urban spaces. Need to go to college, major in design or math, then grad school for architecture.

2. **What ignites or uplifts you to make the world a better place? (250 words)**

    Reading, especially history and fiction by Black authors

    Nature

    Solid, elegant buildings

    Parks and gardens

    Cristiano Ronaldo (soccer player)

3. **How would you use your education to improve the world? (250 words)**

    By designing urban spaces that take people into account, I can improve the quality of life for people living in the city.

    I want to start a nonprofit that promotes literacy in my community, Southeast DC.

4. **What is the importance of equity in education? What does a fair chance and equitable access to education mean to you? (250 words)**

Equity means everyone getting a fair shot.

It means help understanding how you prepare for college.

It means having the ability to pay for college.

It means having help and support to succeed academically—tutoring when necessary.

I could talk about my mother and how she started college but didn't finish because money ran out and she had to work.

Videos

1. **What dreams would you like to follow that this scholarship would help you attain? (2 to 5 minutes)**

   Becoming an architect

   Raising a family

   Giving back to my community

2. **Tell us about a personal achievement that has empowered you. (2 to 5 minutes)**

   Could talk about skateboarding: mastering the dark slide

   Making the varsity soccer team

   Helping to start a literary magazine at my high school

3. Make a plan and outline each essay

In some of the essays, this student ended up writing about exactly what he came up with during the brainstorming. In others, however, he had to narrow the topic down down.

For example, in essay 2 he chose to focus on the first two items: reading and nature. From his research he could tell that reading was tied to the NAACP's goals, and he chose to talk about nature in this essay because he knew he was going to focus on architecture in essay 3 and video 1. (Cristiano Ronaldo, the soccer player, would be a good choice for a scholarship focused on sports.)

For the equity essay (number 4), he decided to organize the essay around the story of his mother, which was an idea he surfaced at the end of the brainstorming. Finally, in the second video he decided to talk about the literary magazine. His hunch was that it would resonate better with the NAACP scholarship committee than an essay about skateboarding—and he was probably right!

4. Write and revise

Once he'd settled on his topics, he briefly outlined the essays, wrote drafts, and revised. Here are the final essays.

What is the end goal of your education/career journey and how do you plan to get there? (100 words)

Growing up in Washington, DC, I've seen a lot of architecture: the good, the bad, and the ugly. When I was young, my mom took me on walks around the National Mall, where I was inspired by the giant buildings and museums, both modern and classical. What a contrast from the stark brick apartment blocks at home.

I believe architecture has the power to change people's lives, which is why I want to become an architect who designs urban spaces and neighborhoods. To do that, I'll need to graduate from college and get a master's degree in architecture.

What ignites or uplifts you to make the world a better place? (250 words)

Many things inspire me, from my favorite soccer player to the smile on my aunt's face when I tell a joke. Two forces that never fail to uplift me are books and nature.

I've loved to read ever since I was a child and would jump around the house when my aunt brought home a new picture book from the library. Reading allows me to see the world through someone else's eyes. I first became aware of the power of African American fiction in tenth grade, when we read *Native Son* by Richard Wright. Although the protagonist's story was very different from mine, I identified with how Wright described a life where you don't have many opportunities, where you can't make sense of the world around you. I've felt that way myself at times, and I'm grateful that, unlike Bigger Thomas, I have the benefits of an education and a strong sense of morality.

Another major force that uplifts me is nature. My neighborhood may not seem to have a lot of natural beauty, but it's here if you know where to find it. There are two parks near my house that are filled with trees and grass in the summer. We've had many barbecues there with my aunt's family and her church. On visits to family in South Carolina, I've seen mountains that go on forever. As an architect, I'd like to bring more of the beauty of nature to people living in the city.

How would you use your education to improve the world? (250 words)

One thing I've noticed about Washington, DC, is that the best architecture is all downtown, where the wealthier people live and work. The buildings in my neighborhood are older, poorly maintained, and less inspiring than what you see elsewhere.

Yet one building stands out as an exception: my elementary school. When I went there, it was just a brick building, like every other school in DC. But when I was in middle school, everything changed. Our councilmember was able to get a renovation funded, which meant that the front of the school was entirely rebuilt with glass and metal, and a new library and arts wing was added to one side. Now it stands out like a sore thumb from the buildings around it, but also like a beacon of a hope. It inspires me to see how much change was possible, even when the original building didn't seem to offer much.

That's the kind of change I want to create as an architect and the hope I want to give people. I want to use architecture to show people living in urban communities that they matter and that beauty isn't just for the rich and powerful. I'd love to design buildings that are environmentally conscious, that bring the power of nature into the city, and that respect our Mother Earth.

What is the importance of equity in education? What does a fair chance and equitable access to education mean to you? (250 words)

When I think about equity in education, I think about my mother. She did well in high school and would have been the first in her family to graduate from college, but unfortunately after two years she had to drop out. Her scholarship covered only part of her tuition, and eventually the money ran out. While she intended to go back and finish her degree, a year after leaving school she had me and I became the focus of her life. I'm sad that I never got to know her well—she passed when I was three, and ever since then I've been raised by my aunt, her sister.

To me, equity in education means going to a high school that prepares you for college, that teaches you what you need to know in order to succeed. My mother had that. But it also means being able to pay for college and to see it through to completion. College doesn't do you any good if you go there for only a year or if you're working so hard to make ends meet that you can't pass your classes.

Like my mother, I've been blessed with good teachers and a strong work ethic. I hope that I also have the opportunity to get scholarships, so that I can make it all the way through. Equity isn't just about starting; it's also about having the chance to finish and to pass what you learned on to the next generation.

Video 1: What dreams would you like to follow that this scholarship would help you attain? (2 to 5 minutes)

In this video, the student elaborated on his dreams of becoming an architect, which were introduced in his essays. He also included a montage of photographs and videos of buildings from his neighborhood, as well as the kinds of buildings he wanted to design. Toward the end he articulated one of his goals: to design a new library and after-school center in his neighborhood.

Video 2: Tell us about a personal achievement that has empowered you. (2 to 5 minutes)

This video focused on the student's work during junior year to start a literary magazine at his high school. He talked about how he had worked with other students to find a faculty sponsor, secured a grant from the local community center to pay for it, and reached out to the entire high school to find poems, essays, art, and short stories for the magazine. The video included pictures of the printed magazine as well as photos of him and his friends working on it.

Conclusion: Hang In There!

So there you have it! If you've made it this far, you now have a clear and thorough understanding of what admissions committees at selective schools are looking for and how the process works. You also now have a sense of what is expected in each of the essays, as well as concrete steps for writing them.

If I can leave you with anything, it's a reminder that the most important thing in this process is to be yourself. Yes, it's a polished version of yourself. It's your profile pic, not the embarrassing selfie you sent to friends in the group chat last week. But it's you. And that's what college admissions officers are ultimately looking for. Beyond all the hype and prestige and school spirit and dining halls with farm-to-table menus, a college is a community of people who care deeply about learning and about one another. That community is made up of individuals, and for admissions officers to offer you a place in that community, they need to see who you really are.

I want you to end up in a college where you will flourish, and I want you to end up there for the right reasons. In ten or twenty years, I want you to look back and be proud of the work you put into your essays, proud of how you represented yourself in this process.

As crazy as the admissions process can be, it usually works out okay. In the end, you can accept an admissions decision at only one school, so the goal of the game is to get admitted to at least one school where you will thrive. When kids follow their heart, put their best foot forward, and apply to a balanced list of reaches, targets, and safeties, that's usually what happens. The übercompetitive kids land at the Harvards and Stanfords of the world, while the kids who thrive in warmer communities land in schools that are a better fit for them. The few times I've seen it go wrong and a student ended up in a school where they were truly miserable, it was always because they had misrepresented themselves or tried to manipulate the admissions process in some way, usually to get into a more prestigious college.

Be honest. Be true. Be yourself. Have the courage to be vulnerable. Put your best foot forward. Highlight your accomplishments, and showcase your passions. If you can do these things, you will succeed.

Go forth and prosper!

Acknowledgments

When I wrote my first musical comedy for the stage, a veteran producer gruffly informed me that "a musical needs lots of friends."

The same, it turns out, is true of books, which is why I'm so grateful to the many people who made this one possible. First and foremost is Kathy Edersheim, one of the smartest people I know and the first reader of the book's early drafts. For nearly three years, Kathy has provided direct, clear, pointed-when-necessary, always constructive feedback and support. It's hard to imagine this book being written without her.

I'm also incredibly grateful to my agent, Karen Murgolo, and the entire team at Aevitas Creative, especially Todd Shuster, who has offered wise guidance and support over many years. Huge plaudits also go to my incredible editor, Ronnie Alvarado, her brilliant, professional team at Simon Element, and Noah Chaskin for last-minute citation work.

It would be hard to overstate the impact of the many people who taught me how to write, starting with Chris Weller (to whom this book is dedicated), a legendary English teacher in my hometown of Staunton, Virginia. I also learned so much from Ned Bonfoey, my AP US History teacher, and later from Professor Robert D. Levin at Harvard and Professor Gundula Kreuzer at Yale. I've also had the gift of wise, brilliant colleagues and mentors, many of whom are still close friends, especially Emily Orser Richardson, Doranna Tindle, Priya Sehgal, Nancy Kreloff, Susan Cohen, Tesha Nixon Cunningham, Michael Motto, Minal

Hajratwala (who helped me find the courage and inspiration to finish writing this book), and so many others.

The "lots of friends" behind this book include countless others who have contributed their time, talent, insight, and emotional support over the years, including Ali, Ben, Adam, Andy and Steve, Anne Kline, Charlie Fink (the "veteran producer" mentioned above), Jon Slaw, Jess and Bulent, Patrick and Leon, John, Cliff, Robert, Carol, and my families at Liberty and St. Luke's.

Equally important are the former students who generously allowed their essays to be included as resources and inspiration for the next generation. They include Dani, Jeremy, John, Nikki, Richard, and others who wished to remain anonymous.

This book was fueled by caffeine, so I want to include a plug for the coffee shops and baristas across New York that helped bring it to life. These include Kinship Coffee in Astoria, Cold Spring Coffeehouse in Cold Spring, the Crafted Kup in Poughkeepsie, Stagecoach Coffee in Cooperstown, and the Beacon Daily and Big Mouth Coffee Roasters, both in Beacon.

And finally, I'm grateful to all of my students over the past twenty years, without whom this book would not exist. Everything in these pages comes from them. The magic of teaching is that when you get out of your own way and actually listen to your students—which I try to do and occasionally succeed at—you end up living the dream of everyone who loves school: you get to spend your whole life learning.

Creating Your College List

The following activity is a first step toward creating your college list. After it, you'll find some strategies to start turning your desires into a list of schools.

Activity: Introspection

What do *you* want in a college? Start your search by writing a page or two on your goals and priorities for college. This could be a few paragraphs of written prose or a bulleted list—either is fine. If it's a list, be sure to rank your priorities in order, from most important to least important.

Whichever format you choose—paragraphs or bullets—at the end you want to be able to clearly identify the top three to five attributes you want in a college. Remember: the more clearly you can describe what you're looking for, the more likely you are to find it!

If you're stuck, here is a list of things other students have written about in the past.

- Academic offerings (What do you want to study? What might you major or minor in?)
- Type of community (Intense or more laid back? Do you want to be in a

place where life revolves around academics, the arts, sports, surfing, the outdoors, big football games, Greek life [fraternities/sororities], something else?)

- Type of school (e.g., liberal arts college, private research university, big state school—if you don't know what those are, google them!)
- School size
- Typical class size and type (Big lecture classes? Smaller seminars?)
- Access to professors
- Research and internship opportunities
- Campus diversity
- Activism and politics
- Geographic location (What part of the country do you want to be in? Do you care about hot/cold/snow/having seasons?)
- Urban versus rural environment
- Traditional campus versus campus blended into a city (New York University, for example, doesn't have a traditional campus, whereas Columbia University, which is also in Manhattan, does)
- Sports and athletics
- Visual and performing arts opportunities
- Other extracurricular interests you might have
- And more . . .

Tips for Creating Your List

Once you've identified your top priorities, you can start looking for schools that match them. When applying to selective colleges, your goal is to put together a list of twelve to fifteen schools, roughly an equal mix of reach, target, and safeties. Reach schools are those where you have a less than 25% chance of admission, target schools are where you have a 25 to 75% chance of admission, and likely or "safety" schools are those where you have a greater than 75% chance of admission.

So how do you find these schools? Begin by reviewing the "Hidden Gems" section of this book (page 224), which contains strategies and resources to help you find target and safety schools. Other useful resources include:

Your Counselor

For most students, the college counselor at your high school is the perfect place to start. They are likely to know a lot about colleges, and if you're lucky, your school might even have relationships with colleges you're interested in.

If, on the other hand, your school doesn't send a lot of students to the kinds of colleges you're looking at—maybe because of geography, maybe because of selectivity—you'll need to turn to the internet.

Online Search Tools

There is a whole range of online tools to help you search for schools, including the hotly debated *U.S. News & World Report* rankings, the College Board's "BigFuture" search tool, and many others.

A good starting point is the *U.S. News & World Report* search tool; in chapter 7 (pages 224–228) you'll find strategies for using it to find schools for your reach and target categories. My other favorite search tools are the *New York Times'* "Build Your Own College Rankings" tool* and Niche.com. The *Times* tool enables you to prioritize some very practical factors such as net cost, median income after graduating, and racial diversity. Niche.com is great because it has extensive data on campus life, as well as thousands of reviews by actual students that you won't find anywhere else. My new favorite way of looking for colleges, however, didn't exist two years ago: AI.

AI

College search is a part of the application process where ChatGPT can be very useful. Once you've identified your priorities, try typing

*https://www.nytimes.com/interactive/2023/03/27/opinion/build-your-own-college-rankings.html.

something like "Tell me 5 to 10 colleges that have strong athletics, a good undergraduate music program, a beautiful campus, and a strong engineering program." Of course, you'll need to do your own research about each school it suggests, but so far I've been impressed with the results.

Another approach: Once you've identified a school or two that appeal to you, use ChatGPT to find similar schools. For example, if Wake Forest is your dream school, you can type "What are some college and universities that are similar to Wake Forest?" Or to help find targets and safeties, you can try "What are some college and universities that are similar to Wake Forest but are less selective?"

My (evolving) take on AI is that if you try to use it to think for you, you're setting yourself up for trouble. But if you use it as a thought partner to help you with tasks, it can sometimes be surprisingly helpful. Keep in mind that the technology is new and evolving, and remember the Russian proverb: "Trust, but verify." Not every school it suggests will hit the mark. Ask it for ideas; then do your own research to confirm that the schools it spits out actually have what you're looking for.

Creating Your Résumé and Activities List

Sample résumés and activities list begin on page 272

The Résumé: Another Chance to Tell Your Story

Putting together your résumé is a great way to jog your memory and start putting together a narrative of your high school years. That's why I recommend doing it early in your application process, before you start your essays.

Why start with a résumé, as opposed to the Common App activities list? It's true that the activities list is required, whereas not every college requires you to submit a résumé. But I've found that a résumé, more than the activities list, requires you to think through the last three years of your life and put together the pieces of your story. So it's the perfect starting place for your college applications. In addition, if the college gives you the option of submitting a résumé, I recommend doing so. Why not give them another chance to see who you are, especially when, unlike the activities list, you control the format and can shape the overall narrative?

What Goes into a Résumé?

Your résumé should tell the story of everything you've done inside and outside the classroom from ninth grade to today. As such, it should contain all educational experiences in that time frame, every activity you've regularly engaged in over some period of time (both inside and outside school), and any honors and awards you accumulated.

I always tell my students to put *everything* in their first draft of their résumé—anything they think might possibly belong on it. A club you participated in for only one year, the tenth-grade "Best Citizen in Geography" award—include them all for now (but don't include the club where you went to one meeting and never went back). Start by casting a broad net, and then later you can run it by your counselor; they can help you omit things that truly aren't important.

This is because at most selective colleges, when it comes to activities, both quantity and quality matter. Is this a good thing? No, because it promotes a culture in which kids and parents feel the need to overbook themselves so that they can have a great brag sheet. Happily, some colleges are aware of this; for example, in 2023, Lafayette College in Pennsylvania announced that it will look at only the first six activities in the Common App, a move that I applaud. Hopefully other schools will follow suit. However, the reality is that at most colleges, both quantity and quality do count, and you should take that into account when putting together your résumé.

Putting It Together

Unlike a business résumé, a college application résumé is not limited to one page. In that way, it's a bit more like a CV, or *curriculum vitae*, which is the equivalent of a résumé in academia. For selective schools, two to four pages is a good number to aim for.

Organize your résumé into several sections, starting with "Education" (you are, after all, applying to an institution of higher education!). Some students include their test scores and senior year classes in this section; at minimum, you should list your high school, expected graduation year, and GPA. I generally tell students to include any details they're proud of; it doesn't matter if you include test scores and classes, because admissions officers will see that information in other parts of your application.

After the "Education" section, you have options for how to structure the rest of your résumé. For example, if you've done a lot of summer programs and community service, you might have separate sections for "Activities" (i.e., school extracurriculars), "Summer," and "Service." If you've played multiple sports, you might have a separate "Athletics" section; the same goes for music, theater, or visual arts.

Pick the format that you think best tells your story and highlights the activities and accomplishments you're most proud of. And however you structure the résumé, end it with an "Honors and Awards" section if you have any to report.

In terms of graphic design, aim for simplicity and clarity. An admissions officer will only spend a minute reading your résumé, maybe less. So you want to make it as easy to read as possible. The only "wrong" layout is one where the reader has to squint their eyes and read things two or three times to make sense of them. The odds are that they won't do either; they'll just skip to the next part of your application.

Line by Line

Though you can format your résumé however you like, it's important that each item on the résumé contain all of the following elements.

- The name of the activity, organization, or club
- Your role (e.g. president, first chair clarinet, member, volunteer, intern, and so on)
- The grade level or years you participated in that activity
- A short description of what you did and, if necessary, the organization/club name

For example, this might look like:

Debate Team

President (11, 12) Grades 9, 10, 11, 12

- Attended practice meetings and researched controversial topics; debated at county and regional competitions.
- As president, organized trips and practice sessions and assigned topics to team members.

I recommend this structure because it summarizes the information admissions officers want to see and also because—not coincidentally—it closely tracks the format you will use for your Common App activities list. That means that once you've written a solid résumé using these guidelines, it will be easy to transform it into an activities list.

For the description of each activity, follow the same general guidelines that you would for a professional résumé, including:

- Use active verbs, ideally at the beginning of each line or bullet point.
- Keep it short (omit needless words!).
- Include specific details that show your actions and the impact (numbers, places, events, awards, and so on.).
- Avoid using flowery terms like "prestigious."

Though you have a lot of flexibility in how you tell your story, the overarching rule in a résumé is: **be consistent**. You can choose to write in the first or third person, in phrases or complete sentences, end each line with a period or not, use grade numbers (9, 10, 11, 12) or years (2023, 2024). The key is to make a choice, then stick with it throughout. Admissions officers are often highly attentive to detail, and nothing says "sloppy" like a résumé that doesn't follow its own internal rules.

Finally, when describing each organization or activity, use common sense as to how much detail to include. You don't need to explain to an admissions officer what a varsity hockey team is—or a marching band or drama club. But it could be helpful to write a few words explaining what your Anime Club is all about or what Students for the Environment actually does.

From Résumé to Activities List

At some point before submitting your first application, you'll need to transform your résumé into a Common App activities list. The Common App allows you to include up to ten activities in your general application. For each, you'll include the information discussed above (organization/activity, role, years, and description), as well as the hours per week and weeks per year you spent on each activity. For the latter, estimates are fine; be honest, and make sure your numbers are realistic. If you end claiming that you spent 100 hours per week on activities in your junior year, that will raise some red flags!

There is a strategy to filling out the activities section: you want to highlight certain activities by putting them first. These include the activities that are the most important to you, those you've spent the most time on, and those you've been committed to over the longest period of time, ideally three or four years of high school. (Never lead with an activity that you did only one hour per week in ninth grade!) You also want to be sure that your descriptions are concise, clear, easy to read, and impactful. As with the résumé, active verbs and specific details are your friends. You'll have only 150 characters (not words) to describe each activity, so brevity is key.

Because the software for entering these activities is rather clunky, I recommend organizing your activities and editing your descriptions in a Word document or Google Doc before submitting them; a template for doing so is on my website at www.write-yourself-in.com.

To help you get started, here are two sample résumés and a sample activities list.

Sample Résumé 1

PIPPIN TOOK
p.took.2990@gmail.com, 512.555.1212

142 Bag-End Road, Austin, TX 11106

EDUCATION

Shire Central High School   Austin, TX

Class of 2025, GPA: 3.65

ACTIVITIES

Forensics Team   Shire Central High School

President (11, 12) and Member   Grades 9, 10, 11, 12

- Attended practice meetings and researched topics; debated at county and regional competitions.
- As president, organized trips and practice sessions, assigned topics to team members.

Thanksgiving Home Club   Shire Central High School

President (11, 12) and Volunteer   Grades 9, 10, 11, 12

- Worked with other volunteers to entertain elderly residents at a local nursing home.
- Planned and organized all club trips and events.
- Responsible for communication and management of other student leaders.

Concert Band   Shire Central High School

Clarinet Section Member   Grades 9, 10, 11

- Rehearsed and performed concert repertoire at five concerts per year.
- Helped plan and organize a spring break band trip to Toronto, Canada.

JV Cross Country Team   Shire Central High School
Team Member   Grades 9, 10
- Attended daily practices to prepare for races; competed at the county and regional level.
- Trained independently in the off-season to stay in shape.

SUMMER EXPERIENCE

UVA Advance Summer Program   Charlottesville, VA
Student   Summer before grade 12
- Enrolled in a college-level political science course, "Campaign and Election Politics"; topics included campaign strategy, election security, media and communications.
- Took an additional elective course, "Fake News and Philosophy."
- Participated in athletic activities and met students from around the world.

Camp Mordor   Livingston, TX
Senior Counselor   Summers before grades 9, 10, 11
- Responsible for well-being, care, and activities for 10 middle school–age campers.
- Worked individually with each camper to help them earn merit badges, develop skills, and accomplish their goals.

HONORS AND AWARDS

Honor Roll (9, 10, 11)
- Awarded for maintaining a 3.3 GPA

First Place, Extemporaneous Speaking, Longhorn Classic Forensics Tournament (11)

Spirit of the Band (11)
- Annual award to the student who "most contributes fun and joy to the band community;" chosen by other band members

Geography Award (9)
- Given to the most outstanding student in AP Human Geography

Sample Résumé 2

Berylla Boffin

123 E. 78th Street, New York, NY • (212) 555-1212

Education	**Sackville-Baggins School for Girls (New York, NY)** Expected graduation May 2025 3.95 GPA in an AP/Honors Curriculum
Junior Course Schedule	Honors Precalculus, AP Chemistry, AP United States History, Honors English, Spanish IV, Studio Art
Senior Course Schedule	AP Calculus AB, AP Biology, AP English Literature, Political Philosophy, Advanced Sculpture and Drawing
Standardized Tests	ACT: 34 Composite (35 Superscore: 36 English, 34 Math, 36 Reading, 34 Science) AP Chemistry (5), AP US History (4)
Work Experience	**Intern, Scenic Hudson (Poughkeepsie, NY), Summer 2023 and 2024** • Interned at an environmental preservation nonprofit in the Hudson Valley. • Organized and led a campaign to oppose the construction of a boardwalk in in the Hudson Highlands. • Worked with full-time staff to prepare analyses of environmentally sensitive beaches and other riverside sites.

Community Service	**Ambassador, Billion Oyster Project (New York, NY), 2022–2024**
	• Volunteered weekly at a nonprofit that works to restore oyster reefs to New York Harbor.
	• Conducted wild oyster surveys; worked to engage other high school students on social media.
	Teacher, MAMACITAS (The Bronx, NY), 2023–present
	• Taught a weekly after-school art class for elementary school students at a neighborhood community center.
	Volunteer, Project Amandla (Johannesburg, South Africa), Spring 2023
	• Volunteered for a two-week school service trip to South Africa.
	• Studied local culture and permaculture techniques.
	• Taught classes to elementary school children, participated in workshops with local farmers.
School Activities	**Member, Field Hockey Team, 2021–present**
	• Member of the JV (2021–2023) and Varsity (2023–present) Field Hockey teams
	• Winner of 2023 NYSAIS championship title
	Founder, Environmental Service Club, 2022–present
	• Founded a club to raise awareness of environmental issues in New York State.
	• Started a program that brought 20 Sackville-Baggins students to a day of service for the Billion Oyster Project.
	• Led a schoolwide presentation on the effects of climate change in Manhattan.
	President, Model UN, 2022–present
	• Organized team trips to conferences.
	• Led training to prepare team members for conferences.
	Tutor, Peer Tutoring Program, 2022–present
	• Tutor selected through application to tutor other Sackville-Baggins students.
	• Qualified to tutor in Precalculus, Spanish, US History, and Chemistry.

Summer Programs	**Yale Young Global Scholars (New Haven, CT), Summer 2024** • Participated in the "Solving Global Challenges" program. • Seminars included "Religion, Ecology, and Environmental Activism for a Dying Planet" and "Climate Refugees." • Completed a capstone project with three other students entitled "Sustainable Use of American Marshlands." **Running Start Program (Washington, DC), Summer 2023** • Attended a summer program that equips young women with the skills to run for political office. • Attended workshops by experts on topics including public speaking, fundraising, networking, media training, and advocacy. • Participated in a small-group discussion with Congresswoman Nancy Pelosi. **EF Languages Abroad Program (Barcelona, Spain), Summer 2023** • Four-week immersive language and culture program. • Studied Spanish grammar and literature in classes taught by native Spanish speakers.
Honors and Awards	**Silver Medal, National Spanish Examination, 2024** Awarded by the American Association of Teachers of Spanish and Portuguese for achievement and proficiency in Spanish. **Harvard Book Award, 2024** Given annually to "an outstanding student who displays excellence in scholarship and high character." **Honorable Mention, Yale University Model UN Conference, 2023** **Honorable Mention, Brown University Model UN Conference, 2023** **High Honor Roll (Fall 2022, Spring 2023, Fall 2023, Spring 2024)** Cumulative term grade average of 95.0 or above **Honor Roll (Fall 2021, Spring 2022)** Cumulative term grade average of 90.0 or above

Sample Activities List

This is how an activities list appears to a college admissions officer. You can see your own list in this format by clicking the "Preview" button near the top of the Common App page where you input your activities.

Activities

Athletics: JV/Varsity

9, 10, 11, 12
School
12 hr/wk, 16 wk/yr
Continue

Baseball, Co-Captain (11), Varsity & JV Teams
MVP award junior year. In 2022-2023 we were district and regional champions, advancing to state playoffs.

Athletics: JV/Varsity

9, 10, 11
School
10 hr/wk, 12 wk/yr

Cross-country, Member, Varsity Team
Daily practice after school in the fall. Placed at county and regional meets.

Music: Instrumental

9, 10, 11, 12
School
10 hr/wk, 40 wk/yr
Continue

First Chair Clarinet (11, 12), Symphonic Band
Section leader and first chair clarinet. Performed at district and regional competitions, receiving a I rating each year.

Community Service (Volunteer)

10, 11, 12
School
2 hr/wk, 40 wk/yr
Continue

Member, Special Olympics Club
Play sports with and coach disabled children. Volunteer to manage Special Olympics events.

Community Service (Volunteer)

10, 11, 12
2 hr/wk, 40 wk/yr
Continue

President (11, 12), AIDS Awareness Club
Lead weekly meetings, plan annual schoolwide AIDS Walk, and raise funds for AIDS research (over $15,000 junior year).

Community Service (Volunteer)

10, 11, 12
School
6 hr/wk, 25 wk/yr
Continue

Volunteer, New Horizons Refugee Center
Worked with children aged 5-10 at a center for refugees. Led activities, taught classes, ran games and arts projects.

Academic

11
Break
45 hr/wk, 1 wk/yr
Continue

EPIC-Engineering Possibilities in College, Student
Studied engineering in an intensive summer program at Cal Poly San Luis Obispo. Modules included "VEX Robotics" and "Design of a Green City."

Emergency Backup Brainstorming Exercises

These are for the Common App personal essay. Use 'em if you need 'em!

1. What are your values?

This one is pretty straightforward. Freewrite two to three paragraphs in response to the following prompt.

What are your values? And how did you develop them?

"Values" here could be anything you value, i.e., hold important. For example: family, honesty, academics, integrity, community, etc.—literally anything that is important to you.

For the second question: Did you learn them from your family? From friends or teachers? From your school? From religious communities, or activities you've participated in such as sports, drama, journalism/yearbook, or elsewhere?

Your values can be good "anchors" for a personal essay, and the stories of how you developed them can be excellent material—especially if they involve struggle and vulnerability—because they are stories of how you grew as a person.

2. What are your passions?

Freewrite two to three paragraphs in response to the following prompt.

What are you most passionate about? And how have you pursued that passion?

This passion could be anything; it could be something academic, a hobby, or some random topic you're fascinated with. It's important that it's a passion that you've actually taken some action to pursue, not something you've just dreamed about but not done anything about.

As you're responding, don't try to psych out the admissions committee. Many students have ideas about what they think admissions committees want them to be interested in, and it usually has something to do with science, great books, or the history of some esoteric intellectual idea. If you actually happen to be interested in that stuff, great! But if you're not, remember this: Whatever you think they want you to be passionate about, you're probably wrong.

Admissions officers read a lot of essays in which students fake passions in "academic" subjects, and they're really good at sniffing those out. What they want is authenticity, so even if your passions seem "stupid" or "dumb" or "unimportant," that's just your Censor acting up! Quirky interests can make for fantastic essays. I've seen students get into top schools by writing about vintage video games, clay models, and the *crema* on top of a good shot of espresso.

3. What makes your eyes light up?

The topic that makes your eyes light up is a clear "tell" for what you're passionate about—as well as what you're intellectually curious about—which means it's potentially great material for a college essay. Freewrite two to three paragraphs in response to the following prompt.

What makes your eyes light up when you talk about it, and why? Tell a story about engaging with that passion in some way.

If you're not sure what that "something" is, just ask some of the people around you—parents, teachers, siblings, friends—the following question: "What makes my eyes light up when I talk about it?" The people who know you well will know the answer.

Additional Resources

If you want to learn more about college admissions process or craft of writing, here are some books you may find helpful. Each has had a substantive impact on me over the years as a writer, teacher, and counselor. They're listed here in order of how often I refer to them.

Books on College Admissions

Who Gets In and Why: A Year Inside College Admissions
By Jeffrey Selingo (New York: Scribner, 2020)

If you want to see how the college admissions sausage is made, this is the book to read. The author, a seasoned higher ed journalist, spent a year in the admissions offices of Emory University, Davidson College, and the University of Washington. He came back with revealing insights into why and how college admissions officers make their decisions.

Colleges That Change Lives: 40 Schools That Will Change the Way You Think About Colleges, 4th ed.
By Loren Pope (New York: Penguin Books, 2021)

Colleges That Change Lives is something of a stealth classic. Written by a journalist who was also a college counselor, the book aims to move the college conversation beyond prestige and rankings. First published in 1996, it spotlights forty liberal arts colleges that, in the author's view, offer an excellent, student-centered education. Although many people have never heard of *Colleges That Change Lives*, others have indeed had their lives changed by it. They include a friend of mine who attended one of the CTCL schools after his mom read the book!

The Truth about College Admission: A Family Guide to Getting In and Staying Together, 2nd ed.
By Barnard Brennan and Rick Clark (Baltimore: Johns Hopkins Press, 2023)

This excellent book, coauthored by the head of undergraduate admissions at Georgia Tech and a prominent high school counselor, is a comprehensive, humane guide to applying to college. It gives families an insider view of admissions, and it offers practical tips to help navigate the process as well as the stresses that accompany it.

The Price You Pay for College: An Entirely New Road Map for the Biggest Financial Decision Your Family Will Ever Make
By Ron Lieber (New York: Harper, 2021)

Every parent should read *The Price You Pay for College* long before their child starts their applications. Much like in health care, the finances of higher education are byzantine, opaque, and stacked against families. Lieber breaks down the details of financial aid and "merit" scholarships, helps families understand why tuition costs are so high (or seem to be), and offers pragmatic advice on how to pay for all of it.

The Best 389 Colleges, 2024: In-Depth Profiles & Ranking Lists to Help Find the Right College for You
By Robert Franek, et al. (New York: Penguin Random House, 2023)

This book is here primarily for sentimental reasons. Though it might seem anachronistic to today's teens, it will bring back memories for parents.

In the pre-internet days, you could tell who was applying to college because they suddenly started carrying around stacks of massive paperback books: an SAT prep book, the College Board book of SAT practice tests, and encyclopedic college guidebooks such as the "Barron's Book." The last was a hefty annual tome published by Barron's Media that ranked colleges and supplied data such as average test scores, admissions requirements, and so on. Buying a copy was a rite of passage for many teens.

Nowadays, of course, all of that information is freely available on the internet from college websites, the *U.S. News & World Report* website, the College Board website, and many more. Princeton Review's *The Best 389 Colleges* is the best book I know of from that weighty (*sic*) genre that's still published today.

Books on the Craft of Writing

On Writing Well: The Classical Guide to Writing Nonfiction
By William Zinsser (New York: HarperCollins, 1976)

A classic guide to writing, this book contains storytelling principles that are directly applicable to your college admissions essays. Zinsser has a wonderful, grandfatherly approach to explaining things. He was a teacher and administrator at Yale, so he knows higher education well.

Writing About Your Life: A Journey into the Past
By William Zinsser (Cambridge, MA: Da Capo Press, 2005)

This book, a follow-up to *On Writing Well*, is specifically about writing memoirs. If you're stuck on how to tell your story, he has tips, examples, and strategies for unpacking one's life on the page.

Story Style: Structure, Substance, and the Principles of Screenwriting
By Robert McKee (New York: HarperCollins, 1998)

Considered a Hollywood screenwriting classic, this book outlines principles of storytelling that have been around at least since Aristotle. The ideas are timeless, and while some might be dated, it's worth learning the rules so you can make conscious decisions about why and when to break them.

The Story Grid: What Good Editors Know
By Shawn Coyne (Black Irish Entertainment, 2015)

I consider this book to be a sibling of *Story*. McKee's writing, though brilliant, can be abstract and philosophical. *The Story Grid* breaks down McKee's ideas into clear, actionable steps, so you can apply them to your own work.

The Artist's Way: A Spiritual Path to Higher Creativity
By Julia Cameron (New York: Penguin Random House, 2016)

This book first came into my life when I was a recent college grad, and I've kept a copy of it on my shelf ever since. Full of deep, spiritual wisdom, it offers the best advice I've found for unblocking your creativity and finding your voice as a writer.

Bird by Bird: Some Instructions on Writing and Life
by Anne Lamott (New York: Anchor Books, 1995)

Lamott is brilliant; reading this book changed me forever. It's full of images, hints, and tips that will make you a better writer.

Sample Essays

Part 1: Personal Essays

Hockey Essay: Seeing the Ice

Four players are fighting for the puck. As my teammate gains possession, I race across the ice and receive a hard pass on my stick. Brushing past two defenders, I rush towards the net, drawing the goalie towards me. Then I flip the puck to my teammate, who catches my pass and shoots into the unguarded net. Score!

I've loved the ice since before I can remember. From elementary school onward I lived, ate, and breathed hockey. Mornings began with hockey practice, afternoons with more practice and training sessions, and weekends with travel games. My friends at school knew me as "the hockey player," and some of my best friends in the world are the guys on my team. Hockey is also where I first became a leader. Because of my skill and determination, my teammates looked up to me, and I led naturally. Even when I struggled with school or other parts of my life, the ice gave me confidence.

Then, in eighth grade, the unthinkable happened. My growth spurt was delayed, so while some of my teammates were suddenly 6 feet tall, I was still 4'10". Where before I'd been a confident, dominant player, I suddenly felt like a defenseless minnow surrounded by hungry sharks. Not only was I no longer one of the top players, but I had lost my edge and struggled just to keep up with my teammates.

As eighth grade progressed, things went from bad to worse, culminating in the day when my coach pulled me aside and explained that I might not make the team next year. I was crushed. Not only had I lost the most important thing in my life, I was losing my identity. After all, if I wasn't a hockey player, who was I?

I thought long and hard about what to do. I could have moved down to a less competitive team or quit hockey altogether. But if hockey has taught me anything, it's that when you're faced with a challenge, you dig in and work harder. So I began taking more skating lessons, spent more time at the gym, got up at 5:00 a.m. for extra practice sessions. Since I could no longer rely on speed or strength, my approach to the game became more cerebral. I taught myself how to avoid hits and to use my opponent's size against him. I also developed my ability to "see the ice"—to slow down the game, watch each play develop, analyze options, and think strategically—all in a matter of seconds. As I learned to see the ice, I got smarter. I struggled, but I stayed on the team, and I stayed competitive.

The summer after ninth grade, my growth spurt finally came. I was larger in tenth grade, and by eleventh grade I was on par with my teammates. Now I had both size and skills, and I was proud when I finished eleventh grade as the top scorer on my team and the second leading scorer in the entire league.

Equally important, I found that my new approach was transforming my life. As I started to "see the ice" at school, I realized that with hard work, my potential to learn was unlimited. So I tried harder, participated even more in class, and met with teachers before and after school. In the process, I developed a newfound passion for history, politics, and science. I also found myself taking on leadership roles in the classroom and getting involved in causes I cared about, from cancer awareness to environmental activism.

Now I can't wait to take on new challenges. I'm still "the hockey player," but I'm also a scholar, a leader, a problem solver, and a thinker. Hockey has taught me that our greatest challenges are also the moments that give us the potential to grow the most, and that's a lesson I will carry with me for my entire life.

Science Essay: A Passion for Research

Until the age of 16, I was like any other kid, discovering my interests and passions and pursuing them. Basketball and rugby were high priorities. Jazz piano had become something of a mini-obsession. With a wide range of academic interests, I read everything I could get my hands on from ancient history to the history of contemporary art. Then my mother was diagnosed with breast cancer. That changed everything.

I felt the need to learn everything I could about the disease as quickly as I could. I started by asking my science teachers for information and poring over textbooks. It wasn't enough. Through my mother's treatment, I got to know her oncologist, who became a knowledgeable and encouraging resource. His encouragement prompted me to ask if I could work in his oncology lab. One week after school ended, I began a summer internship that would change my life.

Professor Gandalf's lab is focused on breast cancer research, specifically on the gene LMTK-3. When this faulty gene is expressed, it allows cancer to enter the bloodstream, evade the immune system, and metastasise. His lab investigates how the body regulates LMTK-3 and how its carcinogenic effects might be mitigated.

My first day at the lab was overwhelming. When my new colleagues spoke, the medical terminology sounded like a foreign language, so when I went home that night I read every journal article I could get my hands on. Even then, the following Thursday, when the entire lab met with Professor Gandalf, I could barely understand what the researchers were talking about, and became flustered when Prof. Gandalf started quizzing me about cancer therapies and signalling pathways that weren't even related to the lab's work. But I continued to read papers, conduct research, and talk to the fellows. As the weeks passed, I not only understood the conversations, I contributed to them.

My primary task was to determine the levels of LMTK-3 protein in test cells—an indicator of our treatments' efficacy. Over the six weeks I was there, I ran the test at least 100 times and was fascinated every time. There are no numbers to analyse, just images, and I had to make judgments based on the relative levels of other proteins. Conducting each test and analysing the data to figure out the "right" answer gave me immense satisfaction. I was learning about cancer and participating in the journey of discovery.

I was also growing as a scientist. By the end of my second week, I started passing Professor Gandalf's tests. I began to realize that by quizzing me, he was treating me like a medical student. By the end of the summer, the lab's senior fellow invited me to work with him on a new research paper. Suddenly, I was a colleague, not just an intern, and this year I have returned to the lab as a Visiting Researcher to work for Professor Gandalf full-time.

Thankfully, my mother's cancer is in remission, but I have seen that cancer is a disease of awesome power, both intelligent and deadly. When you try to shut off different pathways, cancer fights back, finding new and increasingly insidious ways to kill you. Treating cancer requires deep clinical knowledge, drawing from science as well as art. It requires both interpretation and imagination. I want to be an oncologist engaged in research, but I also want to be in an environment that will allow me to study other disciplines. A liberal arts environment will encourage me to think broadly and creatively. So many scientists who have made great contributions, from Leonardo da Vinci to Marie Curie to Oliver Sacks, embraced that blend of creativity and scientific rationality. I want to enter into their tradition and make great contributions of my own.

Curiosity Essay: The Power of Questions

Some people say I ask too many questions. As a child, my parents would get frustrated because I never answered their questions with a simple "Yes" or "No." Instead, I would always ask, "Why?" I was fascinated with science, so I peppered them with queries like: Why do our cells divide? Why do I look more like my mom than my dad? But I was also deeply interested in people. Not just helping people—although I care deeply about that—but the "why" of people. I wondered what the biological basis of suffering was and what it meant to be human.

The first time I started to sense some common ground among my questions was two years ago at Camp Dream Street, a summer camp for children with chronic illnesses. The camp's goal is to create a normal childhood experience for its campers by mixing them with healthy children. I was a counselor, and I went into the experience—uncharacteristically—with very few questions. Instead, I decided that I was going to protect my campers from harm, no matter what.

My most exuberant camper was Rebecca. She was always smiling and running around the camp. I, however, feared that she would hurt herself. Sure enough, one day as Rebecca was running to the pool, she fell and scraped her knee. Because the campers' conditions were not disclosed to us, I was terrified. Could Rebecca be a hemophiliac? Did she have a chemotherapy port? My mind went racing through all the potential disasters that could result from that one fall.

Rebecca was fine. The nurse gave her a Band-Aid, and she ran cheerfully to her next activity. But I was shaken by my own response, and by the assumptions I had made about my "sick" camper. Was I thinking of her as a disease or as a person? What makes someone "normal" or "sick"? I wasn't sure of the answers yet, but for the first time I saw that my questions about science and people might be related. I also realized that healthy people have a limited perspective on what it means to struggle with a long-term illness, an insight I've brought into my work with the AIDS Awareness Club and Sackville-Baggins Fights Against Cancer.

My truly transformative experience, however, happened last summer. I enrolled in "The Science of Psychology" at Columbia University by accident—I wanted to take a biology and genetics course, but it was full. The next three weeks changed my life. I loved psychology, but what I loved even more was that it was interdisciplinary, encompassing fields like neurobiology, philosophy, and health care. Psychologists were asking questions that fascinated me, such as: "How do chemical imbalances in our brain cause mental health disorders?" and "How can the behavioral effects of being sick affect the progression of disease?" By the end of the summer, I was able to combine my interests in science, the brain, and even graphic design (a hobby of mine) to create an experiment that used water bottles to measure social influence. My professor was impressed with my work, and I was ecstatic when she invited me to become a research assistant in her lab.

Now I see psychology everywhere. I see it in the billboards on Route 17, the menu options at Starbucks, even the new design of the iPhone 7. More importantly, I now know that the kinds of questions that interest me most are the interdisciplinary ones. In college, I want to reach high, think broadly, and do research that goes beyond traditional ways of understanding the world. I want to ask untraditional questions, and I could easily see myself majoring in biology, or psychology, or even the history of medicine. But whichever direction I pick, I want to continue to ask questions that connect the dots in new ways, and broaden our understanding of what it means to be human.

Yearbook Essay: Hit to the Corners

"Hit to the corners, Rachel!" By tenth grade, I had heard that phrase shouted at me for years. Tennis has been a passion of mine since I was six, but regardless of how long I had played, I was a conservative player. Often I hit to the middle of the court: the safe shot. I wasn't afraid of training hard, but I didn't want to make an unforced error, so I stayed in my comfort zone, on the court and in life.

All of that changed sophomore year when I was selected as co–editor in chief of Lakewood's yearbook. I was honored but apprehensive. Not only was a junior editor in chief unprecedented in my school, but the yearbook class was collapsing. The staff had shrunk from fifteen to three, causing efforts around the yearbook to become nearly nonexistent.

When my advisor told me the harsh reality that if I didn't step up, there would be no yearbook, I knew what I had to do. The yearbook is a living record of students' passions, voices, and opinions. The idea that it would cease to exist was incomprehensible to me, so I gathered up my courage and said yes.

The months that followed were challenging. Creating our 200-page yearbook requires hundreds of hours of coordinated planning, outreach, design, and production. With only three people doing the work of fifteen, I was faced with a reality where if I played to the middle of the court, I was guaranteed to fail.

I began to strategize, starting with how I could expand and retain the yearbook team. The yearbook had never had official leadership roles (aside from editor in chief), so I decided to create new positions, from "Photography Coordinator" to "Business Manager," which I hoped would attract students. Not every student I approached became a major contributor, but for many students, having a title empowered them, and our staff began to grow.

Simultaneously, in hopes of encouraging student involvement, I began to visit classes during my free periods, advocating for the yearbook. Over time, I found that this proved to be successful; for every three or four visits, one or two students would join. Some of my swings were misses, but others were winners, and slowly our team filled to capacity.

As the year progressed, I started taking more risks. When seniors failed to respond to our emails requesting quotes and photos, I decided to try unconventional methods of outreach, using different forms of social media to obtain information. To facilitate greater communication, I created a council of seniors to act as liaisons between the yearbook and the senior class, which enabled us to communicate with the entire class quickly and seamlessly.

I realized that in the long term, one of the only ways to secure student commitment to the yearbook was to make it a credit-bearing class, so I began lobbying the principal. This was especially challenging; he was resistant and skeptical that offering credit would get more people involved. Refusing to be discouraged, I created a survey on yearbook participation, polled my peers, and gathered hard data to support my argument. After presenting the data, I persuaded the principal of the merits of my proposed program, and next fall, for the first time ever, Lakewood plans to offer yearbook as a credit-bearing class.

When I look back on the past year, I feel proud. Not only did we create a yearbook that reflects my school's diversity, but I could have never imagined that the risks I took would transform into an incomparable life lesson. Although I can easily be content sticking to the safe shots, the only way to reach my goals is to complement those shots with a hit to the corners. I know that sometimes I may fail, but if I continue to work hard, persist through adversity, and try creative approaches, I can accomplish what would have otherwise been impossible.

Poetry Essay: Language and Confidence

I was sweating. A lot. But I wasn't running a marathon or playing tennis. I was getting ready to stand for my rebuttal speech, and I heard everything—the creaking of the wooden floors, the judge's exhales, my opponents' persistent pen clicking. I walked to the podium and, for the next four minutes, stumbled through a disorganized volley of words. "Thank you, Ben," the judge said. Although I liked the name "Ben," it was not mine. I couldn't even find the words to correct her so, head down, I shuffled back to my desk.

I've always been the "tech guy" and can usually be found in the robotics lab or behind a computer. If I ever needed to give a speech on stage, though, fear of public speaking stifled my voice. So, two years ago, I signed up for debate to tackle this issue. My knack for logic and mathematics helped me think through the issues, but after my first few debates, the truth became clear: I wasn't very good.

A few weeks later, something unexpected happened. My English teacher asked us to make an "airplane poem": open *Pride and Prejudice* to any page, select a line at random, copy it down, and repeat until we had a poem. Although I was doubtful, I nevertheless followed his instructions and was amazed as a poem formed in front of my eyes. Somehow, these randomly selected words had meaning. Did my interpretation of the words bring them to life? Was meaning present in the very words themselves? Was it both? I wasn't sure, but I had felt the power of words and I was hooked.

Hungry to learn more about poetry, I started with poets I knew. As I read Edgar Allen Poe's dark and twisted tales, Elizabeth Bishop's precise descriptions, and Robert Frost's conversational depictions of nature, I felt that I was beginning to see life through their eyes. Later, as I discovered Billy Collins's quirky language and Wallace Stevens's grand phraseology, I began to amass a collection of voices and perspectives in my head. Anthologies piled up on my shelf, and I even tried writing poems in the voices of my favorite authors. The more I read, the more I wanted to learn.

As I explored this world of poetry, I found my debate speeches changing. They became more personal, more understandable, more impactful. Over time, the process of immersing myself in the work of authors who had found ways to express their inner selves changed me: it pushed me to find language to express who I truly am. I realized that I, too, have a style, a way of using words to describe the world as I see it. Sometimes I may pair corny jokes with the cold clarity of logic, or I may simply reveal my emotions. As the debate season continued, I read my speeches over and over to my family, then to my friends, until the speeches felt natural and I felt comfortable. I was finding my voice.

A year later, at another debate tournament, I found my heart racing as my opponent delivered his speech. This time, however, I took notes with a steady hand. When the judge called time, I spent thirty seconds preparing for my rebuttal, leapt to the podium, and began. In that moment, I forgot that I was in a lecture hall. Instead, I was at home, in my room, writing a poem, creating a combination of words that worked. Each idea led to the next; the poem made sense, and my words rang true.

Will I ever be a Poe or a Frost? Probably not, and in truth I don't know if I want to be—I want to be an engineer. But I'll always be an engineer who understands the beauty of poetry, and I'll always be grateful for the voice that poetry has helped me find.

Part 2: Supplemental Essays

Long Why Our School Essay 1: Science Geek

Prompt: Describe the unique qualities that attract you to the specific undergraduate College or School (including preferred admission and dual degree programs) to which you are applying at the University of Michigan. How would that curriculum support your interests? (550 words)

The first time I visited Michigan's campus, I felt at home. The students I met were enthusiastic and engaged and shared a sense of intellectual curiosity that resonated strongly with me. I would love to be a student at the University of Michigan's College of Literature, Science, and the Arts. At LSA, not only could I pursue my interests, I could pursue interdisciplinary studies that explore how they intersect.

First and foremost, I am a science geek. I love biology and genetics, and after last summer at Columbia University, I'm passionate about psychology. I want to go to Michigan because it has one of the best psychology programs on the planet, and I'm particularly drawn to the Biopsychology, Cognition, and Neuroscience major. This unique program would allow me to explore my fascination with how humans think, process, and remember information. I can't wait to take classes like "Psychology of Thinking," which would give me a foundation for understanding the complex pathways of the mind.

When I think about college, I'm especially excited to do research, and there is no better place for scientific research than Michigan. I would love to work with Professor Brenda Proudfoot and help expand our understanding of the biological mechanisms that humans use to store memories. I would also love to participate in research at the Brain, Cognition, and Action Laboratory, perhaps as part of a UROP. Professor Bolger's research on how we multitask, process information, and remember images is fascinating and would allow me to deepen my understanding of the both cognitive psychology and neurobiology.

Michigan is also a place where I could learn broadly. This year I'm taking a microeconomics class and have become fascinated by economics. Through LSA, I could take classes that explore how economic principles play out in the real world, like "International Economics" and "Industrial Organization and Performance." I'm also intrigued by the relationship between science and society. I would love to participate in the Science, Technology, and Society program, which offers a uniquely interdisciplinary approach, and even to minor in STS.

Beyond the classroom, Michigan is a place that I want to call home. My work as president of my school's HIV/AIDS Awareness Club has taught me the importance of taking a stand on issues I care about. I was excited to learn that Michigan has a GlobeMed Organization that focuses on both local and international improvements in health. I would love to get involved with GlobeMed, as well as service groups such as University Students Acting Against Cancer. Working on my school's newspaper and as editor of the yearbook has been extremely rewarding, and I would be thrilled to write for *Blueprint Literary Magazine*, where my passion for literature could shine. In my free time, I know that I would often be found jogging around Ann Arbor, hopefully with members of the MRun running club. Michigan has everything I could want from a college and more, and I can't imagine a better place to spend the next four years.

Long Why Our School Essay 2: Rubik's Complex

Prompt: How does the University of Chicago, as you know it now, satisfy your desire for a particular kind of learning, community, and future? Please address with some specificity your own wishes and how they relate to UChicago.

When I was fifteen, my biology teacher told me I had a "Rubik's Complex." He was right. I love science because I love the puzzles, the complexities, the possibility of discovery. But I also love the humanities, especially history, art, poetry, and jazz. The University of Chicago is the perfect school for me because it is an incredible place to study science, and is also one of the best places in the world to engage with the liberal arts tradition.

Academically, I would plan to major in biochemistry. I want to study in ways that connect basic science to medicine, and the biochemistry major addresses the molecular level of biology I most enjoy. Most exciting are the extraordinary research opportunities at UChicago. The Ben May Department for Cancer Research, where biochemists, pharmacologists, and doctors work as a team, epitomises the kind of interdisciplinary work I want to pursue. I'd love to work with faculty members like Dr. Lily Cotton. Her research into tyrosine kinase signalling is fascinating and would allow me to further investigate the cellular mechanisms I'm currently exploring through my research internship.

Chicago is also exciting because scientists there are using the latest technology to fight cancer. I want to be part of the effort to make cancer therapies more targeted, and researchers at the Institute of Molecular Engineering are using immuno-bioengineering to rewire faulty immune systems, a common hallmark of cancer. I'm extremely interested in pursuing the bioengineering minor offered through the Institute. Creative approaches to cancer are important, because as my mentor Professor Adalgrim Took often says, "The dumbest cancer cell is smarter than the world's best oncologist."

It's not just science, however, that draws me to Chicago. The liberal arts focus, in particular the humanities-based structure of the Core, would allow me to pursue the broad education I crave. I want to work with inspired, inquisitive people who, like me, want to ask questions and challenge views. The Core would be an incredible place to have those conversations. I'd love to continue studying the Western classics and to take classes such as "Islamic Thought and Literature" that engage with other cultures. I also find the "Big Problems" curriculum fascinating. Coming from Great Britain, where we have universal health care, I'm interested in classes like "Health Care and the Limits of State Action." Not only would I be curious to discuss these issues with Americans, but this class addresses a contemporary, relevant topic that encompasses both the philosophical and the practical. That is the kind of education I could experience only at Chicago.

Outside of the classroom, the city of Chicago is an incredible attraction. Chicago is culturally rich, from the remarkable postwar architecture of Walter Gropius to the Art Institute of Chicago, with its great paintings from Rembrandt to Kandinsky. The ability to see these masterworks and live in a new city would be a second education in itself. UChicago combines the academics I want with the cultural experiences I crave, and I can't imagine a better place to spend the next four years.

Short Why Our School Essay 1:
Computer Science

Prompt: If you are applying to the Trinity College of Arts and Sciences as a first year applicant, please discuss why you consider Duke a good match for you. Is there something particular about Duke that attracts you? (150 words)

Duke's strength in the sciences, incredible interdisciplinary opportunities, and groundbreaking AI research make it the ideal school for me. I'm deeply fascinated by the ethical challenges raised by artificial intelligence technologies. By pursuing a BS in computer science with a minor in artificial intelligence, I could gain a strong foundation in data science while diving deep into algorithms and machine learning. I'd be thrilled to participate in the interdisciplinary research at Duke's unique Moral AI Lab, perhaps by pursuing a C-SURF on racial and gender bias in large language models. In addition, courses like "Philosophy of Language" would give me tools to examine generative AI from a philosophical perspective. Outside of the classroom, Duke's emphasis on service and community is an enormous draw. I hope to continue playing cello in the Duke Symphony Orchestra while building on my volunteer experience with Education Through Music as a member of ArtsConnect.

Short Why Our School Essay 2: Global Health

Prompt: If you are applying to the Trinity College of Arts and Sciences as a first year applicant, please discuss why you consider Duke a good match for you. Is there something particular about Duke that attracts you? (150 words)

Throughout high school, I've been inspired by opportunities to develop my skills, think big, and solve global problems. Duke is the perfect fit because it's a world leader in the health sciences that also offers a uniquely global perspective.

I experienced a taste of Duke's incredible opportunities through my two summers at Global Public Service Academies for Health, where I met and worked with Duke students and faculty. As a Global Health major at Trinity College, I'd love to continue doing research on HIV transmission in the developing world with GPSA's founder, Duke Professor Robert Malkin. I'm particularly drawn to Duke's Global Health Institute, where I could pursue research on strengthening health-care systems throughout the world.

Beyond academics, Duke's campus offers the perfect blend of scholarship, athletics, and community. From club lacrosse to groups like Women in Science and Engineering, I know Duke is a place where I would thrive.

Why Our School Engineering Essay: Robots!

Prompt: Cornell Engineering celebrates innovative problem solving that helps people, communities . . . the world. Consider your ideas and aspirations and describe how a Cornell Engineering education would allow you to leverage technological problem-solving to improve the world we live in. (650 words)

Over the past four years I have partnered with friends to create a new robotics team, collaboratively built machines that will change lives, and co-founded an entertainment magazine highlighting student voices. I love bringing people together around ideas that spark change; that's how we tap into the power of technology to create a better future. Cornell Engineering is my top choice for college because it actively encourages the impactful, interdisciplinary work that I love, and will help me become the kind of engineer I aspire to be.

I've spent much of the last six years building robots, and I want to major in Mechanical Engineering with a focus on robotics. Robots fascinate me because they are physical, combining logic with the power of mechanics. I have also seen firsthand the positive impact they can have on people, especially children. Last summer I began working in UVA's Mechatronics Lab, researching human-robot interaction alongside a team of graduate students. I worked to design and build DAMEON, a robot that displays emotions and can teach social skills to autistic children. I also worked on a multirobot swarm that educates children about robotics. In the process I've learned ROS (Robot Operating System) and MATLAB; I've also learned how to contribute in a professional environment and participate in high level discussions. Our lab uses technology every day to improve lives, and this sense of purpose drives me to continue this work.

In college, I can't wait to take classes that will deepen my understanding of robotics. Through Cornell courses like "Human-Robot Interaction—Research and Design," I could continue the work I began at UVA this summer, exploring how robots communicate and interpret their user's needs. I would enjoy taking Professor Petersen's "Bio-Inspired

Coordination of Multi-Agent Systems" and, with any luck, work in her Collective Embodied Intelligence Lab. There, I could contribute to the control of advanced robotic swarms as they coordinate in completing complicated tasks.

While I love creating new technologies, I know that my creations won't have an impact unless I connect with the people who need them. One of my favorite things about Cornell Engineering is the Dyson Business Minor for Engineers. Not only would Dyson give me a strong foundation in business, but courses like "Entrepreneurship for Engineers" would teach me how to collaborate on entrepreneurial teams. In "Social Entrepreneurs, Innovators, and Problem Solvers," I could examine how inventors before me have unpacked social challenges and solved them with technology. These classes and conversations would prepare me to take my creations out into the world, where they can change peoples' lives.

Beyond Dyson, Cornell is a place to explore all of my passions. Even though I'm focused on robotics, computer science is at the heart of my work. Cornell's computer science courses would help me expand my coding skills, while classes like "Foundations of Artificial Intelligence" would allow me to explore human-robot interaction in the context of AI, a new and exciting subject. Exploring computer science in further depth would offer even more tools to be able to create and innovate disruptive technologies.

When I visited campus, I was thrilled to see how Cornell's entrepreneurial culture supports innovations of every kind. I could create a technology magazine that makes engineering more accessible to children, or sign up for an engineering project team like CUAir or Seismic Design, making friends while learning about autonomous movement or safe structures. Cornell's Engineering Innovation Award Competition would be an incredible space to build on my robotics team experience, creating and competing alongside other engineers. Within these programs, every creative solution advances the world of engineering—I want to be a part of that movement.

Cornell Engineering has the innovative atmosphere and free-flowing ideas that will help me make an impact on the world. I can't imagine a better place to spend the next four years.

Lived Experience Essay: Finding an Orchestra

Prompt: Reflect on an element of your personal experience that you feel will enrich your college. How has it shaped you? (400 words)

In seventh grade I began playing the bassoon in band, and a dream quickly developed in my mind: to play in an orchestra. Having listened to classical music from a young age, I knew that I loved the orchestral sound, and I believed strongly (if inaccurately) that all the "serious" music was written for orchestras. There was just one problem: I live in rural Virginia, and there is no orchestra in my town.

So I started asking every adult I met—at church, at school, while doing volunteer work—how I could play in an orchestra. Eventually I learned about a small youth orchestra on the campus of Eastern Mennonite University, about 30 miles north of my town. As soon as I got my driver's license (my parents work nights and weekends, and they can't afford to take time off to shuttle me around), I called the orchestra's conductor, auditioned, and was accepted.

As a gay teen, I was nervous about being on the campus of a conservative, Christian school, but people there turned out to be very open and welcoming. The experience was incredible, and the following year, it led to an offer to play in the campus orchestra of Washington & Lee University, which is 40 miles south of my town (more driving!). Playing the exposed second bassoon part in Mozart's A-major piano concerto was terrifying, especially because all of the other players were college students or professors. But the feeling of being totally surrounded—literally and figuratively—by such beautiful music was one of the most thrilling experiences of my life.

Reaching beyond my local community has not only made me a better musician, it's transformed me as a person. It's meant less time for friends, schoolwork, and other activities, so I've had to get much better at managing my time. I've also become more resilient, learning to trust my inner voice, persist in the face of challenges, and to keep asking questions even when I don't know the way forward. In college, I can't wait to continue playing orchestral music. I also want to bring the spirit of this experience to the Yale community, not only for myself, but to support my classmates in following their dreams and creating meaningful experiences that enrich their lives.

Intellectual Engagement Essay: Understanding FDR

Prompt: Tell us about an intellectual or creative passion you have pursued; what did you learn about yourself through that pursuit? (350 words)

For as long as I can remember, American history has fascinated me. When I was in elementary school, I loved visiting Washington, DC, with my family and driving past the massive limestone buildings where democracy actually happened. As I've grown older, I've been inspired by the multiple generations of women in my family who have served in the Navy.

So last year, when I had the opportunity to do an extended research project for AP US History, the obvious choice was my favorite president: Franklin Delano Roosevelt. Although I didn't know much about him at the start, his fireside chats and leadership through World War II had always intrigued me. As I started to learn more about him by reading biographies, analyzing primary sources, and watching interviews with scholars, what began to captivate me were the inherent contradictions in his character. Roosevelt projected strength and boldness, yet he was crippled and often went about in a wheelchair. He was a passionate advocate for the common man, yet he came from a wealthy, aristocratic background. And while he was a staunch defender of democracy, some of his political maneuvering—say, the court-packing plan or his promise in the 1940 election to keep America out of war despite his intention to do the opposite—seemed frankly undemocratic, almost authoritarian.

While this project taught me a lot about our 32nd president, it taught me something much more important about myself: I'm passionate about psychology. My high school doesn't offer a psychology class, but after finishing the paper I found myself checking out books on psychology from the library, watching YouTube videos on personality and character traits, and reading articles on new psychological discoveries when they appeared in the *New York Times* and my local newspaper. Looking forward, I can't wait to take psychology and sociology classes in college or perhaps even major in the social sciences. History will always be a source of fascination, but I now know that my true interest is in people: how they see the world, why they do what they do, and what makes them tick.

Activity Essay 1: Yearbook

Prompt: If you could only do one of the activities you have listed in the Activities section of your Common Application, which one would you keep doing? Why? (100 words)

For the past three years I've constantly looked forward to sitting down, grabbing my mug of coffee, and diving in on the yearbook. I love yearbook because it ties together three of my favorite activities: writing, graphic design, and organization. This year, as editor, I'm especially excited because I'm responsible for everything from the overall theme to cover design. After we publish this spring, I look forward to passing on my experience to the rising class of editors. Next year, I can't wait to join another student publication where I can channel my inner writer, designer, and manager.

Activity essay 2: Ultimate Frisbee

Prompt: If you could only do one of the activities you have listed in the Activities section of your Common Application, which one would you keep doing? Why? (150 words)

I love ultimate Frisbee. Not only is the sport physically challenging, but it also forms incredible relationships, requires quick decision making, and brings out the best in people. Since ultimate is self-officiated, anyone can call a foul at any time, with obvious potential for abuse. However, ultimate players also follow an unwritten code known as "Spirit of the Game." This code promotes respect and sportsmanship, from honesty in foul calls to complimenting opponents on a nice play. Thanks to this honor system, ultimate can be fiercely competitive while also creating an ethos of community and inclusivity.

Ultimate has enriched my life immensely, and I hope to keep playing in college. At Michigan, joining the MagnUM ultimate team would give me an instant community of new friends, help me stay in shape, and—given that I'll spending most of my time at North Campus—offer regular opportunities to enjoy the outdoors and nature.

Community Essay 1: *Tzedakah* and *Mitzvah*

Prompt: Everyone belongs to many different communities and/or groups defined by (among other things) shared geography, religion, ethnicity, income, cuisine, interest, race, ideology, or intellectual heritage. Choose one of the communities to which you belong, and describe that community and your place within it. (250 words)

Judaism is at the core of my identity. I was raised in a Jewish household, and at age thirteen I officially joined my synagogue as an adult. While I'm only seventeen, I take my "adult" responsibilities seriously. Two Jewish concepts in particular are central to how I approach the world.

One is *mitzvah*, which literally means "good deed" and also translates to "commandment." The other is *tzedakah*, or charitable giving.

Through Torah study and service work at temple, my community has given me a hands-on understanding of both terms. *Tzedakah*, I've learned, comes in many forms: donations of time, knowledge, and passion. *Mitzvah*, as well, is a social obligation to alleviate suffering and pain. These concepts inform everything I do. For example, I see my work as president of the AIDS Awareness Club at my school as *tzedakah*, whether we're organizing fundraisers to support AIDS research or raising awareness around the disease. In another club I lead, Helping Out People Everywhere (HOPE), the principle of *mitzvah* inspired me to expand the scope of our volunteer work to nursing homes, community centers, and other places where we can directly relieve suffering.

One of the many things I love about Judaism is that it immerses me in multiple communities. Locally, I'm part of my synagogue and the Jewish Community Center, yet I'm also a member of the global Jewish community. Giving back, through both *mitzvah* and *tzedakah*, connects me to all of these communities and to the human community at large.

Community Essay 2: Teen PEP

Prompt: Everyone belongs to many different communities and/or groups defined by (among other things) shared geography, religion, ethnicity, income, cuisine, interest, race, ideology, or intellectual heritage. Choose one of the communities to which you belong, and describe that community and your place within it. (300 words)

Last fall, I never would have imagined that a group of juniors, who at first glance have little in common, would become so important to me. The Teen Prevention Education Program (Teen PEP) is a peer-to-peer sexual education program that equips students with knowledge and skills for sexual health. Through interactive workshops that include skits, talks, and group discussions, we create safe environments to educate students about topics like gender and homophobia, while teaching skills to make healthy decisions and resist peer pressure.

The work I've done for Teen PEP has been incredibly meaningful, and I'm proud to have had a positive impact on the next generation of Westlake High students. What surprised me, however, was how close I became to the other peer educators in my cohort, and how we became a community.

Our cohort contains students from a variety of social, ethnic, and economic backgrounds. We practice different religions and come from different cultures, but through the hours of honest and personal discussions that PEP demanded, we found that we shared a deep desire to help others, and to bring more justice into the world. Often, we would stay late at night after our Teen PEP meetings, discussing current events, world politics, and social change.

This community, with its diversity of thought and opinion, has changed me. It has exposed me to new ideas, and led me to broaden my circle of friends. Over time, I even surprised myself with how vocal I became about my own ideas and passions, especially around gender and equity.

Although we will soon split up to follow our own paths, I'm grateful for what my Teen PEP community has given me, and I know I will find similarly inclusive and engaging communities at the University of Michigan.

Diverse Perspectives Essay: COVID Conversation

Prompt: At Princeton, we value diverse perspectives and the ability to have respectful dialogue about difficult issues. Share a time when you had a conversation with a person or a group of people about a difficult topic. What insight did you gain, and how would you incorporate that knowledge into your thinking in the future? (250 words)

Last year, while hiking near my home, I ran into a man who wanted to talk about COVID. Despite the fact that he worked in health care, he wasn't getting vaccinated. In fact, he believed there was a conspiracy and that vaccines caused COVID.

My initial reaction was anger. I knew he was wrong, and I had statistics to challenge his unscientific views. Yet as he spoke, I began to notice something else: he was afraid. Thinking back to my own vaccination the previous month, I remembered that when the National Guard medic stuck that needle in my arm, I, too, had an irrational fear that it might give me COVID.

So instead of reiterating the facts, I listened. When he was done, I told him about my vaccination, how scared I had been. Sure, I felt sick for a few days afterwards, but I got better. Today, I had just hiked a mountain!

He nodded, and I think he heard me. While I'd like to think that my empathy helped persuade him to get the vaccine, I do know that I learned a valuable lesson: there is power in simply listening to someone's story and sharing your own.

I love science, and I'll always believe in the power of truth and reason. Yet I now know that facts are not the only way to persuade. If I truly want to have an impact, I need to continue listening to others' stories and finding the courage to share my own.

Notes

Preface

xii   *already a top factor in admissions:* Melissa Clinedinst, "2019 State of College Admission," National Association for College Admission Counseling, https://nacacnet.org/wp-content/uploads/2022/10/soca2019_all.pdf, 15.

xii   Source: Michelle N. Amponsah and Emma H. Haider, "Harvard College Accepts 3.41% of Applicants to Class of 2027," *Harvard Crimson*, March 31, 2023, https://www.thecrimson.com/article/2023/3/31/admissions-decisions-2027.

xiii   *colleges began experimenting with AI:* Scott Jaschik, "Admissions Offices, Cautiously, Start Using AI," *Inside Higher Ed*, May 15, 2023. https://www.insidehighered.com/news/admissions/2023/05/15/admissions-offices-cautiously-start-using-ai.

xiii   *"the first full academic year of the post-ChatGPT era":* Kevin Roose, "How Schools Can Survive (and Maybe Even Thrive) with A.I. This Fall," *New York Times*, August 24, 2023, https://www.nytimes.com/2023/08/24/technology/how-schools-can-survive-and-maybe-eventhrive-with-ai-this-fall.html.

xiii   *her professors gave ChatGPT:* Maya Bodnick, "ChatGPT Goes to Harvard," *Slow Boring*, July 18, 2023, https://www.slowboring.com/p/chatgpt-goes-to-harvard.

xiii   *Harvard Class of 1999:* Valerie J. Macmillan, "12 Percent Accepted into Class of 1999: News: The Harvard Crimson," *Harvard Crimson*, April 5, 1995, https://www.thecrimson.com/article/1995/4/5/12-percent-accepted-into-class-of/.

xiii   *University of Pennsylvania Class of 2004:* Dana Klinek, "Penn Accepts Just 22% of Applicants," *Daily Pennsylvanian*, April 5, 2000, https://www.thedp.com/article/2000/04/penn_accepts_just_22_of_applicants.

xiii *University of Michigan Class of 2002:* "University of Michigan–Ann Arbor Common Data Set 1998–99," published by University of Michigan, https://obp.umich.edu/wp-content/uploads/pubdata/cds/cds_1998-1999_umaa.pdf.

xiii *Harvard Class of 2026:* John S. Rosenberg, "Harvard College Admits Class of 2026," *Harvard Magazine*, March 31, 2022, https://www.harvardmagazine.com/2022/03/harvard-college-class-2026-admissions.

xiii *University of Pennsylvania Class of 2025:* "University of Pennsylvania Class of 2025," *University of Pennsylvania Almanac*, May 11, 2021, https://almanac.upenn.edu/articles/university-ofpennsylvania-class-of-2025.

xiii *University of Michigan Class of 2025:* "University of Michigan–Ann Arbor Common Data Set 2021–2022," December 15, 2021, published by University of Michigan, https://obp.umich.edu/wp-content/uploads/pubdata/cds/cds_2021-2022_umaa.pdf.

xiii *"A number of years ago":* Jim Jump. "Ethical College Admissions: Admit Rates," *Inside Higher Ed*, April 3, 2022, https://www.insidehighered.com/admissions/views/2022/04/04/how-sincere-are-colleges-dont-release-their-admitrates-opinion.

Chapter 1: Know Your Audience: AdCom Psychology 101

16 *In a classic* Simpsons *episode: The Simpsons*, Season 5, Episode 3, "Homer Goes to College," written by Conan O'Brien, aired October 14, 1993, on Fox.

17 Source: Shutterstock.com (stock photo ID 1613072653).

21 *which brings with it:* David Brooks, "In the Age of A.I., Major in Being Human," *New York Times*, February 2, 2023, https://www.nytimes.com/2023/02/02/opinion/ai-human-education.html.

21 *it also created:* Tess McClure, "Supermarket AI Meal Planner App Suggests Recipe That Would Create Chlorine Gas," *Guardian*, August 10, 2023, https://www.theguardian.com/world/2023/aug/10/pak-n-save-savey-meal-bot-ai-appmalfunction-recipes.

22 *More quietly, admissions offices:* Scott Jaschik, "Admissions Offices, Cautiously, Start Using AI," *Inside Higher Ed*, May 15, 2023. https://www.insidehighered.com/news/admissions/2023/05/15/admissions-offices-cautiously-start-using-ai.

23 *"Colleges want applications":* Rick Clark, "Seniors, Can We ChatGPT?," Georgia Institute of Technology, July 27, 2023, https://sites.gatech.edu/admission-blog/2023/07/27/seniors-can-we-chatgpt.

23 *"In the same way":* "Personal Essays," Georgia Institute of Technology, https://admission.gatech.edu/first-year/personal-essays.

Chapter 2: The Top Ten Qualities Admissions Officers Look For

30   *"Will she contribute":* Quoted in Delano R. Franklin and Molly C. Mc-Cafferty, "Here's How the Harvard Admissions Process Really Works," *Harvard Crimson*, October 29, 2018, https://www.thecrimson.com/article/2018/10/29/how-to-get-in-toharvard/.

33   *There are hard skills:* Tami Simon, e-mail message to the Sounds True community, "One of the most empowered leaders I've ever met," April 8, 2021.

37   *"capacity to recover quickly":* New Oxford American Dictionary (Oxford: Oxford University Press, 2010), s.v. "Resilience," via *Apple Dictionary*.

38   *President Joe Biden issued:* President Joe Biden, "Remarks by President Biden on the Supreme Court's Decision on Affirmative Action," The White House, June 29, 2023, https://www.whitehouse.gov/briefing-room/speeches-remarks/2023/06/29/remarks-by-president-biden-on-the-supreme-courts-decision-on-affirmativeaction.

38   *"describe a barrier":* Eric Hoover, "An Early Peek at How Admission Applications Are Changing After the Supreme Court Ruling," *Chronicle of Higher Education*, August 1, 2023, https://www.chronicle.com/article/an-early-peek-at-how-admissionapplications-are-changing-after-the-supreme-court-ruling.

43   *"Nothing in this opinion":* Supreme Court of the United States, *Students for Fair Admissions, Inc. v. President and Fellows of Harvard College*, 600 U.S. 181, preliminary print, June 29, 2023, https://www.supremecourt.gov/opinions/22pdf/600us1r53_n7io.pdf, 230–31.

Chapter 3: Your Plan of Action

53   *"Follow the correct order":* Marie Kondo, *The Life-Changing Magic of Tidying Up: The Japanese Art of Decluttering and Organizing* (Berkeley, CA: Ten Speed Press, 2014), 64.

53   *"warrior princess":* Richard Lloyd Parry, "The Japanese Way to Declutter Your Home . . . and Your Life," *The Times* [London], April 7, 2014, https://www.thetimes.co.uk/article/the-japanese-way-to-declutter-your-home-and-your-life-5qpjkkccmhc.

Chapter 4: Writing the Common App Personal Essay

62   *"At its heart":* Robert Lee Brewer, "What Is a Personal Essay in Writing?," *Writer's Digest*, May 8, 2021, https://www.writersdigest.com/write-better-nonfiction/what-is-a-personal-essay-in-writing.

66 *"We are victims":* Julia Cameron, *The Artist's Way* (London: Penguin Publishing Group, 2002) (Kindle), 11.

67 *"Make this a rule":* Ibid.

68 Source: Shutterstock.com (image ID 1337030075).

73 *Below are the Common App prompts:* "First-Year Essay Prompts," Common App, https://www.commonapp.org/apply/essay-prompts.

81 *a whopping 42%:* Editorial Board, "America's Teens Are in Crisis. States Are Racing to Respond," *Washington Post*, April 1, 2023, https://www.washingtonpost.com/opinions/2023/04/01/teen-mental-health-state-programs/.

84 *Yale University:* Susan Svrluga and William Wan, "Yale to Update Policies After Lawsuit over Student Mental Health," *Washington Post*, August 25, 2023, https://www.washingtonpost.com/education/2023/08/25/yale-set tlement-mentalhealth-lawsuit/.

92 *"The first draft of anything":* Arnold Samuelson, *With Hemingway: A Year in Key West and Cuba* (New York: Random House, 1984), 11.

115 *"a phrase or opinion":* New Oxford American Dictionary, s.v. "cliché."

Chapter 5: Supplemental Essays, Part I: The Why Our School essay

121 *"Thirty years ago":* Anne Lamott, *Bird by Bird: Some Instructions on Writing and Life* (New York: Anchor Books, 1995), 18.

122 *"genre": New Oxford American Dictionary*, s.v. "genre."

123 Source: "My Colleges," Common App, accessed November 1, 2023, https://apply.commonapp.org/mycolleges/445/about.

Chapter 6: Supplemental Essays, Part II: The Contributions/Lived Experience, Intellectual Engagement, Activity, Community, and Diverse Perspectives Essays

152 *your experiences as an individual:* "Application Deadlines and Requirements," Johns Hopkins University, https://apply.jhu.edu/how-to-apply/application-deadlines-requirements.

Chapter 7: Supplemental Essays at Highly Selective Schools: The Ivies and Ivy Adjacents

196 *"There's a river of power":* Richard Ben Cramer, *What It Takes: The Way to the White House* (New York: Vintage Books, 1993), 501.

196 *"Ivy-covered professors":* Tom Lehrer, "Bright College Days," track 2 on *An Evening Wasted with Tom Lehrer*, Reprise, 1990.

196 *at $50 billion:* Adam Vaccaro, "Harvard's Endowment Is Bigger than Half the World's Economies," Boston.com, September 25, 2014, https://www .boston.com/news/business/2014/09/25/harvards-endowment-is-bigger -than-half-theworlds-economies/.

200 *"The mission of Harvard College":* "About: Mission, Vision, and History," Harvard College, https://college.harvard.edu/about/mission-vision-history.

204 *In 2001, it was the first:* "Twenty Years Later: Princeton's Visionary Financial Aid Program," Office of the President, Princeton University, January 5, 2021, https://president.princeton.edu/blogs/twenty-years-later-princetons -visionary-financial-aid-program.

204 *"In the nation's service":* "Princeton in NJ's Service," Office of State Affairs, Princeton University, https://stateaffairs.princeton.edu/princeton-nj /princeton-njs-service.

209 *Some would add:* "About the Ivy Plus Libraries Confederation," Ivy Plus Libraries Confederation, https://ivpluslibraries.org/about/.

210 *"can be approached":* "UChicago Supplemental Essay Questions," University of Chicago, https://collegeadmissions.uchicago.edu/apply/uchicago -supplemental-essay-questions.

216 *schools that are owned or heavily funded:* Richard Moll, *The Public Ivys: A Guide to America's Best Public Undergraduate Colleges and Universities* (New York: Viking Press, 1985).

216 *According to data:* Emma Kerr and Sarah Wood, "The Cost of Private vs. Public Colleges," *U.S. News & World Report,* June 8, 2022, https://www.us news.com/education/best-colleges/paying-for-college/articles/2019-06-25 /the-cost-ofprivate-vs-public-colleges.

Appendix II: Creating Your Résumé and Activities List

268 *in 2023, Lafayette College:* Liam Knox, "The Common App Enters an Uncommon Era," *Inside Higher Ed,* August 2, 2023, https://www.inside highered.com/news/admissions/traditional-age/2023/08/02/colleges -change-essay-prompts-after-affirmative-action.

277 Source: Generated from Common App, October 30, 2023, https://apply .commonapp.org/common/7/232.

About the Author

ERIC TIPLER holds degrees from Harvard (AB) and Yale (MA) and has spent the past twenty years working with teenagers, first as a high school teacher and more recently as a writing coach, tutor, and college admissions counselor. Throughout his career, Eric has taught writing to students from a wide range of socioeconomic backgrounds. He taught social studies at Friendship Public Charter School in inner-city Washington, DC, and at Thomas Jefferson High School for Science and Technology in Alexandria, Virginia, often ranked the number one public high school in the United States. Eric also taught and advised Yale undergraduates as a teaching fellow and served as an Assistant Head of College for Yale Summer Session. As a writing coach and admissions consultant, Eric currently works with students across the country, as well as doing pro bono work in New York City and rural New York. In addition to teaching and tutoring, Eric writes musical theater and works as a story consultant for Broadway-bound musicals.